LEADING FOR TOMORROW

Unlocking Human Potential in the Era
of *Continuous Change* and *Endless Possibility*

Edited by **Scott Barry Kaufman** and **Chris Shipley**
Foreword by **Rita McGrath**

WILEY

Library of Congress Cataloging-in-Publication Data is Available:

ISBN 9781394366279 (Cloth)
ISBN 9781394366286 (ePub)
ISBN 9781394366293 (ePDF)

Cover Design: Jon Boylan
Cover Image: © Khulqi Design/stock.adobe.com

Printed and bound by CPI Group (UK) Ltd, Croydon, CR0 4YY

C9781394366279_120526

*This book is dedicated to the transformational
leaders who put humans at
the center of their organizations.*

Contents

Contents

We stand at a peculiar moment in history. The digital revolution that began with the microprocessor has now changed virtually every aspect of life and work. It is gradually challenging every element of the previous technological regime, anchored on mass production, cheap energy, and abundant materials. As economic historian Carlota Perez has argued, we are at the turning point.[1] This is the turbulent, unpredictable situation on which the old regime clings, huge financial rewards have accrued to just a few, income inequality is cruel, and, for many, capitalism has lost its legitimacy. Populists rise and the old order shows its limitations. What her framework suggests, however, is that we have the potential to unleash a new golden age, a harmonious period when technology, business, capital, and society align to create broadly shared prosperity. Until then, we find ourselves suspended in what feels like perpetual turbulence, where each wave of innovation crashes into the next before we've learned to ride the first.

Every major technological revolution—from the first industrial revolution through the age of steel, electricity, oil, and mass production—has followed a predictable pattern: installation, crisis, turning point, and deployment. The installation phase brings creative destruction, speculative bubbles, and growing inequality. The deployment phase, when it arrives, delivers the golden age: broad-based prosperity, social progress, and human flourishing. But between these phases lies the crucial turning point, where societies must consciously choose to reshape their institutions, values, and leadership models to harness technology for the common good.

Unlike the age of steel or electricity, the digital revolution doesn't just transform how we make things. It transforms how we think, connect, and organize ourselves. It collapses time and space, accelerates change beyond human adaptation rates, and creates what Kaufman and Shipley aptly call continuous disruption. It introduces exponential change when human brains operate with linear thought processes.

This is where the wisdom gathered in this anthology becomes essential. The Silicon Guild's contributors understand something profound: In an era where artificial intelligence can replicate and accelerate nearly every technical skill, the uniquely human capacities—creativity, empathy, purpose, meaning making—become not just valuable but indispensable. These leaders recognize that the bridge to our next golden age won't be built by algorithms or automation but by humans working together in new ways.

It won't be the technology that determines the outcomes. Rather, as Perez notes, "the sociopolitical form we give to technology will define whether we enter a golden age." The choice isn't predetermined. We could use AI to create a hyperquantified society where every human interaction is optimized for measurable outcomes. Or we could deploy it to create the abundance and efficiency that enables a flourishing of precisely those immeasurable aspects of human experience that make life worth living.[2]

The Last Golden Age Didn't Just Happen: It Required Leadership

History offers us a crucial lesson here. The last great deployment phase, which was the post–World War II era of mass production and consumption, wasn't inevitable. Franklin Roosevelt's New Deal, the Bretton Woods system, the Marshall Plan, the GI Bill, the rebuilding of Japan, the establishment of the United Nations, government-backed housing loans, the construction of highways, and more were the result of conscious choices to reshape institutions and redirect capital toward human development and shared prosperity. Leaders like Roosevelt, Truman, and their international counterparts designed institutions with human welfare at their center.

The business leaders of that era acted in concert with these government policies. An incredibly influential business group was the Committee for Economic Development. Early members included Paul G. Hoffman (Studebaker), William Benton (advertising), and Marion B. Folsom (Eastman Kodak). Thomas B. McCabe, the chairman of the Board of Governors of the Federal Reserve System, made a speech in November of 1949, reflecting on its remarkable history. The committee, he said, was launched "in the dark days of 1942 with one outstanding immediate objective, namely, to enable us to do everything in our power as businessmen to see to it that the economy did not collapse when the war effort was over and the war contracts were cancelled."[3] The message here is that a group of aligned, motivated leaders conceived of and built a system that served the majority of people well.

Today's challenge is both similar and more complex. We need leaders who can navigate continuous disruption, who can build resilience rather than just efficiency, who can foster human agency in an age of algorithmic decision making. The Theory Z that Maslow

Foreword

envisioned—where work becomes a source of transcendence and peak experience—could be an imperative. When machines handle routine tasks, humans must do what only humans can: imagine, connect, create meaning, and care for one another.

Toward the Permissionless Organization

The leaders featured in this book understand this imperative and believe that a better future for all of us can happen only when we build better organizations, teams, and careers. They're inventing entirely new kinds of organizational forms. These are characterized by different organizing principles than the mass production bureaucracies of the past. They are increasingly "permissionless," in which consequential decisions can be made by those closest to the edges of the organization, where the most information exists. Their fundamental unit of operation is not a hierarchy but a network. They are, in many cases, motivated by a compelling larger purpose to have an impact on the world. Organizations built this way can thrive in perpetual change. In a world where competitive advantages are transient, the only sustainable advantage is the ability to continuously learn, adapt, and innovate.

This brings us to the essential insight that runs through these pages: The next golden age won't be measured by GDP growth or stock market returns but by human flourishing. The deployment phase we seek is a true socioeconomic revolution. It's about fundamentally redefining what we mean by value, success, and progress. It's about creating organizations and societies where people can bring their unique talents and capabilities to creatively solve problems without laboring under onerous controls.

The path forward requires what might seem like a paradox: using our most advanced technologies to become more deeply human. It means building AI systems that augment rather than replace human

Foreword

judgment, creating virtual workspaces that strengthen human connection, designing economic models that value contribution over extraction. Most important, it means leaders who can hold the tension between acceleration and reflection, between efficiency and empathy, between individual agency and collective purpose.

We have many of the tools we need to realize this future. What we lack, and what this book provides, is the leadership vision and moral imagination to build the bridge from installation to deployment, from painful disruption and disengagement to flourishing.

Collaborating for Impact

This book was inspired by a combustion of ideas shared between two remarkable organizations. The first is Thinkers50, which for 25 years has recognized the critical importance of management thinking to influence management practice and consequently societal outcomes. Their biannual list of leading management thinkers brings new concepts to light and influences the practice of management. The other is the Silicon Guild, a loosely organized group of nonfiction authors who regularly share important ideas, provide each other with support and advice, and influence the way the world works with their writing. Many members have written bestsellers and are household names. Indeed, as one newly selected member observed, "It's almost as if having imposter syndrome is a requirement for belonging to this group." Our mission is to "unlock and support human voices."

Several members of the group met up during the most recent Thinkers50 conference and, remarking on how aligned the missions of the two groups were, conceived of assembling a joint project, which eventually became this book. The project evolved from a description of different aspects of humanity today to a sharp focus on what kind of human-centered leadership we need for the future. The submissions reflect a delightfully diverse set of perspectives on how leaders can leverage uniquely human qualities. The core themes of the book have to do with purpose, creating a mindset suitable for shifts, learning, resilience, and addressing human needs.

The contributors to this volume aren't just theorizing about transformational leadership. They are actively shaping the ideas that will inspire it. In their organizations and communities, they're demonstrating that human-centered leadership isn't soft or sentimental but rigorously practical. They show us that psychological safety drives innovation, that purpose attracts talent, that trust reduces transaction costs, that diversity enhances decision making. They're proving that the most successful organizations in an age of continuous change are those that invest in human potential.

As you read these chapters, consider them not as prescriptions but as invitations. Each author offers a piece of the larger puzzle. They cover how to lead when the ground keeps shifting, how to build trust in virtual spaces, how to foster creativity under pressure, how to go from knowledge to wisdom, and, most important, how to maintain humanity in an algorithmic age. Together, they paint a picture of leadership that is both revolutionary and deeply rooted in timeless human values.

A Leader Is Not a Position

The last golden age emerged from the conscious choices of leaders who understood that technology's promise could be realized only through institutional innovation and human development. Today, we face a similar choice. We can continue on a path to greater fragmentation, inequality, and anxiety. Or we can choose to collaborate, to share resources, and to create calm.

The stakes couldn't be higher. The convergence of artificial intelligence, biotechnology, climate change, and geopolitical tension creates both existential risks and unprecedented opportunities.

The leaders who guide us through this transition will determine not just economic outcomes but the very nature of human experience in the coming century.

We don't need to wait for great leaders to emerge. In an age of distributed networks and democratized tools, leadership itself is being democratized. Each of us, in our own sphere of influence, can embody the principles outlined in this book. We can create psychological safety in our teams, pursue purpose alongside profit, and foster creativity and connection. We can choose to see disruption not as threat but as opportunity to rebuild our organizations and institutions around human flourishing.

The journey from our current turbulence to the next golden age won't be automatic or easy. It requires the kind of leadership explored in these chapters—leadership that is simultaneously humble and ambitious, grounded and visionary, analytical and empathetic. It requires leaders who understand that in an age when machines can think, the greatest value lies in helping humans become more fully human.

This, then, is the call to action that echoes through these pages: to recognize that we stand at a turning point not unlike the 1940s, when visionary leaders chose to rebuild the world around human dignity and shared prosperity. The technologies are different, and the challenges are new, but the fundamental choice remains the same. Will we use our unprecedented capabilities to amplify what divides us or what connects us? Will we optimize for efficiency or for resilience? Will we automate away human agency or augment human potential?

The contributors to this anthology have made their choice clear. They're building organizations and systems that treat humans not as resources to be optimized but as creators to be empowered. They're demonstrating that the path to the next golden age runs not through soulless algorithms but through the human heart and mind.

Foreword

As you engage with their insights, remember that you too are part of this transformation. Every interaction, every decision, every moment of leadership—no matter how small—contributes to the larger pattern. We are all parties to writing the next chapter, determining whether this technological revolution will deliver on its promise.

Welcome to this conversation. Welcome to this movement. Welcome to the work of building the bridge to our next golden age. The future is not something that happens to us; it's something we create together, one human connection, one purposeful decision, one act of courageous leadership at a time.

—Rita McGrath
Founder and CEO of Acumen
Princeton, New Jersey
December 11, 2025

Notes

1. Carlota Perez, *Technological Revolutions and Financial Capital: The Dynamics of Bubbles and Golden Ages* (Edward Elgar, 2002).
2. Carlota Perez, Leo Johnson, and Art Kleiner, "Are We on the Verge of a New Golden Age?," Strategy+business, August 28, 2017. www.strategy-business.com/article/Are-We-on-the-Verge-of-a-New-Golden-Age
3. Thomas B. McCabe, "The Committee for Economic Development - Its Past, Present and Future," Address before the CED Board of Trustees, November 17, 1949. https://fraser.stlouisfed.org/files/docs/historical/federal%20reserve%20history/bog_members_statements/mccabe_19491117.pdf

Introduction: Toward a Human-Centered Future

Scott Barry Kaufman and

Chris Shipley

By the 1930s, nearly 90 percent of America's urban households were electrified. It would take another 30 years—and an act of Congress—for electricity to reach most, but still not all, of the country's rural and remote homes. In other words, the adoption of this life-changing technology was slow.

In those days, a factory foreman (and it would have been a man) could supervise line workers from a perch above the factory floor, noting who was performing and who was not, each worker a replaceable cog in a production process. Over decades, both products and the lines that produced them became more complex and moved more quickly. The Industrial Era gave way to the Knowledge Era. Adoption curves compressed. Thirty-year cycles became ten. Digital technologies transformed the way much work is done. The pace of change quickened, yet the fundamentals of production remained the same: Leaders directed people to perform known tasks toward known outcomes. And, generally, that leadership style worked.

Until now.

Today, change comes so fast that adoption curves have collapsed onto one another. Generative artificial intelligence systems reached 100 million users in under two months. By the fall of 2025, ChatGPT—just one of several large-scale generative systems—was processing 2.5 *billion* queries a day. Each new disruptive wave arrives faster than the one before, compressing the time between invention and ubiquity so significantly that leadership has no time to adapt before the next wave hits.

We no longer live through disruptions; we live *inside continuous disruption*. And that demands a wholly different kind of leadership—one measured not by productivity but by the capacity to harness the human potential to think, connect, innovate, and act meaningfully and purposefully even as the ground keeps moving beneath us.

Over much of the last 100 years, productivity was the holy grail of business. In the industrial age, productivity meant producing more with less—standardizing processes, optimizing labor, and eliminating waste. Leaders optimized output, their workers a necessary, if often messy, part of that process. If the process worked efficiently and cost-effectively, profitability followed, and all was well. If conditions changed, leadership might swap out people like broken gears in a machine, in search of greater efficiency and higher returns. In effect, people were parts.

Even in the knowledge economy that followed, productivity remained the organizing principle, albeit measured through output of ideas and data rather than physical goods. But productivity is rooted in a world of predictability. It presumes that work can be measured, optimized, and repeated. The system worked well enough for business—if not always so much for workers—when environments were predictable and the time between transformative disruption was measured in decades rather than days.

That is no longer our reality.

Introduction: Toward a Human-Centered Future

Our new world requires new tools, new values, and a new way of defining success. This book emerges from this pivotal moment. It brings together a chorus of leading thinkers and practitioners who understand that, in the face of perpetual disruption, the most effective leaders are those who serve as anchors of stability and sources of growth and empowerment. This book's chapters reveal how leadership must evolve—not through rigid control or outdated hierarchies but through empathy, adaptability, and a commitment to nurturing the full potential of every individual.

Human Adaptability Beats Operational Efficiency

In a world of continuous disruption, efficiency alone loses its value. Performance is no longer the sum of individual outputs but the quality of human interaction that generates new insight and value. It is the art of responding collectively and intelligently to the unknown. And in an economy defined by uncertainty, it is the new foundation of profitability. Efficiency gains are quickly commoditized. AI systems can already produce code, analysis, and content faster than humans. What matters now—what remains scarce and uniquely valuable—is the human capacity to adapt, sense, connect, and create together in real time. This is profoundly *human* work.

This, then, is the essence of leadership in the age of continuous change: to move from directing work to empowering humans who keep an organization learning, adapting, and creating new value. The leaders who thrive are those who recognize and elevate human capacity over production capacity. They see collaboration and purpose not as vague ideals but as core principles that keep organizations cohesive, adaptive, and high performing, even as the world around them changes.

Introduction: Toward a Human-Centered Future

The Age of Agency

That this dynamic environment follows so closely on the heels of the COVID-19 pandemic only deepens the urgency for leadership transformation. In a matter of weeks, workers shifted from in-person, command-and-control workplaces to autonomous, virtual organizations. In the face of a genuine existential crisis, leadership discovered the power of empathy and compassion, not simply to be kind but to unlock the human capacity for performance amid uncertainty.

By shifting agency from the organization to the individual, leaders tapped new reserves of adaptability and creativity. And that agency, once ceded to workers, is impossible to reclaim. The workforce has learned what it means to perform with agency and purpose, and no amount of managerial control can return it to the old order.

How, then, are leaders to proceed?

In every corner of our interconnected world, organizations and individuals alike confront challenges that are more complex and unpredictable than ever before. The traditional management playbooks, built for stability and certainty, no longer suffice. Instead, we find ourselves called to a new ethos—one that places the human experience and the complexity of human needs at the very center of leadership.

The next generation of leaders must recognize that human collaboration and shared purpose have become the primary sources of value. The companies that thrive will not simply be the most productive but the most adaptable: organizations where people work together fluidly, creatively, and meaningfully in the face of constant change.

Redefining Human Success

The famous MIT management professor Douglas McGregor once contrasted two different assumptions managers hold about workers, arguing that these assumptions impact their management style.[1]

According to "Theory X," people inherently dislike their work and are primarily motivated by carrot-and-stick incentives, such as money and security. Work environments operating under Theory X value efficiency, structure, and routine and are high in control, strict rules, and even routine threats of punishment.

In contrast, "Theory Y" assumes that people find work intrinsically enjoyable and have the capacity to be self-directed. In a Theory Y work environment, workers are motivated by intrinsic rewards such as creativity and personal growth. Theory Y environments tend to be autonomy-supportive and collaborative. There is a lot of trust in employees, and workers feel empowered to nurture their inherent inclinations for personal growth and professional development.

These managerial assumptions reflect attitudes about work and leadership that are losing validity in a world of continuous change and disruption. Today's environment requires a dramatic redefinition of success, one based not on the measurement of productivity but rather on the *fulfillment of human needs*, including the opportunity for people to connect, serve a higher purpose, and experience self-transcendence in their work.

That is the essence of humanistic psychologist Abraham Maslow's "Theory Z."[2] Maslow argued that people are also motivated by *self-transcendence*, the need to look beyond oneself to connect with something larger and more meaningful. In a Theory Z work environment, workers strive for connection, purpose, and peak experiences. Theory Z environments are those that bring out this higher human potential in everyone.

A New Hierarchy of Human Needs

Maslow realized the immense potential of the workplace to test his ideas. The experience of observing the workplace, he said,

> *opened up to me a body of theory and research which was entirely new to me and which set me to thinking and*

Introduction: Toward a Human-Centered Future

theorizing. . .only recently has it dawned on me that as important as education, perhaps even more important is the work life of the individual since everybody works. . .The industrial situation may serve as the new laboratory for the study of psychodynamics, of higher human development, of ideal ecology for the human being.[3]

When many people think of Maslow, they typically think of the pyramid of needs. But Maslow never actually drew a pyramid.[4] A static pyramid where needs are stacked upon one another, the climb to the top a measure of fulfillment, departs significantly from Maslow's concept of the journey of self-actualization. Maslow, a developmental psychologist at heart, repeatedly emphasized the nonlinear nature of human development.[5] Adaptation, he believed, requires going back and forth between needs.[6]

A better metaphor for self-actualization is a sailboat charting its course in the vast unknown of the sea.[7] (See Figure I.1.) The boat itself represents security: safety, connection, and self-esteem. When these human needs are deficient, attention shifts to the boat simply to make sure that it doesn't sink. But just being secure will not take you anywhere. Eventually you will have to open the sail and move with a sense of creative exploration, love, and purpose. Opening the sail is inherently vulnerable because it means you're moving in the great unknown of the sea, with ever-changing winds and tides. But that's life. Our need to grow is just as important as our need for security. In order to grow, we must learn to adapt.

If we're really lucky, we can even enter a transcendent flow state of consciousness where we feel a profound connection to the world, a state where what is good for you is automatically good for the world. Maslow called it synergy. The flow state is a beautiful place to be, often arising when we feel secure *and* when we are growing into our higher potential.

Introduction: Toward a Human-Centered Future

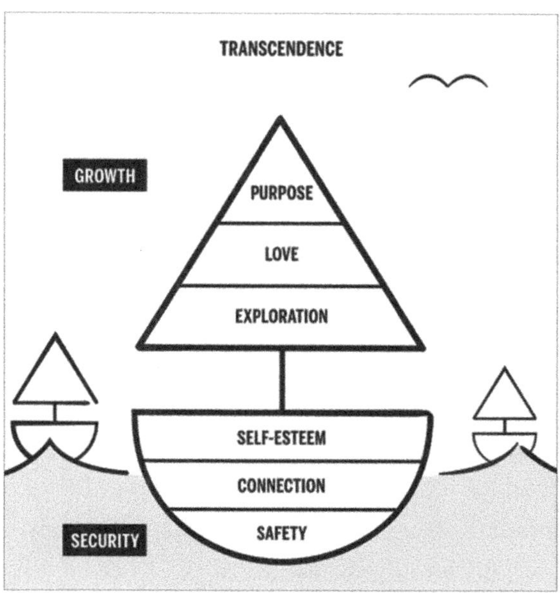

Figure I.1 The Sailboat Metaphor of Human Needs

Maslow's vision of humanistic leadership emphasized that humans want more than just security. They need to grow and seek transcendence. To ignore those needs is to strip the workplace of humanity and severely limit its potential to change the world for the better.

This, then, is the new mandate for leadership: to become a catalyst for human achievement, trusting that better humans create better workplaces.

Leading for Tomorrow

The emerging model of leadership enables humans to perform under dynamic conditions. This requires new priorities and competencies:

- **Shift in mindset.** In uncertain times—and face it, all times are uncertain now—leaders must create the conditions for collaboration and adaptability. Trust, empathy, and psychological safety

Introduction: Toward a Human-Centered Future

must become the infrastructure of human performance, serving as the safe base to tap a diversity of talents and strengths.

- **Address multiple human needs.** Recognize that humans need creative exploration, love, purpose, and even transcendent experiences, such as flow and peak experiences.

- **Centering purpose.** A clear and well-articulated purpose aligns values and goals and enables teams to make effective and autonomous decisions and respond to rapidly shifting conditions.

- **Learning as core competence.** Organizations must learn at the speed of change, and leaders must foster the curiosity, experimentation, and vulnerability to reflect on and incorporate new and emerging ideas.

- **Resilience as performance metric.** The true measure of performance is not output but *recovery*—how quickly and creatively a team can bounce back, reframe problems, and find new paths forward.

Across these pages, readers will discover fresh perspectives and practical wisdom for creating workplaces where human flourishing is not only possible but prioritized. The contributors illuminate a path toward a human value economy, in which organizations thrive because their people do. As you journey through these chapters, you'll find that to lead for tomorrow is to champion the possibilities within each of us, forging a future where exceptional achievement and collective well-being go hand in hand. This is leadership for the new world, a world that demands nothing less than our humanity, courage, and imagination.

This is a profound reorientation. It redefines leadership from an act of *control* to an act of *curation*. The leader's role is to design and sustain environments where people can do their best thinking and most meaningful work—spaces of trust, challenge, and shared purpose.

Introduction: Toward a Human-Centered Future

The Human Frontier of Value

As technology takes over more of what humans once did, the differentiating factor will be what technology cannot do: **build trust, imagine possibility, and find meaning in uncertainty.** The next great business advantage will not come from algorithms or automation but from *the depth and quality of human collaboration.*

This insight reframes leadership as a profoundly human act. In a world driven by data and disruption, leaders must reassert what makes organizations truly alive: empathy, creativity, and shared purpose. The goal is not to resist technology or rapid change but to humanize both to ensure that the systems we build amplify human potential rather than diminish it.

Notes

1. Douglas McGregor, *The Human Side of Enterprise* (McGraw-Hill, 1960).
2. Scott Barry Kaufman, *Transcend: The New Science of Self-Actualization* (TarcherPerigee, 2020); A. H. Maslow, *The Farther Reaches of Human Nature* (Penguin, 1993/1971).
3. Abraham H. Maslow, *Eupsychian Management: A Journal* (Richard D. Irwin, and the Dorsey Press, 1965), p. 6.
4. Todd Bridgman, Stephen Cummings, and John A. Ballard, "Who Built Maslow's Pyramid? A History of the Creation of Management Studies' Most Famous Symbol and Its Implications for Management Education," *Academy of Management Learning and Education* (April 2018): 18. doi.org/10.5465/amle.2017.0351
5. Andrew M. Bland and Eugene M. DeRobertis, "Maslow's Unacknowledged Contributions to Developmental Psychology," *Journal of Humanistic Psychology* 60, no. 6 (2017): 934–958. doi.org/10.1177/0022167817739732
6. Abraham H. Maslow, *Motivation and Personality* (Harper & Row, 1954).
7. Kaufman, *Transcend*, pp. xxxiii–xxxv.

Chapter 1

The Human Touch: Why Leadership Still Matters Most

Tom Kelley

Growing up near Akron, Ohio, one of my summer jobs was working the night shift at Oak Rubber, a factory boldly claiming to be "the world's largest manufacturer of toy balloons."[1] My boss there was never mean to me, but he was also never motivational. At the start of my first midnight shift, he explained that I must make no less than my quota of 1,800 toy footballs each night; my coworkers urged me not to make *more* than 1,800. My foreman was perfectly adequate for the job of supervising me, and I made my quota every day by 8 am.

If "adequate" is good enough, and your work never changes, maybe you don't need human-centered leadership. But if your company aims higher, the right kind of leadership makes all the difference. After seeing a wide range of leadership styles across more than a thousand client organizations during my career at IDEO, I found that human-centered leaders are the ones best equipped to help organizations learn and innovate at the pace of change.

> Human-centered leaders are the ones best equipped to help organizations learn and innovate at the pace of change.

What makes a human-centered leader? The question is best answered by example and by contrasting such leaders with other, very different management styles. I sincerely hope you have had firsthand experience with human-centered leaders who are distinguished by the cultures they create around them. They lead with empathy in a way that enhances employee engagement and loyalty. They enable team members to speak up without fear of punishment or repercussion. They listen with care and then lead with confidence. They inspire others to do their best, most creative work. They model integrity and purpose. Even at moments when you disagree, they still convey a sense of being on your side.

Those characteristics may seem universally desirable, and yet most of us have also dealt with managers or coaches with polar opposite leadership styles: tyrants, taskmasters, narcissists, or weak managers who are just muddling through.

That old balloon factory faded away, and tasks like the ones at Oak Rubber have been offshored or outsourced to robots and algorithms. Now, decades later, artificial intelligence promises to be even more disruptive than offshoring and automation, opening the door to both threats and opportunities.

A couple of years ago, *Wired* produced a thought-provoking video titled "A.I. Tries 20 Jobs," featuring people from 20 different careers as they each did a self-assessment of how vulnerable their jobs were to encroachment from AI.[2] One by one, they looked into the camera and explained why they thought their job would be safe for the moment. An advertising copywriter showed how a ChatGPT response couldn't quite match her at writing the tagline for a new product. A graphic designer compared her own logo design favorably to AI-generated versions. A translator pointed to subtle flaws in the current AI translations. Even at the time, however, their jobs seemed more vulnerable than they realized. Only the firefighter and

2

Leading for Tomorrow

the circus performer seemed truly safe from AI, and even the firefighter should already be looking over his shoulder at the firefighting robots and drones racing to encroach on his job.

Leadership as a Future-Proof Skill

In the short time since that video was made, I have experienced dozens of worried conversations in which people are wondering: "Will my job survive?" A better question might be: "Which human qualities can't easily be replaced by AI?" There's a lot of speculation on this topic, and of course, no one—including me—can claim to have the definitive answers. My current take, however, is that there are a handful of human-centered leadership skills that can improve your chances of surviving and succeeding in the age of AI.

- *Inspiring a shared vision.* AI can't instill passion, create purpose, or cultivate a company culture where people genuinely care about their work. Nor can it make people feel connected to a company's mission. As a human-centered leader, you can paint a positive picture of the future with your ideas in it.

- *Building trust.* Trust is an essential element of thriving organizations. AI can provide unbiased analysis, but it cannot build relationships, mend conflicts, or create a culture of psychological safety.

- *Making tough decisions.* AI is a powerful tool for synthesizing mountains of data and generating recommendations. But good leaders also understand the human emotions, diplomacy, and moral dilemmas that play a role in making the final call.

- *Managing through a crisis.* When crises hit, employees don't look to AI for guidance; they look to their leaders.

The Human Touch: Why Leadership Still Matters Most

- ***Developing people.*** AI will inevitably automate many tasks, but it cannot develop the leaders of tomorrow. And when AI does encroach on many jobs, leaders can create pathways for reskilling the people affected.

- ***Making employees feel valued, trusted, and motivated.*** A human-centered leader can look someone in the eye at the end of a tough project and say, "I believe in you." Such leaders can also be present at times of need and roll up their sleeves to help at critical moments.

So, what does this future-proof human-centered leadership look like in practice? I found answers in one-on-one interviews with remarkably human-centered leaders, including a Fortune 50 CEO, an expert in professional development, and the inspirational founder of a life-changing nonprofit.

First, however, here's a story closer to home:

Straight out of college, my son Sean began his career as a mechanical engineer at Varian Medical Systems in Palo Alto, working on advanced technologies for cancer care. His job there had special meaning for our family because Varian's radiation oncology machines had helped save my brother's life during a long and scary cancer journey. One day, his boss unexpectedly called Sean into his office for a conversation. Although Sean liked his boss, the sudden meeting made him wonder if he was in trouble. He wasn't. His manager said something like this:

> Sean, this may sound funny to you, but your happiness is important to me. You represent the next generation of leaders here, and I want to help you on that path. So, let's make a social contract between the two of us that you won't come into my office a few years from now and say you're leaving because one thing is annoying you or

another thing is frustrating you. If things start to annoy or frustrate you, let's agree that you'll come to me *first*, before it gets to be too much, and we can fix it together, so that you can continue to be happy and energized here.

That one-on-one conversation with a promising young employee exemplified the best of human-centered leadership. The older man didn't speak about the company's metrics or even his own expectations, though both the senior leader and the young engineer knew that those were essential. Sean's boss centered the whole proposal on Sean, and the two of them exchanged promises. Although I never met that leader, I greatly admired him, and almost a decade later, I borrowed his idea to make a similar social contract with a young, wise-beyond-his-years venture capitalist at D4V, our Tokyo-based VC firm.

Lessons from Remarkable Leaders

As I set out to write a chapter about human-centered leadership, the first senior leader who came to mind was Jim Hackett, former CEO of Ford Motor Company. As much as any CEO I have ever met, Hackett both appreciated the value of human-centered design and practiced the art of human-centered leadership. In his previous role as CEO of Steelcase, Hackett had an open-door policy that allowed anyone in the company the possibility of bringing an issue to his attention. Looking at each individual topic of those meetings, some might have seemed trivial, but at a macro level, the open door signaled that Hackett was approachable and willing to listen. Throughout Steelcase's history prior to Jim becoming CEO, the company had been family-owned and operated, so Hackett's approachability preserved that same spirit, even inside a publicly traded company.

Hackett always emphasized that integrity was an essential element of human-centered leadership. Shortly after meeting him decades ago,

The Human Touch: Why Leadership Still Matters Most

he handed me a book on ethical management and emphasized the importance of doing the right thing. "People don't have to agree with you," Hackett explained, "They don't even have to like you. But if you have deep integrity, they will still follow your lead." He mentioned the name of a prominent Fortune 500 CEO who blamed employees whenever the business results were bad. By contrast, Hackett felt his role was not to put people in their place but to help them thrive.

Having been a strong advocate for human-centered design both at Steelcase and Ford, Hackett has immersed himself in the world of AI, even advising executives on the topic, in working sessions he calls "CEO Labs." Drawing a connection between human-centered design and AI, Jim says that it used to be enough to design products or experiences with a human-centered perspective, but with the growing influence of AI, we should be designing systems for human agency. In other words, he believes leaders should design the organization to engage the capabilities of AI while still having humans at the center, like conductors of a complex symphony that includes both human and AI resources.

> Leaders should design the organization to engage the capabilities of AI while still having humans at the center.

When asked about success stories from his own CEO leadership roles, Hackett modestly shifted the focus to other human-centered leaders. Hackett, a former college athlete and athletic director of the University of Michigan,[3] immediately thought of fellow athlete Junior Bridgeman, an NBA player who went on to even greater success in food and beverage businesses. After retiring from the NBA, Bridgeman started buying Wendy's restaurant franchises, growing his business year by year until he amassed more than 400 fast food outlets.[4] By then, he was a wealthy entrepreneur, but as Hackett reports, you could still drop into a Wendy's and find Bridgeman flipping burgers.

If the owner of hundreds of restaurants shows up to work the grill, what signal does that send to the team? It says he still understands the business, all the way down to the grassroots level. In the process, he becomes more familiar to the employees, not just some faceless boss whom they have never met. It also lets people know that he remembers what it's like to be a regular guy, born the son of a steelworker in the Midwest.

On the basketball court, Bridgeman had been a solid player, more often serving as the sixth man coming off the bench than as a starter for the team. In his role as a leader and entrepreneur, however, he was a superstar. In the long history of the NBA, only four players have ever become billionaires. Three of them are household names: Michael Jordan, Magic Johnson, and LeBron James. The fourth was Junior Bridgeman.[5]

Cultivating Human Potential

The late Sir Ken Robinson never ran a Fortune 500 company, yet his ideas about learning and development have influenced leaders and educators around the world. Among his many accomplishments, Robinson is best known for his iconic 2006 TED Talk, "Do Schools Kill Creativity?"[6] Watched more than 100 million times, it is the most-viewed talk in TED's history.[7] Two decades later, the talk still holds up remarkably well, losing none of its original impact.

Watch even the first 60 seconds of Robinson's presentation, and you encounter a human-centered thought leader with an extraordinary ability to build rapport and trust. He takes the stage as a stranger to most people in the room, yet within his opening moments he has the audience firmly on his side. His warmth, humor, and humility are not performance tricks. They are expressions of how he understands people. In that talk and throughout his later career, Robinson focused primarily on K–12 education. Yet his message for the business world is both relevant and unmistakable: Leaders create living ecosystems in which people either flourish or quietly shut down.

"There are lots of different styles of leadership," Robinson once observed. "If you were just after efficiency, then you may need to go into command-and-control mode."[8] But he was adamant that this logic breaks down when the goal shifts to innovation or cultural transformation. In those moments, he argued, the leader's job is not simply to tell people what to do. Leadership may include direction, but great leaders also create what he called a climate of possibility, an environment where people feel safe to experiment, challenge assumptions, and discover capabilities they didn't know they possessed. Creating a climate of possibility may be Robinson's most concise articulation of human-centered leadership.

When I interviewed Robinson years ago near his home in Los Angeles, he displayed the same warmth and authenticity millions have witnessed in his talks. I never had the opportunity to ask him about the leaders who shaped his early life, but in later public interviews he shared a telling example. As a teenager in the United Kingdom, Robinson was unexpectedly asked to direct a school play. "It had never crossed my mind that I could direct a play," he recalled. But a high school teacher saw latent potential and nudged him toward the role. "Sometimes other people see in you things you don't recognize in yourself," Robinson reflected. "They can see a strength or ability that you didn't know you had."[9]

The play was a success, and decades later Robinson still spoke of the experience with gratitude.[10] That long-ago teacher was demonstrating human-centered leadership in microcosm: taking a risk on another person, expanding what was possible, and quietly changing the trajectory of a career and a life.

8

Leading for Tomorrow

Leading with Empathy

Interviewing executives for this chapter, I often asked them who comes to mind when they think of human-centered leaders. Over lunch at Café Borrone in the heart of Silicon Valley, I asked that question of Greg Warman, cofounder at Toronto-based ExperiencePoint, one of the world's leading experiential training companies.[11] I was pleasantly surprised when the first person he mentioned was a senior leader at my firm, IDEO.

Warman is very skilled at leading lively, interactive workshops, and one day several years ago, he was hosting an all-day event at IDEO's San Francisco office. There was just one problem. The printed handout materials for his workshop were nowhere to be found, and his clients would be showing up at any minute. Just then, an IDEO partner was passing by and noticed that something was up. "Are you OK, Greg?" the partner asked. "Not really," replied Warman, and explained his predicament.

With time running short, the IDEO partner urged Warman to get started while he searched for the missing materials. Warman took a leap of faith, starting a high-stakes workshop while still unsure how he would finish it. Luckily for all parties, the IDEO leader showed up in time, carrying the boxes of handouts. Warman said that, for him, that whole sequence of events epitomized human-centered leadership. "It wasn't only that he delivered the crucial materials just in time," Warman explained. "It was that he noticed my problem in the first place. He had enough empathy to sense that I needed help, and he cared enough to ask 'Are you OK?' He took time on a busy day to make my problem his own. The world needs more leaders like that."

Empowering Future Leaders

My last interview was with Emily Pilloton-Lam, an architectural designer, author, TED speaker, educator, and nonprofit founder. Pilloton-Lam gained a surge of public attention when she was the

The Human Touch: Why Leadership Still Matters Most

focus of the documentary film *If You Build It*, about an innovative design program she created for high school students in rural North Carolina.[12] By then, however, she had already started a design firm, written her first book,[13] appeared on late-night TV, and traveled 6,000 miles in her Airstream trailer to share her unique design exhibit with schools across America—all before she turned 30.[14] Pilloton-Lam is now the founder and executive director at Girls Garage, a nonprofit design and construction program that helps students aged 9 to 18 build not only their skills but also their confidence.[15]

Pilloton-Lam emphasized the idea that leaders can be found everywhere, regardless of the organizational structure or the power dynamics. As she put it in a June 19, 2025, interview with me, "The people that I think of as leaders in my own life are pretty quiet about it. I don't even know whether they self-identify as leaders." If a leader is simply someone who helps make others successful, then there's room for all of us to be leaders in our own way. At Girls Garage, Pilloton-Lam feels the need to pay attention to the tiny details of every individual while simultaneously crafting her vision for the whole organization. She values both granular and global views, knowing that the small details shape the big picture.

> Leaders can be found everywhere, regardless of the organizational structure or the power dynamics.

I've had the honor of working with many human-centered leaders in my life, but Pilloton-Lam takes her leadership one step further than any I have ever met. More than 1,000 students have gone through the Girls Garage program so far, and Pilloton-Lam feels connected to all of them. In her farewell address to graduating seniors, Pilloton-Lam tells students to "open your phone and make sure you have my number. If you need me, even at 2 am, *you call me*. No judgment."

And they do call, on an incredible range of topics, including "Can I use you as a reference for my first apartment?" Sometimes her

Leading for Tomorrow

alumni have big questions, like "Should I stick with my first job, even if my boss is a little toxic?" And sometimes the questions are much narrower, like "I'm at Home Depot. Can you remind me of the name of the screws we use?" Emily Pilloton-Lam patiently answers them all, taking human-centered leadership to a whole new level.

An Early Role Model for Business and Life

Like many kids in my generation, I looked up to my father as a primary role model for business leadership. My siblings and I got to witness his work ethic at home and to sense the importance he placed on doing a good job, but we never actually got to see him in action at Goodyear Aerospace because of security restrictions at his plant. Halfway through his career, however, the company magazine featured him in a profile that gave me the first glimpse of what he was like at work:

> *Getting James Bernard Kelley to talk about himself is not easy. One way or the other, Jim keeps shifting the talk toward the nearly 400 engineers, scientists, technicians, and administrators who make up his division. Ask him what he's doing, and he tells you what they've done.*[16]

The profile clearly suggested that he was a human-centered leader, and more confirmation followed decades later, at the end of his career. When Dad retired after 38 years with the company, Goodyear celebrated his achievements with a 20-page booklet titled "A Gifted Leader with the Human Touch." The long tribute wrapped up with a description of his management style:

> *Jim also played another equally memorable leadership role during his years at Goodyear. Throughout it all, he maintained a remarkable human touch and was richly endowed*

> *with a concern, compassion, and caring for people. This*
> *role endeared him in the hearts of all his associates, and for*
> *this, he will always be treasured.*[17]

As my father's career ended and the heart of my own began, Goodyear's profile of him inspired me to seek my own path to human-centered leadership.

Leaders Who Matter

With every leap forward in AI, new possibilities emerge, sparking predictions of the future that range from utopian to apocalyptic. Talking with human-centered leaders has given me cause for optimism, pointing toward the possibility that we can use artificial intelligence to amplify the best of human capabilities. The leaders who will matter most tomorrow may be the ones who care most today: the ones who know how to read the room, who show up with empathy, who act with integrity, who unlock hidden talents in their people. If you can be an effective human-centered leader, you can thrive in the age of AI and help shape a brighter future.

Notes

1. *Ravenna, Ohio: Rich in History with an Eye to the Future, Business View Magazine* (February 2023): p. 4.i. https://businessviewmagazine .com/brochures/feb-2023/Ravenna-OH/12/
2. *A.I. Tries 20 Jobs* [Video], *Wired*, March 17, 2023. www.wired.com/ video/watch/ai-tries-20-jobs
3. Anthony Broome, "MNB: Hackett Repaired U-M During His Short Tenure," *Detroit Free Press*, December 7, 2015. www.freep.com/story/ sports/college/university-michigan/wolverines/2015/12/07/jim-hackett-michigan-football/76928280/

4. Mary Vinnedge, "From NBA to Fast-Food Empire: Junior Bridgeman Dies at 71," *Franchise Wire*, March 18, 2025. www.franchisewire.com/from-nba-to-fast-food-empire-junior-bridgeman-dies-at-71/

5. Richard Sandomir, "Junior Bridgeman, N.B.A. Player Turned Mogul, Dies at 71," *New York Times*, March 15, 2025. www.nytimes.com/2025/03/15/sports/basketball/junior-bridgeman-dead.html

6. Sir Ted Robinson, "Do Schools Kill Creativity?," TED2006, February 2006. www.ted.com/talks/sir_ken_robinson_do_schools_kill_creativity

7. TED Talks, "Do Schools Kill Creativity?" by Sir Ken Robinson, YouTube [Video], January 7, 2007.

8. HundrED, "Sir Ken Robinson Compares Human Organisations to Organisms: Education Is a Dynamic System," 2017 Innovation Summit, April 3, 2017. https://hundred.org/en/articles/5-sir-ken-robinson-compares-human-organisations-to-organisms-education-is-a-dynamic-system

9. Ibid.

10. Tim Bogatz, "An Interview with Sir Ken Robinson," *Art Ed Radio*, June 6, 2017 (Audio podcast episode 68). https://theartofeducation.edu/podcasts/interview-sir-ken-robinson-ep-068/

11. Training Industry, "Announcing the 2024 Training Industry Top Training Companies Lists: Experiential Learning Technologies," August 29, 2024. https://trainingindustry.com/top-training-companies/learning-technologies/top-experiential-learning-technologies-companies/

12. *If You Build It* [Film], directed by Patrick Creadon, produced by Christiene O'Malley and Neal Baer (2013). O'Malley Creadon Productions. https://ocpmedia.com/project/if-you-build-it/

13. Emily Pilloton, *Design Revolution: 100 Products That Empower People* (Metropolis Books, 2009).

14. "Live@ICFF: Emily Pilloton's Design Revolution Road Show," *Metropolis*, May 15, 2010. https://metropolismag.com/programs/liveicff-emily-pillotons-design-revolution-road-show/

15. "Emily Pilloton-Lam," Girls Garage Team, n.d. https://girlsgarage.org/about/team/emily-pilloton-2/

The Human Touch: Why Leadership Still Matters Most

16. "A Study in Motion," *Profile*, Goodyear Aerospace Corporation, 1968, p. 18.

17. "A Gifted Leader with the Human Touch" [Unpublished corporate booklet], Goodyear Aerospace Corporation, 1987, p. 19.

Chapter 2

Extraordinary Possibility in Extraordinary Times

Scott D. Anthony

On June 7, 2025, Matt Slaughter, the dean of the Tuck School of Business at Dartmouth College (where I teach), stood before the graduating class of 2025. The nonstop rain felt appropriate for the world the newly minted MBAs would enter, one in which technological disruptions coupled with the shredding of rules and norms governing the global economy for the past 80 years meant spiraling uncertainty that bordered on the edge of constant chaos.

Despite the weather, Slaughter struck an optimistic note appropriate for a graduation.

> The world today stands at the crossroads of extraordinary possibility: advances of artificial intelligence, the interdependence of global systems and the persistent challenges of fractured trust and deep social divides that are all reshaping societies in real time. In this dynamic landscape, you, the wise and decisive leaders of tomorrow, are called to not only apply your hard-earned knowledge but also to steward your communities and institutions, with vision, with integrity, and with care. Go be awesome.[1]

The "crossroads of extraordinary possibility" graduates face, however, is one shrouded by a deep, dense fog. Technologies are advancing exponentially; lines between industries are blurring; expectations of consumers, employees, and stakeholders are shifting; and global shocks are happening with increased frequency. It is the era of predictable unpredictability, where yesterday's strengths become tomorrow's weaknesses.

In this fog, the would-be wise, decisive leader must confront complex challenges that feel paradoxical. Protect the present and create the future. Enable empowerment and autonomy and decisively lead in new directions. Build a high-performance meritocracy and provide equitable opportunities. *In the fog, it's hard to know right from wrong.*

When we encounter fog while driving, we slow down. If it is too dense, we stop and wait for it to pass. Today's world demands that we accelerate.

In the fog, leaders need the wisdom to see the invisible and the decisiveness to let go.

The Wisdom to See the Invisible

Wisdom. Experience. Knowledge. Good judgment. These take time to develop in stable times. Doing so requires something different in uncertain times. It requires being able to see things that otherwise would be invisible.

The fog of uncertainty presents two unique challenges.

First, leaders face the information-action paradox. By the time there is enough data to justify a decision, it is too late to act. Leaders are told that change requires a burning platform, but by the time the platform is on fire, it is too late. That means leaders need to do something equally paradoxical: They need to act when the data tells them not to.

That doesn't mean they should *ignore* data. Rather, that means they need to seek out early warning signs of change and amplify those signals using a good model or framework.

That's exactly what Berkeley Cox and Michelle Mahoney did when they were leading a change initiative at the Australian arm of King & Wood Mallesons (KWM), a leading global law firm. By all external measures, in 2018 KWM Australia looked healthy. However, Cox, the organization's leader at the time, had a sense that important forces promised dramatic change over the medium and long term.

He asked Mahoney, who led KWM's innovation team, to investigate further.

"Lawyers are risk-averse by nature," Cox said. "That's why they're good at what they do. They also look for perfect information to make decisions, but in this environment, as in many environments, information is not perfect."[2]

Mahoney and a small team (that received support from Innosight, a consulting company where I worked at the time) looked beyond traditional data like revenue and client satisfaction. They interviewed clients to find "near misses" where clients considered but ultimately chose not to switch to an emerging technology provider. They investigated early-stage startups. They ran surveys of frontline lawyers. They looked at more granular cuts of revenue and saw that there was erosion in customer segments that often are susceptible to more disruptive offerings.

Using Clayton Christensen's disruptive innovation model (see "Disruptive Innovation" at the end of the chapter) allowed the team to amplify these weak signals, because they fit past patterns that suggested a high likelihood of significant change. In the end, publicly available data suggested staying the course; the unique data KWM unearthed suggested sweeping changes.

KWM made the decision to infuse technology like artificial intelligence in the practice of law well before it was obvious to the broader market. The decision allowed it to significantly outpace its competitors and prepare it for the wave of technological change that affected the industry in earnest over the past few years.

17

Extraordinary Possibility in Extraordinary Times

Second, leaders face the challenge that their teams are often less aligned than they think. Research led by Don Sull at MIT shows that only 50 percent of top management teams can even *name* their organizations top three priorities, showing a stunning lack of leadership alignment.[3] What's behind the data? A range of individual and group biases mean that individuals aren't sharing their real feelings in group settings.

> A wise leader listens to the voice that doesn't speak.

A wise leader listens to the voice that doesn't speak. That starts with following practices that surface divergent opinions. Back when I was at Innosight, we pioneered a technique called a strategic sparring session designed to do just this.[4] Just like a boxer uses a sparring session to get fighting fit, a strategic sparring session allows dynamic exchanges of discordant ideas.

The intent of a strategic sparring session is to bring lingering disagreements to the surface. It doesn't seek to get false alignment; it seeks to pinpoint where there is the sharpest misalignment to focus further research and experimentation.

It sounds emotionally wrought, but it doesn't have to be. One trick is to shift from battles of beliefs to battles of assumptions.

A battle of beliefs generally involves people starting statements with phrases such as, "I think" and "I believe." Battles of beliefs are personal. Someone wins and someone loses.

A battle of assumptions, on the other hand, involves people starting statements with phrases such as, "What must be true is," "The critical assumption is," or "The data suggests that." In psychological terms, this shift splits an individual from an argument. The assumptions can have fierce fights without any personal repercussions.

Another technique that surfaces disagreement is called walk the line. The idea, which draws on cognitive science research into the impact of motion on thinking, is to make disagreement visible. Here's an example from one of my MBA classes.

A divisive topic at Tuck relates to the culture. Tuck has a relatively small, full-time MBA program with about 300 students per class. Nestled in a bucolic portion of New England, the closest major city is more than two hours away. There is strong cohesion among students who all choose to spend two years in this remote setting. One of the social norms goes by the name "Tuck Nice."

The positive side of this norm is students caring for and helping each other. The perceived downside to it is a lack of direct confrontation and passive aggressive behavior, which can stunt the kind of productive disagreement that spurs fresh thinking.

Students used a polling app to rate the degree to which they agreed with the statement "Tuck Kind should replace Tuck Nice" on a scale of 1 (highly disagree) to 7 (highly agree).

The average score was 4.33, with 31 percent of students giving a 1 or 2 and 13 percent of students giving a 6 or 7.

I then asked for student volunteers for each of the numbers. Seven students came to the front of the room and stood on a place on a line representing their answer. Everyone could see exactly where they stood. I then went down the line and asked students to share the rationale for why they were standing where they were standing without using the pronoun "I" to encourage battles of assumptions not beliefs.

Students shared different definitions, assumptions about how niceness might be more expectations-oriented and kindness more empathy-oriented, results from student surveys, and recent research that showed too much niceness blunts psychological safety. The rest of the class had a chance to adjust their votes in real time. About 20 percent of students revised their answers. The average score of those students was 3.80, with 40 percent giving a 1 or 2 and 20 percent

Extraordinary Possibility in Extraordinary Times

giving a 6 or 7. There was no clear answer, but that wasn't the point. The point was to see where people stood, and why.

Walk the line is a powerful technique. Practitioners should keep three tips in mind. First, ask people to cast their vote first before they physically array on the line. Otherwise, they are more susceptible to groupthink. Second, have the top senior leaders either go last or act as observers, lest the hierarchy bias impact people. Third, plan to run it at least twice. The first run sets a research and experimentation agenda. Let the assumptions battle before seeking convergence.

Remember, *you can't hear the voice that doesn't speak unless your ears are open.* In 2020, I had a chance to interview one of my heroes: Ed Catmull, the cofounder of Pixar. Catmull is one of the most successful leaders of his generation (and one of the early members of the Silicon Guild). He's won multiple Academy Awards. He won the Turing Award for his pioneering work on computer animation. He led Pixar through a stunning run of successful movies and, after Disney acquired Pixar in 2006, helped to revive Disney's legendary animation studio. It would be easy for that run of success to convince Catmull he was always right.

Far from it.

"I realized that about two thirds of the things that I tried to do were right and one third of them just were wrong," Catmull told me. "It is very good for leaders just to say to themselves, 'I'm experienced, I'm here for a reason, but a third of what I'm thinking, or what I believe, is a complete crock.'"[5]

He went to note the importance of listening.

"What it did for me was to walk into meetings and say, 'OK, I might be wrong,'" he said. "So, I have to listen."

Acting when the data tells you not to and hearing the voice that doesn't speak allows a wise leader to see what would otherwise be invisible forces, setting the stage for decisive action.

20

Leading for Tomorrow

The Decisiveness to Let Go

A decisive leader makes effective decisions around tough issues. Should we invest in this product or that one? Respond to this shareholder or that one? Promote this person or that one? Provide incentives to individuals or teams?

In the fog, the most critical decision a leader makes is what *not* to do.

It starts with their own involvement in decisions. An important and undervalued decision is about which decisions a leader will participate in personally and which decisions are best taken by other people in the organization.

In his 2015 letter to shareholders, Amazon.com founder Jeff Bezos drew an important distinction between two very different types of decisions.[6] Some decisions are high stakes, complex, once-in-a-generation decisions. They are, in essence, one-way doors, so Amazon calls them "Type 1" decisions.

Because they are "consequential and irreversible," Bezos noted, they "must be made methodically, carefully, slowly with great deliberation and consultation." Senior leaders need to be deeply involved in these decisions.

Most decisions, in contrast, are low stakes, straightforward, day-to-day decisions that are safely made quickly, even automatically, by "high judgment" individuals or small teams. These "Type 2" decisions are two-way doors where, Bezos wrote, "if you've made a suboptimal . . . decision, you don't have to live with the consequences for that long."

The challenge, Bezos noted, is that larger organizations tend to follow the same heavyweight process for all decisions. "The end result of this," he wrote, "is slowness, unthoughtful risk aversion, failure to experiment sufficiently, and consequently diminished invention."

How Tuck thinks about new courses and new teaching methods demonstrates how to avoid this trap.

Extraordinary Possibility in Extraordinary Times

A major revision to the core curriculum, which every first-year MBA student goes through, is a Type 1 decision. That would, appropriately, be a slow process, involving Dean Slaughter and other senior leaders.

Adding an elective course is a Type 2 decision. There, a small group of academic leaders quickly (but carefully) considers course proposals by faculty. If the course goes badly, various feedback mechanisms will catch it quickly, and the course will be sunset. Minimal damage done.

A few years ago, to encourage faculty experimentation, Tuck adopted an even speedier two-way door: a "sprint" format. Where a full-term class has 18 90-minute sessions, a sprint class is four-and-a-half hours of instruction split however the instructor deems appropriate. Classes are graded credit/no credit. Sprints have included decision biases in professional basketball, the pricing of wine, and using generative AI as a consultant (I designed and taught that one).

In-classroom shifts, such as adding a new reading or activity or using AI in a different way, are left in the hands of individual professors, subject to basic guidelines and principles.

This thoughtful approach allows Tuck to be structured where it needs to be and experimental where it must be. If a 125-year-old business school can do it, any organization can.

Scott Cook, the cofounder and still-active board member at Intuit, a leading financial services company, goes even further. When he served as board chair, he viewed his role as the "experimenter-in-chief." That meant his role when Intuit was exploring new opportunities was to *not* make decisions.

Cook observes that when you innovate, no one knows what the right answer is. And a leader of today's business often lacks intuition about new and uncertain territory. Therefore, the job of the leader isn't to make decisions; it is to encourage experiments that surface the direction in which to go.

"We teach our leaders that it's your job to put in the systems that enable your people to run your experiments fast and cheap and to keep making them faster and cheaper," Cook said. "Yield as many of your decisions off to the experiment as possible."[7]

In the fog, sometimes you lead by letting go. Sometimes that's not just of decisions, but of entire pieces of the business.

> In the fog, sometimes you lead by letting go.

In 2010, Mark Parker was early into what turned into a hugely successful run as CEO of Nike. At a conference that year, he described receiving a congratulatory call from the legendary Steve Jobs. Parker asked Jobs for advice. At first, Jobs resisted, saying he was just calling to offer his congratulations. Parker pushed, and Jobs relented.

"Nike makes some of the best products in the world," Parker said Jobs told him. "Products that you lust after. Absolutely beautiful, stunning products. But you also make a lot of crap. Just get rid of the crappy stuff and focus on the good stuff."

Parker told his audience, "I expected a little pause and a laugh. There was a pause but no laugh. He was absolutely right."[8]

The mythology of Steve Jobs centers on *Jobs the Creator* who took Apple to new heights with the introduction of the iPod, iPhone, iPad and the revolutionary App Store. We forget that what enabled this was *Jobs the Destroyer*. When Jobs came back to serve as the CEO of Apple in the late 1990s, his first act wasn't to create new products and services; it was to winnow down Apple's product portfolio to create capacity to innovate and grow.

Get rid of the crappy stuff and focus on the good stuff. It sounds so easy. But it can be painfully hard for a company to stop a project that has champions and supporters, and even harder for it to shed a part of the business that was part of its heritage.

One of the most powerful rituals to help with this is one followed by Finnish gaming company Supercell. Every time a team successfully launches a new game, everyone gets together and

Extraordinary Possibility in Extraordinary Times

cracks open a beer. Every time a team admits defeat and decides to shut down, everyone gets together and pops a bottle of champagne. The "reward" for the failure is greater than the reward for success.

Saying cheers to failure has two clear benefits. First, it shows that a good, not bad, thing has happened, encouraging other teams to continue to push frontiers. Second, it shows that the effort is finished. Many organizations suffer from what I call zombie projects.[9] The walking undead. Projects that everyone knows will not move the needle, but they shuffle and linger on, sucking all of the life out of the organization. Saying cheers to failure stops zombies from spawning.

Leaders who decide to remove themselves from some decisions and say cheers to failure set their organization up for future success.

The Extraordinary Possibility in the Great Unfreezing

One of the pillars of change management is a three-stage model attributed to German American psychologist Kurt Lewin, who did his work in the 1930s and 1940s. At any given time, the model goes, an organization is frozen. That is, it does things a certain way, and change is hard. Then the three stages: unfreezing (precipitated by a crisis or dynamic leader), change, and refreezing.

You can argue that the 2020s represent the Great Unfreezing. Where sure facts are revealed to be assumptions before becoming open questions. To push the model to its breaking point, the unfreezing is so profound that the phase change goes from solid (ice) to liquid (malleable water) to gas.

Not only is that gas hard, nigh impossible, to grab hold of, it adds to the dense fog that makes it even harder to determine what to do next.

But the Great Unfreezing also creates the extraordinary possibilities Slaughter mentioned on graduation day. Change of unprecedented scale is within a leader's grasp. It is a moment where leaders can refresh, reimagine, and reinvent their organizations.

That requires fresh thinking and innovation. That's hard.

Consider an example examined in detail in my book *Epic Disruptions*[10]: gunpowder. In 1620, Sir Francis Bacon said gunpowder—along with the printing press and the compass—was one of three technologies that changed the appearance and state of the whole world.

Gunpowder's coming-of-age moment was in 1453, when a cannon cast by a mysterious figure called Orban enabled the Ottoman Empire to topple the Theodosian Walls that had protected Constantinople for a millennium. The Byzantine Empire ended in the 47 days it took for the city to fall.

The first reference to gunpowder appears in *The Book of the Kinship of Three*—in 142. Its development over the centuries involved alchemists, blacksmiths, peasants, gunners, philosophers, and scientists. There were farmers and fighters experimenting with different uses. There were leaders allocating time and money and directing work. As one historian noted, success required the work of "daredevils, visionaries, madmen," many of whom found "not fortune but disfiguring burns and death."[11]

The burns are more metaphorical today, but they still sting. Doing new things is hard. Having things not work out as expected is painful. Innovators question the status quo. Some people inside organizations love it, some are indifferent to it, some actively seek to subvert or sabotage it. It casts a shadow.

Bring light to the shadow. When you see someone who is pushing against orthodoxy, who is driving change, look them in the eye,

25

shake their hand (or hug them if it is socially acceptable), and thank them for their work.

As ordinary as that seems, it helps to make the extraordinary possible.

Disruptive Innovation

Clayton Christensen discovered the concept of disruptive innovation during his doctoral research in the early 1990s. In 2022, *Harvard Business Review* named disruptive innovation one of the four most influential ideas in business history.

Across a vast literature examining disruptive change, three findings stand out.

Disruptive innovations drive transformational growth. At its core, a disruptive innovation transforms existing markets and creates new ones by making the complicated simple and the expensive affordable. Disruptive innovations range from gunpowder and the printing press to military drones and generative AI-driven coaches and therapists. Disruption is an engine of progress, transforming how we work, live, communicate, and play.

Market-leading incumbents underinvest in disruptive innovations for logical reasons. Companies tend to allocate resources toward opportunities that allow them to offer better performance to their best customers. A disruptive innovation trades off performance that historically mattered to mainstream customers to offer improvements on overlooked dimensions such as simplicity and price. Mainstream customers don't want inferior products, at least initially. So even if a company spots an opportunity to disrupt, its customers don't want it to do so.

The innovator's dilemma can be the innovator's opportunity. The innovator's dilemma is a failure of success. Market leaders do what they are supposed to do: Listen to their best customers, innovate to

26

meet their needs, push prices up, push margins up, and fail in the face of disruptive change. However, companies ranging from Microsoft to Schneider Electric have shown how the right leadership actions turn disruptive innovation from a threat to an opportunity.

Notes

1. Matthew J. Slaughter, "Speech—Dartmouth Tuck School of Business MBA Class of 2025 Investiture," June 7, 2025. www.youtube.com/watch?v=MTbrvVzRwyo

2. Pontus M. A. Siren, Scott D. Anthony, and Utsav Bhatt, "Persuade Your Company to Change Before It's Too Late," *Harvard Business Review* (January–February 2022). https://hbr.org/2022/01/persuade-your-company-to-change-before-its-too-late

3. Donald Sull, Charles Sull, and James Yoder, "No One Knows Your Strategy—Not Even Your Top Leaders," *MIT Sloan Management Review*, February 12, 2018. https://sloanreview.mit.edu/article/no-one-knows-your-strategy-not-even-your-top-leaders/

4. Scott D. Anthony, Natalie Painchaud, and Andy Parker, "Building Consensus Around Difficult Strategic Decisions," *Harvard Business Review*, October 27, 2023. https://hbr.org/2023/10/building-consensus-around-difficult-strategic-decisions

5. Ed Catmull, cofounder of Pixar, with Scott Anthony, *Eat, Sleep, Innovate: Virtual Book Club—Pixar's Ed Catmull on Creativity*, Innosight [Video], November 19, 2020. www.youtube.com/watch?v=Ts3C8fYgWgw

6. Jeffrey P. Bezos, 2015 Letter to Shareholders, Amazon.com, Inc. https://s2.q4cdn.com/299287126/files/doc_financials/annual/2015-Letter-to-Shareholders.PDF

7. Drake Baker and Scott Cook, "Why Intuit Founder Scott Cook Wants You to Stop Listening to Your Boss," *FastCompany*, October 28, 2013.

Extraordinary Possibility in Extraordinary Times

www.fastcompany.com/3020699/why-intuit-founder-scott-cook-wants-you-to-stop-listening-to-your-boss

8. Carmine Gallo, "Steve Jobs's Strategy? 'Get Rid of the Crappy Stuff,'" *FastCompany*, October 8, 2010. www.fastcompany.com/1693832/steve-jobss-strategy-get-rid-crappy-stuff

9. Scott D. Anthony, David S. Duncan, and Pontus M. A. Siren, "Zombie Projects: How to Find Them and Kill Them," *Harvard Business Review*, March 4, 2015. https://hbr.org/2015/03/zombie-projects-how-to-find-them-and-kill-them

10. Scott D. Anthony, *Epic Disruptions: 11 Innovations That Shaped Our Modern World* (Harvard Business Press, 2025).

11. Jack Kelly, *Gunpowder: Alchemy, Bombards & Pyrotechnics: The History of the Explosive That Changed the World* (Basic Books, 2005), p. 22.

Chapter 3

Rethinking Maslow's Hierarchy of Needs: Dignity Must Come First

Jacqueline Novogratz

It is time to rethink Maslow's pyramid and place dignity as the foundation of all human needs. In my work investing in companies and leaders dedicated to solving problems of poverty, I'm struck time and again by how Maslow's hierarchy—which suggests that before we can pursue higher aspirations like self-actualization, meaning, and purpose, we must first secure our physiological needs, then safety, then love and belonging, and then esteem—omits this truth.

Dignity is agency. It derives from being seen, valued, and trusted. It entails having the freedom, power, choice, and opportunity to influence one's own life. Dignity requires seeing no one above or below you but treating others—and being treated—with humanity. Dignity is the most fundamental of our yearnings.

> Dignity is agency. It derives from being seen, valued, and trusted.

In an interdependent world, our connected systems become more effective, resilient, and humane when we design them from a place of our shared humanity. Yet our dominant approaches to problem solving, especially regarding low-income communities, too often see people as objects of aid or control rather than as individuals with agency over their own lives, overlooking, underestimating, and thus stifling the potential of an enormous population of human beings.

And as increasing climate shocks disproportionately impact the most vulnerable, widening inequality and deepening uncertainty, we must ask: What kind of leadership can meet the demands of this moment? Basic needs like food, shelter, education, and security are essential, but the crises we face today are too complex for simple solutions. We need human-centered leadership rooted in moral imagination—placing humanity and the Earth, rather than profit or efficiency, at the very core of our priorities.

My understanding of this has deepened over four decades of walking alongside low-income individuals and communities. They have modeled for me what dignity looks like, even in the harshest environments. And they have taught me the profound truth that my dignity is entwined with theirs.

When we invest in dignity, communities transform. Broken systems heal. Companies and organizations grow and sustain. I've had a front-row seat as an investor in the dreams and operations of hundreds of social entrepreneurs focused on solving problems of poverty. Since 2001, my organization Acumen has invested more than $343 million in pioneering enterprises impacting nearly 800 million low-income people with solutions in clean energy, resilient agriculture, quality education, and healthcare. Our best companies are those that work to earn the trust of their customers through continually showing up, listening to voices unheard, fighting the status quo, and executing with operational excellence. In time, both founders and those they serve transform.

Human-Centered Leadership

Maslow's hierarchy of needs has shaped how we think about human development since he first penned "A Theory of Motivation" in 1943, defining self-actualization as "the desire to become more and more what one is, to become everything that one is capable of becoming."[1]

Possibly because of its seemingly linear structure, many teach it without nuance. Yet Maslow himself understood that human beings are complex: "We have spoken so far as if this hierarchy were a fixed order but actually it is not nearly so rigid as we may have implied. . . . It is not necessary that a need be 100 per cent satisfied before the next need emerges."[2] Contemporary psychologists, such as Scott Barry Kaufman, in his book *Transcend: The New Science of Self Actualization*, have since deepened this interpretation, showing that self-actualization is less a fixed ladder than a dynamic process continuously unfolding.[3]

Despite this subtlety, many systems still back away from a genuinely human-centered approach. I saw this firsthand in the mid-1980s when I was cofounding Rwanda's first microfinance bank.

The experience taught me that access to markets is necessary but not sufficient; what truly empowers people is recognizing their inherent dignity and building systems that support their confidence and agency. It taught me that low-income communities around the world offer enormous potential to be part of the transformation the world needs.

During this time, I came across a bakery operated as a charity project by nuns to help 20 unwed mothers. The women were paid 50 cents a day just for showing up. Although run with good intentions, I couldn't shake the feeling that good works by good people were resulting in dependency, which ultimately was the opposite of dignity. The women "beneficiaries" had few skills, earning just enough to keep them in desperate poverty. Pity disguised as kindness can be corrosive, speaking first to helplessness rather than to human possibility.

I offered to turn the project into a real business, guaranteeing for one year to pay women at least what they had been earning, regardless of how the business did. We began weekly training and established systems to reward hard work and honesty. We painted the bakery bright blue so the women could feel proud of their space. I resolved to think of the women as employees, not beneficiaries.

31

Rethinking Maslow's Hierarchy of Needs: Dignity Must Come First

The risk of overempathy and the importance of accountability became clear. When the women got a whiff that I had lower expectations, they lived down to those. When I raised the bar almost impossibly high and was willing to accompany them through the hard work, they—in time—rose to the challenge. The experience for me reinforced the power of enthusiasm as a management tool. The more the women believed in themselves and had the results to prove it, the more their business flourished.

Within months, the women earned minimum wage, and by year's end, we had cornered the local snack market, and the women were earning four times the minimum wage.

The microfinance bank and the bakery opened my eyes to the power of human-centered development. When the bakery was operated as a project, the women internalized that they were needy, undervalued, and, ultimately, helpless. The bakery's success grew from the deep belief that their dignity was not a gift but something to claim and nurture. The systems we built affirmed their agency— and their capacity to lead change. And that made all the difference. How we see others is often how they see themselves.

Yet, all around me, traditional aid continued to keep low-income people caught in the endless emergency of poverty. Thousands of cookstoves, maize mills, and other women's labor-saving devices were distributed "to help" without consulting the recipients to understand what they needed or wanted. Consequently, most programs failed. I founded Acumen in 2001 partly because of those early experiences, resolving to create an institution that builds solutions with and for people.

Forty years after my experiences in Rwanda, the pattern persists. Too many top-down programs, often designed by outsiders (and sometimes local elites), overlook local wisdom and values rather than starting by listening. Governments slash funding for the arts and sports in inner-city schools, not thinking about the message this sends to the

Leading for Tomorrow

young people who walk through doors staffed by security guards and who have few opportunities for creativity during chaotic days.

Public health officials promote "best practices" without understanding how people make decisions or what they value. When Acumen invested in a mosquito net manufacturer in Tanzania, we saw that women preferred bright blue nets. They wanted beauty, status, dignity. Yet many donors felt uneasy when we spoke about aesthetics, implying that beauty is a luxury relegated to some, not all, of us.

Impact investing echoes these mistakes. Entrepreneurs and investors often prioritize scale and financial returns, assuming solutions devised in boardrooms will seamlessly meet the needs of underserved communities. But when growth takes precedence over listening and efficiency over equity, systems intended to serve the poor can end up exploiting or excluding rather than empowering.

It doesn't have to be this way. Throughout the human experience is a yearning to be seen, to belong, and to matter. When we honor that yearning and build systems that recognize dignity as the foundation, not the reward, we unleash the full potential of individuals and communities to transform themselves and, in turn, the world around them.

"I Want to Be a Somebody"

After my first book, *The Blue Sweater: Bridging the Gap Between Rich and Poor in an Interconnected World*, was published,[4] I received a message from Kevin Otieno, a young man in Nairobi's slums. Kevin was given the book by a local Acumen fellow, and he saw himself in my story—not because of my achievements, but because I had failed and lived to tell about it from a place of strength, not weakness.

"I'm just like you," Kevin said. "Like you, I have failed many times. I only completed third grade. I am HIV-positive and out of work. But if you have failed and still made so many changes, it gives

Rethinking Maslow's Hierarchy of Needs: Dignity Must Come First

me hope I can, too. And I want to help bridge the gap between rich and poor."

Kevin didn't ask for charity or trite affirmation. He wanted purpose. He and his friends organized a 100-person book club and hosted TEDx events highlighting graffiti artists, organic gardeners, and young entrepreneurs. "We're tired of our communities being known only for AIDS and violence," they told me. "There's so much more to us."

At one of these gatherings, his friends and I exchanged ideas from my book. After contemplating Dr. Martin Luther King Jr.'s wisdom, Alex, a young man living in the slums, looked at me and said, "I don't want to be a Nobody. I want to be a Somebody."

I asked what that meant. He replied, "To be a somebody means that people see you. They respect you. They don't make you pay bribes for the smallest things. It means they recognize you as someone who can contribute."

Alex's words captured the core of human dignity: being seen and valued and given the chance and indeed the expectation to contribute.

Listening Is the First Act of Moral Imagination

Social entrepreneurs embody human-centered leadership. They start by listening, by immersing themselves in the realities of others. They build *with*, not *for*. Their models may be slower to grow, but they are more just, resilient, and sustainable.

> Social entrepreneurs embody human-centered leadership. They start by listening.

Take electricity access. Despite Edison's invention of the lightbulb in 1879, as late as 2007, 1.5 billion people still lacked reliable power, one of the greatest market failures of our time. Nedjip Tozun and Sam Goldman, fueled by moral imagination, decided to do something about

Leading for Tomorrow

it and built a solar company called d.light. They began by seeing low-income people as customers whose trust they had to earn.

I remember visiting Theresa, a tiny grandmother in rural Kenya, who had recently bought a simple solar lantern with her daughter's help. It took time to convince people like Theresa, who lived with limited income in rural areas, to trust d.light enough to purchase a lamp—so many charities and cheats had come and gone, and people had too little to take risks on newfangled technologies. But watching her speak with a company representative inside her two-room house was an affirmation of the power of recognizing human beings' desire for agency.

Theresa said the lantern was life-changing, offering concrete reasons: It kept away wild animals, and it let her read her Bible and find things after dark. "Great, but there must be ways the companies can improve this product," I said. I had heard so many rural women tell donors what they wanted to hear that I wasn't sure what to expect.

This time was different. Without missing a beat, she suggested four tangible upgrades. In that moment, I realized I was finally doing the work I had come to do by supporting enterprises that were not there to solve problems for people but to build solutions *with* those who have been overlooked.

Theresa viewed herself as a partner. She had saved her money to be a customer and had earned the right to give feedback. Equally, the company had to work to earn her trust. In the interaction between the d.light representative and this tiny grandmother, the seeds of their mutual dignity were planted.

A few years later, I visited Bahawalpur in rural Pakistan, an area known for its fertile land and deep feudal roots, on a day when temperatures neared 120°F. I spent time outside with women weavers married to low-income farmers, most of whom were indentured. Their homes lacked toilets, electricity, and clean water. The heat was oppressive, yet these women worked tirelessly.

35

I asked if they would be interested in purchasing solar lights for their homes, explaining how they could save money on kerosene and improve their safety. After a pause, a woman with a dupatta around her head, sweat dripping down her face, leaned forward and said, "We're hot. We don't want a light. We want a fan."

Of course, I didn't have a fan to offer. Instead, I explained the benefits of the light—how it could help save money, reduce smoke, and let their children study at night. But she repeated: "We don't want a light. We're hot. We want a fan."

The key to human-centered leadership is deep listening. You'll hear what people actually want, not what you assume they should have, if you ask the right questions and demonstrate that you take the answers you hear seriously. This kind of listening—and leadership—is not about having all the answers but about building relationships and, critically, trust. As the adage goes, progress moves at the speed of trust.

For the record, today, in markets where the climate is the hottest, most solar home systems come complete with fans.

Making the Invisible Visible in Supply Chains

Too often, our farmers cannot feed themselves with the income that they make from growing our food. Six hundred million smallholder farmers (who typically work on less than five acres) produce about one third of the world's food. Yet nearly half live in poverty, and a quarter in extreme poverty. It is no wonder that the average age of a smallholder farmer is above 55 years old worldwide: Young people want dignified jobs and don't see that in the sweat and toil of their parents. Our food system is one that too often treats human beings as mere inputs rather than active, dignified participants.

Tyler Youngblood, founder of Azahar Coffee Co., understood this dynamic well. He asked: What if we reimagined a system of capitalism that started with the farmer rather than focusing solely on profitability for the shareholders? After spending years with farmers, he built a business model that bases its prices on the actual costs farmers expend to produce the best coffee in the world. He made the entire supply chain—from the farmer's coffee trees to the retail cup—visible to all players, including the farmers themselves. Based on the company's accumulated knowledge, Tyler created a "sustainable coffee buyers' guide" so that coffee roasters could decide whether they wanted to pay the farmers minimum wage or a "prosperous price"—a living wage.

Premium companies like Blue Bottle are now choosing the prosperous wage, wanting to please their customers with the best available coffee and also treating the farmers with equity and dignity. A new generation of consumers recognizes that for capitalism to be sustainable, it needs to do more to recognize the farmers and the factory workers, as well as the Earth itself, not as assets to be used at whim but as critical stakeholders in our shared future.

The Power of Beauty as a Path to Dignity

Beauty is often dismissed as superficial, yet it is fundamental to our resilience and hope. Florence Nightingale, in her groundbreaking *Notes on Nursing*,[5] observed that the sick suffer from seeing the same bleak walls and environment. She believed that beauty—bright colors, flowers, uplifting surroundings—heals the spirit and speeds recovery.

Systems aimed at the poor too often are structured, unsurprisingly, through the lens—and values—of those who create them. Decision makers also get trapped in ideology rather than learning about what works from the perspective of those the systems are intended to serve. Prioritizing "basic education" in our public schools is often a justification for cutting spending on arts, music, and sports. Not only is the unintended consequence a lack of critical thinking in our young people, but society sends a message that these kids don't matter.

Rethinking Maslow's Hierarchy of Needs: Dignity Must Come First

How we see others directly impacts how others see themselves.

How we see others directly impacts how others see themselves. Similar dynamics exist in public health and sanitation. One in three people on Earth lacks access to a toilet. Charities have responded in slums with pit latrines that, once filled with human waste, are abandoned, unsightly, unhealthy, and often dangerous places. With their company, the Sanergy Collaborative, Lindsay Stradley, David Auerbach, and Ani Vallabhaneni took a human-centered approach, one that used markets without being controlled by them.

Sanergy's founders needed to construct a toilet that would remain clean and fresh—and thereby healthy. They listened to entrepreneurial leaders in Mukuru, a dense urban community in Nairobi, and designed a bright blue toilet that separated liquid from solid waste. They created a system that relied on local community entrepreneurs to invest in individual toilets as microbusinesses. This provided an incentive to ensure the toilets were constantly cleaned and stood as inviting, safe places. The company then collected the waste daily, ultimately composting it and converting it into animal feed and fertilizer.

The end result is a flourishing system of sanitation entrepreneurs, employees with dignified, important work, and communities that have experienced a reduction in disease and a significant increase in cleanliness. Sanergy now operates in multiple cities across several nations, often partnering with local governments to turn waste into gold.

It Will Take All of Us

The attributes, skills, and tools of human-centered leadership I've described are applicable to all leaders, including those who feel beholden to quarterly returns, to policymakers weighing the best use

Leading for Tomorrow

of public resources, and to local communities. Indeed, these skills are needed for all aspects of leadership in a world changing in increasingly dramatic ways, especially when it comes to inequality and climate change. Especially when a new generation is tiring of the impact of unbridled capitalism and searching for *practical* solutions toward building a more sustainable world.

Corporate leaders can practice such leadership and enlist moral imagination in redesigning their business models and supply chains to be more transparent, just, and fair. Hamdi Ulukaya, founder and CEO of Chobani, himself an immigrant to the United States, made a commitment to build operations in old factory towns where jobs were in decline. He gave 10 percent of his company to employees and modeled belief in a greater sense of purpose. The results show up in all aspects of the company.

Griffith Foods is a Chicago-based company operating in more than 30 nations, with a commitment both to carbon reduction and to significantly increasing its use of regenerative practices in its supply chain. I visited our investee company, SiembraViva, in Colombia, which is partnering with Griffith, and was thrilled to see a sense of collaboration, experimentation, and dedication to healing the soil.

"In the end, Nature wins," Diego Benitez, founder of SiembraViva, told me. "We've poisoned the soil with chemicals for too long, and it shows up in a lack of agricultural productivity and in the poor health of our children." Social enterprises can show the way, but corporate leadership is critical for that change at scale.

We remember leaders who have the courage to make change. When I think of those companies run with a human-centered leadership model today, the first that come to mind are private—Chobani and Griffiths, and I would add the likes of IKEA and Patagonia. Think of these companies as hope spots, showing what more we can do if we lead with an insistence on giving more to the world than we take from it. But to make our economic system fully work for us, public

Rethinking Maslow's Hierarchy of Needs: Dignity Must Come First

companies, too, have to adopt this ethos. That means acknowledging value created for workers and farmers, putting nature on the balance sheet, and moving away from the single-minded pursuit of quarterly financial returns.

And what if this same ethos transcended all sectors? Everything would change.

Leadership that puts our humanity first is not confined to nonprofits or certain sectors; it can thrive in for-profit, competitive markets. When leaders choose to anchor their approach in dignity, fairness, and moral imagination, they prove that profitability and purpose are not just compatible; they reinforce each other. All of us can change the systems we inhabit because, ultimately, we are the system.

So in this time of confusion and uncertainty, when it can seem that those committed to unbridled power keep winning, remember that change rarely happens in a straight line. It will take a new generation that understands that dignity is the most fundamental of human needs and our unequal, divided yet beautiful world deserves a radical moral rejuvenation. This renewal starts with a belief in human dignity and commits itself to listening to those who are unlike ourselves. It insists on the profound truth that our lives are interconnected. And it is a renewal that needs all of us.

We are each other's destiny—and the seeds of transformation are rooted in one another. Maslow provided a map, but the terrain we walk today is more complex. It's time to draw a new map—one that begins with dignity, not ends with it.

Notes

1. Abraham H. Maslow, "A Theory of Human Motivation," *Psychological Review* 50, no. 4 (1943): 370–396, p. 382. https://doi.org/10.1037/h0054346
2. Ibid., pp. 386, 388.
3. Scott Barry Kaufmann, *Transcend: The New Science of Self-Actualization* (TarcherPerigee, 2020).
4. Jacqueline Novogratz, *The Blue Sweater: Bridging the Gap Between Rich and Poor in an Interconnected World* (Rodale, 2009).
5. Florence Nightingale, *Notes on Nursing: What It Is, and What It Is Not* (Harrison, 1859; repr., Dover, 1969).

Rethinking Maslow's Hierarchy of Needs: Dignity Must Come First

Chapter 4

Futures-Centered Leadership: How Leaders Build Tomorrow Today

Lisa Kay Solomon

Forever—is composed of nows.

—Emily Dickinson

In December 2022, visitors to the Smithsonian's Arts + Industries Building encountered FUTURES, a 32,000-square-foot interactive exhibit. It centered on a profound provocation: "Everyone has a role to play in building the future. In the next year, I will . . . In the next month, I will . . . In the next day, I will . . ."

These prompts are simple yet revelatory. They embody a truth that has become more urgent as each year delivers accelerating change: The future doesn't have to be something that happens to us.

We live in an era where uncertainty is the only constant. Traditional business strategies crumble in the face of technological disruption. Climate change reshapes industries overnight. Global conflicts create humanitarian crises that ripple across generations. Democratic institutions strain under the weight of polarization and distrust. While we can't predict what will unfold in the next five, ten, or 25 years, we can assume that the world will become increasingly ambiguous and complex, not less. In this context, leaders face a fundamental choice: Retreat into the illusion of control or learn to take a different stance toward the future.

Most leadership development focuses on managing the present: quarterly results, team dynamics, operational efficiency. But the most consequential leadership challenges of our time—climate change, technological disruption, social inequality, global migration—require a different approach. They demand leaders who can navigate profound uncertainty while making decisions for futures they may never see.

The Problem: Outsourced Agency

The challenge isn't that leaders lack vision. It's that we've begun outsourcing our agency and ceding our imagination to others. When I ask my students "Who shapes the future?," I hear the same answers: CEOs of big tech companies, successful entrepreneurs, venture capitalists. Rarely do I hear "We do." In our prevailing narrative, the future belongs to a select few visionaries while the rest of us wait to see what they decide.

This mindset extends beyond individuals to entire organizations and communities. Our organizations and incentives reward measurable returns on investment, immediate payoffs, and quick decisions and lack processes that foster the longer-term investments that seed the futures to come.

The cost of this outsourced agency is everywhere: organizations that chase trends instead of creating them, communities that solve yesterday's problems while tomorrow's crises build, and leaders who feel overwhelmed by forces they can't control.

But here's what gives me hope: Agency can be learned. At the end of my classes, many students report, "I used to think that the future was something other people control, and now I think I have the tools and practices to shape it for myself." This isn't just feel-good feedback; it's evidence that futures-centered leadership is something we can learn, not an innate gift bestowed on a few.

What if we helped more leaders and learners develop the capacity to shape better futures rather than just practice reacting to them?

Four Foundational Mindsets

Leaders who embody futures-centered thinking are all around us. They're not just in boardrooms or government offices; they're artists, coaches, entrepreneurs, and activists who understand that today's choices create tomorrow's possibilities. We can learn from them—if we tune ourselves into noticing.

Futures-centered leadership starts with a radical reframe: The future isn't something that happens to us; it's something we actively create. This isn't about prediction or crystal ball gazing. It's about developing the capacity to sense emerging patterns, imagine multiple possibilities, and take purposeful action even when outcomes remain uncertain.

> The future isn't something that happens to us; it's something we actively create.

At its core, futures-centered leadership rests on four foundational mindsets. These are beautifully demonstrated by Taylor Swift and Dolly Parton, two artists who have shaped culture and community far beyond their music.

Agency over Anxiety

Futures-centered leaders move away from "This is happening to me!" to "What can I create from this?"

Shortly after Taylor Swift left her original record label in 2019, the "masters" of her first six albums were sold to a private equity firm, a move Taylor publicly disapproved of. She didn't spiral into victimhood. She announced she would rerecord them all—a massive, multiyear undertaking. As she shared in an Instagram post, "Artists should own their own work for so many reasons."[1] Instead of being paralyzed by what happened to her, she charted a completely new path forward.

When Dolly Parton recognized that children in rural areas had limited access to books because their communities lacked public libraries, she didn't wait for someone else to solve the problem. She created the Imagination Library, which has shipped more than 300 million books directly to children's homes.

Abundance over Scarcity

Futures-centered leaders operate from abundance, knowing that power shared is power multiplied and that today's investments in others become tomorrow's foundation for collective success.

Time and time again, Taylor Swift broke the mold of outdated business models and relationships. In late 2023, she decided to give $55 million in bonuses to her tour crew for their hard work on the first leg of her Eras Tour. It wasn't just generous; it was strategic. She understood that investing in people creates compound returns across time.

Opportunity over Obstacle

Futures-centered leaders see disruption as creative material, not crisis management.

When torrential rain threatened Swift's concert in Massachusetts, she didn't cancel or apologize endlessly. She turned it into one of the most memorable shows of the tour, with fans dancing in downpours and sharing joyful videos that went viral.

Dolly Parton turned the challenge of vaccine hesitancy into an opportunity for education and connection. She helped fund COVID-19 vaccine development through her $1 million donation to Vanderbilt University Medical Center. But she didn't stop there. She filmed her own vaccination and playfully adapted one of her most famous songs—from "Jolene" to "Vaccine"—to encourage others, making the experience relatable and removing the fear factor.

Becoming over Being

Futures-centered leaders embrace the ongoing journey of becoming, understanding that in a rapidly changing world, the ability to adapt and grow matters more than having all the answers.

Perhaps more than any of their specific actions, Swift and Parton have given their fans—and all of us—permission to keep evolving. Their music chronicles their growth, their mistakes, their learning. They model that mastery includes the humility to change.

Essential Leadership Practices

These four mindsets create the foundation, but futures-centered leadership requires translating mindset into action. The following practices help leaders operationalize these mindsets in their daily work and long-term strategy.

Cultivating Long-Term Thinking

In his book *The Good Ancestor*, cultural philosopher Roman Krznaric builds on a profound question posed by immunologist Jonas Salk: "Are we being good ancestors?"[2] Krznaric's research into long-term thinking suggests that this question should be framed on every leader's desk. Each decision a leader makes—a budget allocation, strategic priority, hiring choice, policy change—either serves future generations or burdens them.

This isn't just abstract philosophy; it's practical wisdom that changes how we make everyday decisions. When leaders ask: "How will this decision look in 20 years?" or "What would the next generation want us to prioritize?," they make fundamentally different choices. They invest in infrastructure over quick fixes, in people development over cost-cutting, in systemic solutions over Band-Aids.

What if we measured success across generations rather than quarters?

Being a good ancestor requires what Krznaric calls "long-term thinking in a short-term world"—and that's the challenge. Our brains are wired for immediate rewards. Our organizations measure quarterly performance. Our attention gets hijacked by whatever crisis feels most urgent today.

But futures-centered leaders have learned to cultivate their "acorn brain," the part (the dorsolateral prefrontal cortex) that thinks in decades, not quarters. They create space for contemplation in a world of constant action. They ask different questions, measure different outcomes, and define success across generations, not just fiscal years.

Our greatest leverage lies not in controlling immediate outcomes but in creating conditions for future flourishing. This requires moving beyond numerical "discounting" formulas that apply artificial rates to future possibilities, devoid of empathy or human understanding.

Instead, we need new forms of accountability for the future. Wales has appointed a Future Generation Commissioner to ensure political decisions don't compromise tomorrow's citizens. The European Commission recently appointed a Commissioner for Intergenerational Fairness, Youth, Culture and Sport whose task is "to give young people more freedom, say and responsibility."[3] The World Futures Society calls for a UN Ombudsperson for Future Generations. These initiatives point toward systemic changes that embed long-term thinking in governance itself.

> We need new forms of accountability for the future.

But the transformation begins with each of us asking: How do we prevent forests from burning after years of drought and underfunded response? How do we rebuild trust in science to guide policy? How do we strengthen democratic institutions against destruction? How do we stop technology companies from knowingly eroding children's mental health? How do we address deep inequities in education, opportunity, and healthcare revealed by pandemic and racial justice reckonings?

The key may be empathy—our most uniquely human trait and our greatest tool for building personal connections with future generations. This experiential learning doesn't require special technology, resources, or expertise. Just the willingness to do things differently.

Rewarding Clarity over Certainty

Bob Johansen, former president of the Institute for the Future, offers one of the most important insights for leaders navigating uncertainty: "The future will reward clarity, but will punish certainty."[4] This distinction between clarity and certainty is crucial for understanding how to lead effectively in ambiguous environments.

Certainty is about knowing exactly what will happen and when. It's the illusion that we can predict and control outcomes with precision. Leaders who chase certainty often become rigid, defending their predictions and plans even when evidence suggests they should adapt.

Clarity, by contrast, is about understanding what matters most—your values, your purpose, your nonnegotiables—while remaining flexible about how you achieve them. Clarity allows you to make decisions and take action, even when you can't predict outcomes with certainty.

This leads to a crucial leadership distinction: the difference between what futurist Paul Saffo calls "strong opinions weakly held"[5] and my belief in having "strong values strongly held." Strong opinions strongly held represent positions we defend regardless of new evidence or changing circumstances. We become attached to specific

Futures-Centered Leadership: How Leaders Build Tomorrow Today

strategies, predictions, or solutions, even when they're no longer serving us well.

The alternative is cultivating strong values, strongly held, combined with strong ideas, loosely held. Your values should be nonnegotiable. These are the stable foundations that allow you to adapt everything else. But your strategies, tactics, and specific methods should remain provisional, subject to revision as new information emerges.

Consider Stanford's women's water polo coach John Tanner, who has won ten National Collegiate Athletic Association (NCAA) championships in 18 years. If you ask anyone on his team what the program is about, they'll give you the same answer: "Inspire Stanford to inspire the world." Notice this isn't "win games." It's a clear statement of values and purpose.

Everything Tanner does connects to this foundational principle. Each spring, his players host a "favorite faculty dinner." Each player invites and introduces their faculty guest, explaining who the person is and the impact they've had on the player's life. Tanner takes time away from pool training for this practice because, as he puts it, "When you give players the chance to become better teachers, it helps them become better learners, too." They also become better teams, he asserts.[6]

This clarity of mission—strong values, strongly held—allows the team to adapt their methods while staying true to their purpose. They already know what matters most when facing new challenges.

Anticipating Possible Futures

It can be hard to imagine what's ahead when so much is in flux. Yet we can't build a future we haven't first imagined.

Shifting mindset is crucial, but mindset without methods remains wishful thinking. Futurist and author Octavia Butler famously wrote, "There's nothing new under the sun, but there are new suns."[7] Butler's insight captures something essential about futures work: While we may draw on familiar patterns and precedents, the future we're building is fundamentally novel—a new sun that demands we look beyond what we already know.

This kind of imaginative work requires what we might call "anticipatory leadership"—the ability to sense emerging patterns, imagine alternative scenarios, and act on insights about what's coming before it fully arrives. Concepts of anticipatory leadership have been evolving since the 1970s when futurist Alvin Toffler, author of *Future Shock*,[8] and Jim Dator, creator of the Manoa School of Futures Studies at the University of Hawaii, began talking about "anticipatory democracy," which emphasized using methods and disciplines to envision alternative futures. Anticipatory leadership isn't about predicting the future with certainty; it's about developing the cognitive flexibility to work effectively with uncertainty.

Anticipation isn't fortune-telling; it's pattern recognition across time. Futures-centered leaders develop peripheral vision, scanning for weak signals that others miss. They notice when small changes in one area might create big impacts elsewhere. They ask questions like: "What's happening at the edges of our industry?," "What would we do if our biggest assumption turned out to be wrong?"

> Anticipation isn't fortune-telling; it's pattern recognition across time.

Most planning assumes one future and tries to optimize for it. Futures-centered leaders imagine multiple scenarios and design strategies that work across various possibilities. They ask: "What if we're wrong about our core assumptions?," "What would we do if this trend accelerated? If it reversed?"

In our "View from the Future" class, we curate vibrant weekly conversations with people who are "living in the future" today. We meet with pioneers, innovators, entrepreneurs, and disruptors who

Futures-Centered Leadership: How Leaders Build Tomorrow Today

are actively shaping tomorrow because seeing possibility expands our capacity to create it. In my "Inventing the Future" class, students create and debate 50-year dystopian and utopian narratives to explore "Should we build it?" rather than "Can we build it?"

By imagining different futures farther out in time, we permit ourselves to unleash our wild imaginations in applied and pragmatic ways and to practice dreaming boldly while staying grounded in action.

Leading with Optimistic Humility

Perhaps the most important shift futures-centered leadership offers is reframing uncertainty from threat to opportunity. In our current moment—with accelerating technological, political, environmental, and social change—uncertainty isn't going away. Leaders who wait for certainty will wait forever.

Instead, futures-centered leaders treat uncertainty as creative material. They develop comfort with not knowing while maintaining commitment to positive action. They build resilience through diversity—of perspectives, strategies, relationships, and possibilities.

> Futures-centered leaders treat uncertainty as creative material.

Leading through uncertainty requires "optimistic humility"—being clear about your values and purpose while remaining open about tactics and outcomes. Like the scientific method itself, this approach combines conviction (the hypothesis is worth testing) with openness (the data may prove us wrong). It's the stance of experimenters who believe solutions are possible while acknowledging they don't yet know what those solutions are.

Futures-centered leaders don't just plan for the future; they build it through purposeful experimentation. They understand that the future emerges through action, not analysis. Instead of trying to predict what will work, they design small experiments to discover what's possible.

This means thinking like scientists: forming hypotheses, testing assumptions, learning from failures, and iterating based on evidence. It means building prototypes before business plans, running pilots before full rollouts, and treating setbacks as data rather than defeats.

In 2020, college basketball coach Eric Reveno at Georgia Tech University put this principle into action. In the wake of the protests following the killing of George Floyd, he was moved to help his players become more civically engaged. Upon learning that none of his team was registered to vote and didn't feel like they had time to get involved, he went on social media and posted a tweet about the idea of taking Election Day off from practice and play to allow time for athletes to vote. He tagged the effort "All Vote, No Play."

Coach Reveno had conviction about his values—civic engagement matters—but remained open about tactics. Within days, over 1,500 athletes and coaches signed his petition. Shortly after, the NCAA passed unanimous legislation for all Division 1 athletic schools to take the day off from athletic activity in order to give time for athletes and coaches to engage civically. Coach Reveno reached out to me for help in creating meaningful civic programs and activities designed to be accessible and relatable to athletes.

Together, through continuous experimentation and rapid testing with coaches and athletes around the country, our nonpartisan efforts have reached over 250,000 athletes and coaches and evolved into an award-winning nonprofit organization called The Team. What began as a single tweet became a movement—not through a perfect master plan, but through optimistic humility: clear values, experimental tactics, and willingness to learn and adapt along the way.

Futures-Centered Leadership: How Leaders Build Tomorrow Today

The Time Is Now

We stand at a moment when the decisions leaders make in the next few years will determine the trajectory of the next few decades. Climate action, technological governance, democratic resilience—they all require leaders who can think beyond performance reviews, fiscal years, and five-year strategic plans.

The good news is that futures-centered leadership isn't a rare gift reserved for visionaries. It's a learnable set of practices, available to anyone willing to shift their relationship with time, uncertainty, and responsibility.

The question Jonas Salk posed decades ago remains urgent today: Are we being good ancestors? Are we making choices that future generations will thank us for? Are we using our brief moment of influence to plant seeds we may never see bloom?

The future doesn't have to be something that happens to us. With futures-centered leadership, it becomes something we actively create—not just for ourselves, but for all the generations who will inherit the world we're building today.

Notes

1. Quoted in Guest User, "Why Taylor Swift Is Recrecording [*sic*] Her Albums and What You Can Learn from It," Stage Music Center, April 18, 2022. https://stagemusiccenter.com/music-school-blog-winchester-acton-ma/ why-taylor-swift-is-recrecording-her-albums#:~:text="Artists%20should% 20own%20their%20work,enjoy%20her%20music%20as%20before

2. Roman Krznaric, *The Good Ancestor: A Radical Prescription for Long-Term Thinking* (The Experiment, 2021).

3. European Commission, "Glenn Micallef, Commissioner (2024–2029)," n.d. https://commission.europa.eu/about/organisation/college-commissioners/ glenn- micallef_en#:~:text=Glenn%20Micallef%20is%20the% 20Commissioner,young%20people%20more%20freedom%2C%20say

4. Bob Johansen, *The New Leadership Literacies: Thriving in a Future of Extreme Disruption and Distributed Everything* (Berrett-Koehler, 2017), p. viii.

5. Educom Review Staff Sequence (1998). Paul Saffo Interview: Betting on 'Strong Opinions Weakly Held. *Educom Review, 33* (3). www.educause .edu/apps/er/review/reviewArticles/33340.html

6. Lisa Kay Solomon, "Coaching Citizen-Athletes," *Stanford Report*, June 16, 2023. https://news.stanford.edu/stories/2023/06/coaching-citizen-athletes

7. Gerry Canavan, "'There's Nothing New / Under the Sun, / But There Are New Suns': Recovering Octavia E. Butler's Lost Parables," *Los Angeles Review of Books,* June 9, 2014. https://lareviewofbooks.org/article/theres-nothing-new-sun-new-suns-recovering-octavia-e-butlers-lost-parables/

8. Alvin Toffler, *Future Shock* (Random House, 1970).

Chapter 5

In Theory There Is No Difference: The Hardest Truth About Leadership

Chris Yeh

In theory there is no difference between theory and practice, while in practice there is.

—Benjamin Brewster[1]

The entire field of leadership development is built on an illusion. The illusion that reading a book or article or taking a course about management theory conveys sufficient information to apply that theory to real-world situations. This foundational illusion supports a colossal industry, estimated to be worth somewhere between $100 and $400 billion in annual revenue. Yet the direct applicability of leadership theory is just that—an illusion that becomes more difficult to sustain or believe the more closely we examine it.

We leadership and management thinkers shouldn't feel too bad about this situation. After all, the theory/practice illusion in leadership is simply a special case of the much broader bias summed up so wonderfully by the Brewster quote that leads this chapter.

Symbolic thinking is the core of human intelligence. The ability to use mental representations, like words and images, to represent objects and ideas is the basis for science, technology, history, literature, and art. Without symbolic thinking, there could be no Apollo moon landing, no iPhone, no *The History of the Decline and Fall of the Roman Empire*, no *Mona Lisa*.

And, yet, symbolic thinking can also become a trap.

Enter "the Perfect Map Paradox"

By definition, a perfect map reproduces exactly all the details of the territory it maps. But the only way this level of perfection is possible is if the map is the same size as the territory it maps, which defeats the purpose of the map itself, which is to serve as a more useful representation of the territory. A truly perfect map is useless because it doesn't save any time in comparison to simply traveling through the territory it maps.

A map's imperfection isn't a bug; it's a feature. Its incompleteness and loss of detail are what make it useful as a navigational aid.

The danger lies in assuming that a given map contains all the information you need to apply its symbolic theory to the practice of navigating the real world around you.

Several years ago, I visited Monaco to attend a conference. At one point during my stay, I checked Google Maps to find a restaurant for lunch. I looked at my computer screen and picked a small Italian cafe that was less than 500 feet away, according to the map. But when I left my Airbnb and began what I expected to be a short walk to lunch, I discovered my error. Monaco is remarkably hilly. What I thought would be a simple straight-line walk between a couple of buildings turned out to be a significant hike because the steep cliff-like rises and drops made it impossible to travel perpendicular to the actual streets. The map was missing the crucial third dimension of height, which rarely comes into play on the streets of Palo

Alto, California, where I live, but is incredibly important on the avenues of Monaco.

As management thinkers, we play the role of organizational cartographers. We try to find the right ways to symbolically represent the businesses we study and provide the necessary frameworks to act on our insights. Yet we must never forget that we are imperfect mapmakers, creating deliberately imperfect maps. Every clean line that we draw likely covers a host of confusing and contradictory features in the organizational terrain. And that is the very essence of human-centered leadership.

> We must never forget that we are imperfect mapmakers, creating deliberately imperfect maps.

Human-Centered Leadership Balances Theory and Practice

The most effective leaders leverage the clarifying power of theory *and* ground their actions in the messy world of practice. They deal with human beings as complex individuals rather than as unnecessary details to be abstracted away.

Human-centered leadership embraces theories of leadership, understanding that abstraction is the necessary precursor to generalization. Yet they also know that operating on "gut feel" and direct analogs to prior personal experiences may be a practical approach to leadership, but it is not a pragmatic one. Instead, these leaders learn from both theory and the experiences of others without slavishly imitating or rigidly applying either. They use this outside knowledge as input for context and decision making.

Striking this balance can be a challenge for leaders, especially early in their careers. I know it was for me.

In Theory There Is No Difference

Theory Can Only Take You So Far

I faced my first real leadership challenges after I graduated from Harvard Business School. I was (and remain) a member of the Class of 2000 during the height of the dot-com boom and the low of its bust. In the summer of 1999, I became convinced that the dot-com boom was unsustainable and would end before graduation day in June 2000. Instead of taking a summer job like nearly every other MBA student, then, I decided to found my first startup and try to sell it before the end of the next school year.

By the time I graduated, I had raised $6 million for my startup, whose team had grown to 38 people, 36 of whom were older than I including every single person who reported to me. I brought in an experienced CEO to run the company while I finished my second year at HBS, and I served as chief marketing officer, overseeing a third of the company.

Unfortunately, things weren't going well. The stock market peaked in March, and by graduation day, the NASDAQ index had already dropped by a third. Meanwhile, the online advertising dollars that flowed into our company coffers so easily in January, February, and March were drying up even faster.

In response, I relied even more on the tools that had made me successful to that point—the ability to read, write, and theorize. I drew on what I had learned in my HBS classes and what I'd read in books and articles, including classics like *The Innovator's Dilemma* and *Crossing the Chasm*.[2] I produced numerous memos, PowerPoint presentations, and spreadsheets to explain ways in which we could make our company more appealing to advertisers, collaborate with partners, and expand into overseas markets. Some of it even worked; we raised additional millions from a prominent Asian investment firm and struck up partnerships across the Pacific, where the markets were still rising.

But while I was focused on developing winning theories and strategies, I was ignoring the reality that my team was nervous and scared. They could see as well as I could that the market had shifted and that the incredible growth we had seen during the first part of the year had given way to steep revenue declines just as venture capital funding was drying up.

It's not that I couldn't sense their uneasiness. I was nervous and scared as well! But I didn't know how to engage with those messy human emotions, which lacked easy resolutions. In contrast, spending hours seeking out the "bowling pin segments" I'd read about in *Crossing the Chasm* that would restore our growth trajectory seemed a lot more appealing. But this retreat into theory was just that— avoidance rather than a real solution.

Practice barged into my office when one of my most trusted lieutenants, Peter, quietly informed me that he had accepted another job at a much larger, more famous, publicly traded startup. I got along with Peter the best of all my direct reports, and it was such a shock when he resigned. (Ironically, that more secure position Peter accepted ended up evaporating when that well-known company went bankrupt and shut down while my little startup was still operating. In theory, Peter found a safer job; in practice, he did not.)

I can't excuse my younger self's overreliance on theory rather than practice, but I can explain it.

I was the product of an educational system and working world that had always rewarded me for my mastery of theory. Getting the answers right on paper tests. Crafting eloquent marketing plans and product requirement documents. Demonstrating my intelligence and eloquence. In other words, I had been taught the art of making elegant, attractive maps. But I had scant experience using those maps to navigate the gritty, dirty, real world of practice.

In Theory There Is No Difference

A huge gulf exists between offering a solution in a classroom and actually dealing with it in the real world.

I'm grateful for the incredible education I received at Harvard Business School, which has benefited me in so many ways, but I can't deny the fact that a huge gulf exists between offering a solution in a classroom and actually dealing with it in the real world.

Practice Is Powerful

One of the most important and practical lessons I learned from my first startup came out of an experience where I felt truly lost and beyond the boundaries of any of my beloved maps. Losing Peter had been a tough experience. But it was a minor pain in comparison to what followed in my next board meeting.

Given the macroenvironment and our declining revenues, I didn't expect an easy meeting. I was completely unprepared for what actually happened. One by one, the experienced venture capitalists and attorneys who sat on my board made it clear that they weren't willing to invest any more money in the company and that it was likely impossible for us to raise money from outside investors. The company had to succeed or fail using the remaining money in the bank, and that meant I needed to lay off as many employees as possible to extend the company's runway.

As I sat across from my board members in the conference room, I was in a near state of shock. Just months prior, we had been discussing possible sales or even going public. Now I needed to terminate nearly 90 percent of my employees. Even in the room, I knew the investors were right. I knew that theory clearly stated that I needed to cut costs to give the company time to pivot. But my mind balked at putting that theory into practice.

My CEO and I worked together over the weekend to put together the termination packets and split up the list of employees to be laid off on Monday morning. It was an awful process, and I felt terrible.

One of the last employees I laid off that day was one of my salespeople, Puneet. Puneet had been one of the first employees to join the company, back when we were operating out of the back storage room of one of our investors' companies. We called it "the refrigerator" because it was so cold that we all had to wear ski jackets in the office. Puneet was one of the true believers in the company, and now I had to let him go.

Puneet was nearly a decade older than me and much more experienced in the working world. He had figured out what was coming, and after seeing the other employees leaving, he knew why I had asked him to join me in the conference room.

At that point, I was physically and emotionally exhausted. That's probably why, as I started the formal layoff process, I also started crying. That's when Puneet came around the table and comforted me. "Don't worry, Chris," he told me, "I'll be all right. You have to do this. It's the only way the company will have a chance to succeed."

I had never taken any class that covered this particular situation in that moment of practice; no theory seemed to apply. But the compassion that Puneet showed me then gave me more comfort than any of the theories I had read.

Puneet and I remained friends. As the years passed, I became the chief advisor for his startup, and he was a cheerful uncle to my children. When my daughter was young, she couldn't pronounce his name correctly, so she called him "Uncle Pete."

Later, I asked Puneet about the day I laid him off and how he was able to set aside his own emotions and support me in that very human way in the moment when *I* was laying *him* off. He didn't cite my brilliant theories or elegant spreadsheets. Instead, he told me about how, a few months earlier, he overheard me talking with my

63

In Theory There Is No Difference

CEO. As the first employee, Puneet had received a special deal, and the CEO wanted to explore renegotiating Puneet's employment contract to be more favorable to the company. Puneet heard me refuse, saying that we were going to be the kind of company that kept its promises to our employees.

There's a coda to this story: Years later, during one of our conversations, I described a situation that was causing me some financial strain. I believed I could manage, but it was stressful. Without hesitation, Puneet, who had achieved considerable financial success since the days he worked for me, loaned me a six-figure sum so that I wouldn't have to worry. He told me that when he overheard my conversation with my CEO, he had resolved then to look out for me the way that I had looked out for him. No theory could have predicted the course of our relationship and the extent to which it would enrich both our lives.

In theory, there is no difference between theory and practice; in practice, there is. I try hard to keep this lesson in mind and nudge others to do the same.

An Elegant Theory Is Still Just a Theory

These days, as the author of multiple business books, including *The Alliance* and *Blitzscaling*,[3] I'm often asked by founders and executives for advice on how to apply my frameworks to their particular situation. I'm happy to answer, but I'm careful to preface my answers by pointing out that "I can give you a general answer, but it's up to you to figure out to what extent it applies to your unique team and your unique situation."

No matter how elegant your theory, no matter how beautiful your presentation, no matter how detailed your spreadsheet, never forget that you are leading human beings, not abstractions. They don't exist just to carry out your plans, no matter how well laid. They have lives

Leading for Tomorrow

beyond the business that can lead to complex and contradictory feelings. They worry. They forget. They break up with their romantic partners. They have a million priorities they have to balance with their work.

If you think your job as a leader ends with formulating a clever plan, articulating a clear vision, and allocating the appropriate resources, think again. You need to learn and take into account the human needs, concerns, and limitations of each of your team members to help them achieve both their goals and those of the business.

It may be tempting (and more comfortable) to focus on the clean elegance of theory, but it is far more effective to practice human-centered leadership by acknowledging and grappling with the messy, confusing, and sometimes surprisingly inspirational nature of individual people.

Notes

1. *"Portfolio: Theory and Practice,"* Yale Literary Magazine 416 (February 1882): 202.
2. Clayton M. Christensen, *The Innovator's Dilemma: The Revolutionary Book That Will Change the Way You Do Business* (Harvard Business School Press, 1997). Geoffrey M. Moore, *Crossing the Chasm: Marketing and Selling High-Tech Products to Mainstream Customers* (HarperCollins, 1991).
3. Reid Hoffman, Ben Casnocha, and Chris Yeh, *The Alliance: Managing Talent in the Networked Age* (Harvard Business Review Press, 2014). Reid Hoffman and Chris Yeh, *Blitzscaling: The Lightning-Fast Path to Building Massively Valuable Companies* (Crown Currency, 2018).

Chapter 6

Deep Connections: The Secret Power of Great Leaders

Jean Oelwang

We spend over 30 percent of our lives working. Sadly, many people waste this precious time in roles where they are disengaged, disconnected, and lack meaning. What a different world we would live in if we made that 30 percent matter for everyone.

Some ten years ago, I was in some trying-to-be-trendy hotel for lunch with a group of CEOs, talking about how we can build 100 percent human workplaces. One of the CEOs asked the team serving food and drinks to join them at the table and share what they think a human workplace should look like. A lively, joyful conversation filled the room with all kinds of ideas, from unlimited leave, to participation in decision making, to more parental leave, to making kindness a performance metric.

As I was leaving the hotel, I saw one of the waiters who had just been in conversation with us sitting in a corner, weeping. She was huddled over and looked like her world had collapsed. I went up and put my arm around her and asked her if she was OK. Through a flood of tears, she shared with me that she was stunned to be invited to sit at the table and to share her views. She never imagined that CEOs could care, could be humble enough to listen. *She had never experienced a human boss.*

The Problem of Compassionless Leadership

We've squeezed humanity out of our workplaces. We've made caring and kindness appear weak rather than central to good leadership.

> We've squeezed humanity out of our workplaces.

I remember having a discussion with a group of MBA students at a university in London about what makes a good leader. At least that's what I thought we were going to discuss. The "good leader" stories ended after a few minutes. The conversation then turned to the many horror stories about bad bosses. Starting with a boss who got so angry and slammed his fists so hard into a glass table that it shattered. Ending with a young leader who shared that her company tested everyone on their leadership traits, and her boss continuously bragged that on his test, compassion was number 30 out of 30—dead last. He was proud of being a compassionless leader.

We've got leadership all wrong. From the time we start to walk, we push people to be the superhero, the one to save the day, to get the gold star and be top of the class. We've shifted the axis of the world from our natural instincts guided by collective well-being to one centered on hyperindividualism, where self-interest rules.

We've mistakenly looked at leadership as a solo endeavor, which is a bit absurd; nothing great ever happens with one single leader who has all the answers.

A Community of Leaders Working Together

The best companies, organizations, and movements understand that the most sustainable and unbreakable leadership is more of a collective approach, where leadership ebbs and flows depending on what is needed in that moment. No one person can be an expert at everything.

Leading for Tomorrow

One community of leaders who instinctively knew this was the group that came together to protect all our lives, the ozone community. This is still one of humanity's greatest achievements. This group saved us by protecting the ozone layer from chemical damage that would have destroyed our food systems, decimated ecosystems, caused unimaginable health issues, and eventually caused the collapse of humanity.

At the center of this great achievement was a group of friends with deep connections who never gave up. Some of them are still doing this work 40 years later. Here are some examples of their successful alchemy of leadership:

- Stephen O. Anderson is a larger-than-life character from Logan, Utah, a "super motivator"[1] who led a network of industry leaders called the Technology and Economic Assessment Panel (TEAP) to work together, often across competitive lines to phase out the chemicals that were destroying the ozone layer. He is a master at bridging across sectors and keeping people focused on their intoxicating purpose—closing the ozone hole.

- Mostafa Tolba was a fiery Egyptian diplomat who was one of the lead architects of the Montreal Protocol. He was a "super negotiator" with a philosophy of "start and strengthen." He was relentless at getting people together in small groups to "take off their cloaks of authority" to have a safe space to debate issues and jointly come up with solutions.

- Ronald Reagan and Margaret Thatcher were two very unlikely environmentalists. As "first-mover politicians," their role was to help convince over 46 countries to sign the Montreal Protocol, eventually leading to its ratification by 197 countries. Still today, it is the single most successful global treaty.

- Scientists Sherwood Rowland and Mario Molina were not just "super experts"; they were beacons of moral courage who set

Deep Connections: The Secret Power of Great Leaders

the values of the community, sacrificing everything to ensure the world listened and acted.

- A cast of other leaders were "network spanners," keeping the connective tissue strong and remaining a flexible, distributed network of global leaders.

Mostafa Tolba summed up the spirit of leadership in this ozone community so beautifully: "What they would implement, and how, has been based on a circle of friends, an ever-growing circle of friends, that has worked tirelessly under conditions of personal trust."[2]

Interestingly, one of the factors that Gallup found increases engagement levels in a company is whether people have a best friend at work.[3]

What Makes 100 Percent Human Workplaces?

Over the last 20 years, we've been building and exploring successful companies and collaborations. What we found surprised us. One of the most important factors for leadership success was not people's breadth of connections, or their experience; it was their ability to build deep connections.

We need a relationship reset in our companies, and in the world. Over the last decade, we've spoken to hundreds of people who articulated what they feel makes 100 percent human workplaces.[4] Five things came out loud and clear: respect, equity, growth, belonging, and purpose. Easy to say, hard to consistently build into your culture. One approach

> We need a relationship reset in our companies, and in the world.

is to build cultures of friendship and service where people feel like they are not "human resources"; they are human beings.

Which brings me to a love story.

Building Companies Based on Friendship and Trust

One muggy afternoon, I sat in a cramped, makeshift studio filming two of the greatest entrepreneurs of our time, Ben Cohen and Jerry Greenfield. The interview was supposed to be an hour and stretched well into the evening. My stomach literally hurt the next morning from laughing so hard. What was most striking was the number of times they used the word "love" to describe their friendship and the culture of the company. An uncommon word in the corridors of companies, yet it was fundamental to their success.

When I asked them how they made Ben & Jerry's so successful, they just cracked up laughing and kept on saying "We were all in, we were all in for each other and for the company." They spoke about how trust and respect were central to everything and that they were "friends before they were partners." One was the marketer, the risk taker, and front man (guess which one), and the other was the operations guy who kept all the trains moving and questioned the ideas that verged on the outrageous. They were bonded in their belief that they were not just building an ice cream company; they were building a company that was going to change the world.

They had the self-awareness to realize that they needed each other, that their skillsets were complementary, that neither of them was the boss of the other one. Their leadership secret was grounded in their ability to build deep connections with each other, their teammates, their customers, and communities all over the world.

Of course, it was not always easy. Their friendship was like an embedded trampoline of resilience. They built tools to help them get to the other side of any disagreements, like the veto card. A simple mechanism where if they disagreed with something and felt so strongly about it, they were able to use the veto card to stop the

Deep Connections: The Secret Power of Great Leaders

decision from going forward. They spoke about how they used it very rarely, but when they did, it saved their friendship—and the company.

The founders of Airbnb—Nathan Blecharczyk, Joe Gebbia, and Brian Chesky, taught me an important lesson about how we consistently deepen our relationships. They built their company on trust. A decade ago, who would have imagined that so many homeowners would welcome strangers into their homes? They also thoughtfully crafted relational infrastructure in their company to create the right environment for trust and deep connections to thrive.

One Airbnb ritual, or magnetic moment as I would call it, is a super-practical, fun way to open safe spaces for communication. It is called "elephants, dead fish, and vomit." Yes, that's correct, three words you never thought you would see in the same sentence. Every month, they would bring together their team and create an opportunity for people to share three things: the elephants in the room that no one was talking about, the dead fish that everyone was talking about but no one was doing anything about, and the vomit, where people just needed to get something off their chest. This simple ritual allowed people to deepen their trust in each other, to talk through the things that were causing friction, and to have truly honest conversations. Basically, bringing humanity into the room.

Investing in a Relationship Reset of Deep Connections

The big question in every room right now is how will AI impact humanity in the workplace? With one extreme fearing that AI will dampen our creativity and disconnect us even further from one another, and the other side painting AI as the chance to build a utopian world where humans will have more free time.

In most of the discussions, what's been missing is the human dimension, the stuff that AI will never be able to do, like build deep connections with each other. We have an opportunity in companies to lead this relationship reset that will move us toward a place where people will come to work each day fully engaged, knowing that they are contributing to something far bigger than themselves. With circles of friends, deep connections serve as centers of resilience and joy in the workplace, and, ultimately, better collective decision making and more sustainable companies that can reimagine their relationships with nature.

We've created a world where leadership is more of a selfish, lonely concept driven, in part, by incentive structures that encourage competition rather than cooperation. The global venture philanthropy firm Draper Richards Kaplan did something unique in the finance sector. It reviewed all its incentive structures and removed the ones causing competition among team members and replaced them with incentives that focused people not on how much money they can make but on where they can make the biggest difference to others. This shift reoriented the dynamics of the organization toward cooperation in pursuit of something way bigger than any singular leader.

The wonderful scientist E. O. Wilson, who studied the collective power of ants, once said, "selfish individuals beat altruistic individuals, while groups of altruists beat groups of selfish individuals."[5] Right now, selfish individuals are often heralded as the best leaders, causing a dangerous race to the top of the short-term profit ladder. What if we turned that upside down and celebrated leaders who build deep connections between people?[6] Who rally around larger missions that will make others' lives better?

Perhaps the answer to making companies more human is a simple one—investing in relationships with each other. Elevating the importance of building deep connections at the center of all we do, building cultures of friendship and service that give people

73

the chance to be engaged in meaningful work. Where leadership is a relational approach rather than an egotistical, individualistic one. With compassionate empathy, kindness, and humility as leadership gold stars.

Focusing on what only we can do as human beings, building meaningful, life-changing relationships with each other and with this wondrous planet.

Notes

1. Quotes in this section are from Jean Oelwang, *Partnering: Forge the Deep Connections That Make Great Things Happen* (Optimism Press, 2022). See also Penelope Canan and Nancy Reichman, *Ozone Connections: Expert Networks in Global Environmental Governance* (Routledge, 2002).
2. Quoted in Oelwang, *Partnering*.
3. Alok Patel and Stephanie Plowman, "The Increasing Importance of a Best Friend at Work," *Gallup Workplace*, August 17, 2022. Updated January 19, 2024. www.gallup.com/workplace/397058/increasing-importance-best-friend-work.aspx
4. 100% Human at Work, a charitable initiative, incubated by Virgin Unite and The B Team, aimed at shaping a future of work, centered on human dignity, purpose, and belonging rather than mere productivity and profit.
5. David Sloan Wilson and Edward O. Wilson, "Rethinking the Theoretical Foundation of Sociobiology," *Quarterly Review of Biology* 82, no. 4 (2007).
6. See John Paul Stephens, Emily Heaphy, and Jane E. Dutton, "High Quality Connections." www.inspiringspace.com/wp-content/uploads/2018/04/Dutton-Heaphy-Stephens-_2011-High_Quality_Connections.pdf. See also Oelwang, *Partnering*; and Plus Wonder, a nonprofit initiative dedicated to helping people cultivate Deep Connections—across families, teams, classrooms, and communities—through intentional practices and story-telling: www.pluswonder.org

Chapter 7

The Fire We Gift: Why Connection Is the Currency of the Future

Sanyin Siang

In the Greek myth of Prometheus and the theft of fire, Prometheus, whose name means "forethought," stole fire from the gods in an act of defiance and gave it to humankind, performing an act of immense generosity that transformed civilization. For this, he was punished eternally, bound to a rock where an eagle devoured his liver each day.

Why did Prometheus do it? He knew that the gift of fire was not about possession but empowerment. Fire gave humanity the means to create, to cook, to forge, and to imagine. His gift sparked progress, but it was also a relational act: a bond between giver and receiver that forever connected Prometheus to humankind.

This is the essence of leadership throughout time. Leaders, mentors, and teachers give their "fire"—their wisdom, perspective, and experience—not simply to complete a transaction or "do their job" but to ignite something enduring in others. The act of sharing knowledge is not just informational. It is *transformational*.

In that myth, the knowledge of fire itself is so valuable that, by giving it to humans, Prometheus was condemned to a life of eternal punishment.

―――――――――

Acknowledgments: The author thanks Charlotte Yew Huixin, Lily Baglio, and Olivia Martin for their help in developing this chapter.

Today, we live in an age of breathtaking technological possibilities when it comes to knowledge. Artificial intelligence can summarize books, generate images, compose music, and even mimic accents and empathy in conversation. Knowledge, once scarce and protected, is now ubiquitous. It's available to anyone, anywhere, anytime.

Yet, amid all this progress, something vital feels increasingly rare: human connection.

This paradox defines leadership today. We have more tools to communicate but less true communication. More data and statistics but often less understanding. More connections on social media, creating the illusion of wider networks, but fewer genuine relationships.

In this world of information abundance, the leaders who will define tomorrow are not those who know the most but those who connect the most. These are the leaders who can make others feel seen, understood, and valued in ways that no algorithm can replicate.

To understand why, we might turn to an ancient idea, one most prevalent among some indigenous tribes far from "modern" civilization: the gift economy.

The Wisdom of the Gift Economy

In a monetary economy, the value of the gift is primarily inherent in the object itself. In a gift economy, value resides less in the object being exchanged and more in the relationship between giver and receiver. A gift is never simply a transfer of goods. It is an act that binds people together through trust, gratitude, and shared meaning.

Anthropologists have noted that in such systems, if someone tries to reciprocate a gift with another gift immediately, they are signaling they want to end the relationship. The magic of the gift lies in its openness, a perpetual cycle of generosity and indebtedness that keeps such communities alive.

Leading for Tomorrow

When I first heard about this idea from my students who took a cultural anthropology of money class at Duke, I was intrigued. Communication is a core aspect of leadership. To lead, one communicates purpose, information, data, vision, ideas, expertise, just to name a few things. But, in a world in which knowledge has become commodified, "received" easily through a search engine or a generative AI model, what does that mean for leadership?

What gives that information weight so that it is credible, or acted upon, has to do with trust in the person sharing that knowledge, conveying the idea. The value no longer lies in a piece of information itself but in the relationship between the person sharing the knowledge and the person receiving it.

Connection is the new currency that augments the value of the gift of that knowledge. That's the essence of the modern knowledge gift economy: Value is created not by possession but by connection. In an age when access to information is abundant, access to trust, networks, and possibilities is what creates exponential value.

When a leader offers feedback, advice, or insight, its impact depends more deeply on the strength of the relationship. A warning about a potential risk or blind spot might be ignored if there's no trust. But when trust exists, that same message becomes invaluable.

So, what if we double down on relationships as value creation? Relationships are how we differentiate. In traditional networking, people exchange business cards and favors. But in a technology-driven era, true connection means creating relationships that generate trust, not transactions.

From Information to Illumination

As a professor and thought leader, I've observed over the years that technology has transformed the way we learn. My students can master coding on YouTube, study economics through open courses, or

The Fire We Gift: Why Connection Is the Currency of the Future

ask ChatGPT to explain complex theories in seconds. But what remains irreplaceable is the human act of learning together: the conversation, the encouragement, the spark that happens when someone truly invests in your growth.

Knowledge, when shared in isolation, is just data. Knowledge, when shared through relationships, illuminates. This is the essence of the gift of mentorship. Mentors don't just transfer information; they shape understanding through empathy, context, and care. The mentee, in turn, doesn't "pay back" the mentor but pays it forward, perpetuating a cycle of generosity that keeps the human ecosystem of learning alive.

In this way, mentorship operates as a modern form of the gift economy. The value of the exchange is not measured by output but by the quality of the relationship.

In the age of commodified knowledge, connection is what makes knowledge valuable again. Consider the relationship between teacher and student, parent and child, leader and follower, and peers on a team. The facts exchanged may be universal but the context—the shared understanding of hopes, fears, and dreams—is deeply personal.

The Human Premium

In organizations, this insight transforms how we think about communication. Too often, leaders obsess over the polish of a speech or the production value of a video. But what gives communication resonance is not the data but the human stories that underlie it.

> What gives communication resonance is not the data but the human stories that underlie it.

I often remind my students that leadership is fundamentally relational, built on a sense of trust. My mentor, Sim Sitkin, had codeveloped a Six Domains of Leadership Model in which the foundational keystone piece is what he terms relational leadership.

In this domain, the leader's behaviors answer for the followers the question: "Does my leader understand who I am, what I care about, and what I fear?"

When followers feel understood, they don't just comply with orders, they commit to the work they are doing. The effect of those behaviors in the relational leadership domain is *trust*.

When people choose to follow a leader, they are giving up precious control and autonomy. The leader's duty is to honor that trust, to ensure that even when disagreement arises, people feel their best interests have been considered. Relational leadership asks: *Do I see you? Do I understand your hopes and fears? Do I make you feel like you matter?*

When leaders operate this way, organizations shift from being systems of transactions to communities of meaning. The result is greater engagement, loyalty, and innovation.

Connection as Sensemaking

We often speak of the information age as a triumph of knowledge, but it is increasingly an age of overwhelm. The flood of information has created confusion, not clarity. The sheer volume of content available today has made it harder, not easier, to discern truth from noise. For every credible study, there's a misleading headline or manipulated statistic circulating alongside it. Deepfakes, for instance, can fabricate realistic videos of public figures saying things they never said, eroding our trust in visual evidence itself. Fake news spreads faster than verified journalism, weaponized by algorithms that reward outrage over accuracy. Even AI-generated text and imagery, once hailed as tools for productivity, now blur the lines between genuine human insight and synthetic imitation.

In such an environment, leaders must do more than share data; they must help others make sense of it. And sensemaking is a deeply human act. It is one rooted in listening, empathy, and connection.

The Fire We Gift: Why Connection Is the Currency of the Future

When people feel connected, they are more receptive. They can hear not just what is said but what it means. Connection allows leaders to filter the noise, to translate complexity into relevance. It turns chaos into coherence.

The Gift of Vulnerability

Connection also requires vulnerability. This is the willingness to be seen as imperfect and to share lessons learned rather than present polished certainty. I recently shared in the *MIT Sloan Management Review* that vulnerability is a way for leaders to meet their followers where they are,[1] creating space that invites their team members to share honest opinions and thoughts. Personal stories of mistakes or uncertainty allow leaders to gain authenticity and relatability.

This aligns with the principle of the gift economy: Leaders can give a part of themselves—their lessons and their honesty—not to gain something in return, but to deepen the relationship. That generosity of spirit creates belonging and trust.

The Power of "Hyperinefficiency"

In our obsession with efficiency, we often overlook that connection takes time. Relationships don't move at the speed of a click. They require presence, patience, and shared experience.

> Connection takes time. Relationships don't move at the speed of a click.

On a visit to Bloomberg's offices, I observed something remarkable.[2] The first elevator only goes up to the sixth floor, and everyone is encouraged to gather in a large open hall on the sixth for breakfast, coffee, and conversation. This deliberate "hyperinefficiency"—people taking time out of their day to gather and connect with people in departments they might not otherwise meet—fuels a culture of connection

It may look inefficient in the short term, but initiatives like this build long-term efficiency through trust, creativity, and collaboration. That face you see every day on the sixth floor might be someone from a completely different division—finance, policy, or marketing—who can turn into a future collaborator, problem solver, or even the key partner who helps unlock your next big idea. Connection, paradoxically, becomes the fastest route to sustainable impact.

The Leadership of Tomorrow

What does all this mean for leaders preparing for the future? It means that leadership for tomorrow will be defined by the ability to foster genuine connection—to make people feel that they matter, that they are understood, and that their contributions have purpose.

The goal of leadership relationships is not friendship; it is trust. You don't have to be best friends with your team, but you must make them believe that you care. As the saying goes: People don't care what you know until they know how much you care.

When we lead with that mindset, we reintroduce the humanity that technology alone cannot replicate.

The Gift That Keeps Giving

The myth of Prometheus ends in eternal punishment. And it surfaces an insight about putting on the leadership mantle. Every act of true leadership carries a measure of sacrifice. When you give knowledge freely, when you invest in others without expecting repayment, you expose yourself to vulnerability, to exhaustion, to misunderstanding.

And yet, you also ignite something enduring. The fire you pass on spreads, illuminating others who, in turn, illuminate others.

Leadership, at its heart, thrives not on scarcity but on generosity, not on efficiency but on empathy. In the age of AI, when knowledge is abundant and connection is scarce, our greatest act of leadership may be the simplest: to give, to connect, and to care without expecting anything in return.

Because when we do, we create not just smarter organizations but more human ones.

Notes

1. Sanyin Siang, "Ask Sanyin: What Does Vulnerability Really Mean for Leaders?" *MIT Sloan Management Review*, June 3, 2025. https://sloanreview.mit.edu/article/ask-sanyin-what-does-vulnerability-really-mean-for-leaders/
2. Sanyin Siang, "In Defense of Inefficiency," *Dialogue Review*, February 18, 2026. https://dialoguereview.com/in-defense-of-inefficiency/

Leading with Empathy in a Whirlwind of Change

Nancy Duarte

Work feels constant now. The pressure to move fast isn't seasonal or tied to a specific transformation initiative. It's nonstop waves of new systems, new tools, new expectations, and new change doesn't come in waves anymore; we're constantly swimming against a current.

In this new reality, traditional change management models are too slow. They were designed for episodic shifts, instead of when change is flowing constantly. Even a multiyear change used to have a beginning, middle, and end. Now there's only one long, messy middle. A long stretch of flux with no obvious finish line.

Leaders try to keep up the pace by applying pressure. But pressure doesn't create alignment, and urgency that isn't rooted in meaning will almost always be met with fear.

It's not the speed of change that exhausts people; it's the uncertainty. The greatest leaders intuit a vision of where to go *and* communicate how to get there. When people can't find the throughline, it feels like they're running hard and fast through zero-visibility fog. Too much time is spent questioning decisions instead of moving in sync with them. Running around bumping into each other while working at an incredible speed only serves to amplify the chaos.

High-change environments need leaders to communicate differently. Not just a message. Not just a deck. Not just a top-down announcement or a carefully worded memo. What's needed is durable and grounding communication powered by empathy. Communication that helps people make sense of what's changing, internalize it, and keep moving forward without losing their footing.

The slog of change is about endurance. To move through sustained change, people need a different kind of fuel: not adrenaline but emotional fuel. When people understand what matters and why, they can keep going even when it's hard. Speeches, stories, ceremonies, and symbols give leaders a structured way to build that clarity and refill people's emotional tanks. When used together, they form a core toolkit that helps people stay grounded and connected while moving fast.

These tools don't make change less urgent. They make it less confusing, and this shift is what makes the speed feel more sustainable.

Speeches Spark It

In moments of change, people look to leaders for signals. Not just about what to do but about how to feel. The first formal communication in a change effort often comes in the form of a speech. It might be part of a town hall or a rollout meeting. It might be just a few sentences in an informal team huddle. But that moment matters and sets the tone.

Too often, speeches are used to share decisions. But during change, the role of a speech is to help people orient within the fog. It helps them understand where they are, what's shifting, and how to navigate it. A well-structured speech marks the steps an audience can take by framing what's possible. It provides enough structure to let people see a small piece of what's ahead so they can act on it.

> During change, the role of a speech is to help people orient within the fog.

Nothing has been foggier than the sudden rise and adoption of generative AI. At Microsoft Ignite 2023, CEO Satya Nadella addressed an audience of developers, IT professionals, and business leaders to help them see the potential in adopting AI. In his speech, he set up the scale of the shift by saying "We're entering this exciting new phase of AI. . . We're at a tipping point. This is clearly the age of Copilots."

Nadella then transitioned to the vision of how AI will integrate seamlessly across Microsoft's existing tools. This assured the business leaders that integrating AI wouldn't be difficult because it is "one experience that runs across all our services. . .bringing the right skills to you when you need them."

To make the tangible benefits of AI clear, he said, "we're able to complete tasks much faster. . .People are spending less time searching for information, they're holding more effective meetings, and that's having a real cascading effect on work and workflow everywhere." Then he described what the future will look like by making AI an integral part of every role. "We believe in a future where there will be a Copilot for everyone and everything you do." The message oriented Microsoft's stakeholders to their commitment to AI-driven productivity.[1]

When my company coaches leaders through communicating change, we often ask: What are you asking people to leave behind? What are you inviting them into? And what belief do they need to adopt in order to cross that threshold?

A good speech isn't pushing people; it's pulling them toward you and your idea by giving them a new frame of reference, helping them see what you see. It names the current reality and points toward a preferred future, building a bridge between the two.

During the Knowledge 2023 keynote, ServiceNow CEO Bill McDermott cited a compelling statistic: "40% of the CEOs in the world today think their companies will no longer be viable in 10 years if they don't radically change course now. So, what does that tell us? It's time to be bold. It's time to be super courageous."[2]

85

Leading with Empathy in a Whirlwind of Change

This stark statistic created an urgency for attendees to act decisively because McDermott framed digital transformation as necessary for survival.

The most effective speeches driving change aren't off-the-cuff remarks or overloaded slide decks. They're carefully crafted, visualized, rehearsed, and delivered for clarity.

When the core concept of a speech is visualized well, it can scale. The CEO of a manufacturing firm introduced a new sustainability framework that everyone could sketch on a whiteboard. Employees could internalize and retell how their individual actions contribute to the shared mission. The unified rollout created the momentum (and alignment) they needed.[3]

Change communication isn't a one-time event; it's a series of intentional moments. Speeches act as pulses that keep energy and belief alive. When leaders treat speeches as transformative rather than performative, they steady the team and help them keep going by reconnecting them to purpose.

Stories Spread It

A speech ignites change, but you need to rely on more tools to sustain it. For the message to become systemic, it has to have momentum beyond the moment it was delivered. That's where stories come in. These are real, factual short anecdotes that generate emotional fuel to keep teams going.

Stories give people something to carry with them that they can retell by taking abstract ideas and making them real. Stories help people adopt change by connecting it to something genuinely human they already care about.

Leaders can design their own story catalog by building a set of stories that motivate teams throughout the change effort. Each story can fuel teams differently by pulling from the past, pointing to the future, or anchoring people in the present.

- **Origin stories** ground people in the organization's identity by visiting formative moments that shaped its values. Use these to remind people of what has always mattered most.

- **Future stories** cast a vision of what's possible by describing a vivid picture of what could be. Share these to help people imagine where the organization is headed.

- **Journey stories** help people understand how they'll get there by highlighting real progress and obstacles that have been overcome. Use these to build momentum and normalize change.

- **Cause stories** define what they're fighting for by surfacing a deeper moral or emotional reason for change. Tell these to create urgency without triggering fear.

- **Moment-of-choice stories** highlight pivotal decisions that reveal what it looks like to choose courage or values when the outcome isn't certain.

- **Hero stories** reinforce what good looks like by spotlighting individuals who model the desired behaviors. Use these to encourage others to follow their lead.

When leaders repeat these story types often and with consistency, something begins to shift. The stories become common language and beliefs. Then belief shapes behavior.

A poignant example of a story follows the long history of Starbucks and its CEO, Howard Schultz. In 1983,

> Stories become common language and beliefs. Then belief shapes behavior.

Leading with Empathy in a Whirlwind of Change

Schultz stood in a Milanese espresso bar, and instead of only seeing the coffee, he saw community. Inspired by the social aspect of coffee, he returned to the United States and communicated a bold future story to transform Starbucks from a coffee bean retailer into a place where human connection comes first. That moment set the course for Starbucks to become a "third place" between work and home. Decades later, amid declining in-store traffic and cultural drift, Schultz returned as CEO in 2022. He pointed back to that original dream by reminding partners that Starbucks is not "in the coffee business serving people" but, instead, is in the "people business serving coffee."[4] By resurfacing his pivotal decision, Schultz created clarity on the company's return to its roots. He conveyed with conviction the courage to make great in-the-moment choices so Starbucks can preserve and protect what it values as it evolves.

Stories add context. In high-speed environments, they provide a thread of continuity when everything else feels in motion. Leaders who apply story well help people understand change so they can embody it and not just comply with it.

Ceremonies Cement It

Change doesn't feel real until it's experienced. That's why leaders need to create moments that mark a transition. These moments don't need to be big. But they need to be intentional.

Ceremonies are how we make meaning through action. They turn invisible shifts into visible ones and signal to people that something old is ending and something new is happening. They demonstrate how all of us are (or were) part of the transformation and invite others to participate in the shift. Ceremonies serve a structural role to launch beginnings, signal milestones, or close out a chapter.

When a leader forces ceremonies, they often feel contrived to others. Instead, ceremonies should occur naturally in your organization, like how Salesforce uses V2MOM (Vision, Value, Methods, Obstacles, and Measures) documents to align vision and priorities at the start of every year. Annual V2MOM meetings act as ceremonial beginnings, where teams commit to shared goals and executives create energy around the direction for the year ahead. Many companies also use ceremonies to sustain change by creating a steady rhythm of weekly gatherings to celebrate milestones or appreciate others. At Duarte, we carve out ten minutes of each monthly meeting so employees can celebrate each other's accomplishments. Feeling seen and appreciated is especially important in continuous and fast-paced change.

Some ceremonies are symbolic, like retiring an outdated process in front of a team. Others are practical, like kicking off change by hosting a shared offsite. Some are personal, like a manager setting aside time to name what the change means to their team. What matters is that the moment is marked, not skipped or rushed.

When ceremonies are used consistently, they create a rhythm that builds confidence. Ceremonies are a powerful tool to leverage a single moment into part of a larger pattern to make it clear that "this is how we do things now."

In periods of constant motion, ceremonies offer stability. They're not a distraction from the work itself but are woven in as part of the work. Leaders who use them consistently create cultures where change gets absorbed and sticks.

Symbols Visualize It

Speeches help people hear it. Stories help people believe it. Ceremonies help people feel it. But symbols help people see it. And once they see it, they start to trust that the change is real.

In high-change environments, leaders can't be everywhere. Symbols matter because they leave a visual mark and create shorthand that says "This matters."

Leading with Empathy in a Whirlwind of Change

Symbols function as visible proof points. Unlike logos or graphic elements, these are symbols in the anthropological sense: actions, objects, spaces, or words that represent something bigger than themselves. They serve as cues that a shift has occurred and that the team is adopting something new.

At Amazon, an empty chair is placed in meetings to represent the customer, ensuring that their perspective is central to decision making. This practice underscores Amazon's customer-centric philosophy. The symbol grounds employees in prioritizing customer needs in all aspects of the business.

There are four types of symbols leaders can use to spread and solidify a message:

1. **Symbolic acts** are actions that embody change. These are things leaders do that communicate the shift more powerfully than words.

2. **Symbolic objects** are physical items that carry meaning. These might be tokens, artifacts, or tools either introduced or retired to mark a new phase.

3. **Symbolic settings** are environmental cues that signal transformation. These include changes to space, location, or configuration that reinforce new ways of working.

4. **Symbolic language** are phrases or terms that act as cultural shortcuts. These can be created intentionally or lifted from stories and ceremonies to become part of everyday dialogue.

Sometimes a single phrase, coined during a speech or ceremony, becomes the shorthand people use to orient around the change, like when Schultz reincorporated the phrase "Third Place" back into the values at Starbucks. Sometimes a symbol becomes the place an offsite was held or a token tied to an event theme.

Symbols are directional. They cue people's attention and behavior. And when used consistently across a transformation, they carry meaning into every corner of the organization. The most highly valued symbols are not generated or imposed by the leaders; they emerge from within the team or organization. A symbol rooted in team identity can travel far.

Sometimes the change is a radical shift, and a ceremony and symbol combine into a symbolic act. In the early 1980s, to develop the original Macintosh, Steve Jobs and the Macintosh team raised a Jolly Roger flag over Apple's smaller building where the Macintosh team worked on Bandley Drive, in Cupertino, California. In a surprise move, they hoisted the flag in the dead of night to demonstrate how this small team was carving a new path within a larger company. To encourage unconventional thinking and risk taking, Jobs would say, "It's better to be a pirate than join the Navy," giving the Mac team permission to break away from Apple's corporate norms.[5]

Clarity Carries It

These tools can help leaders be more human. They create urgency without fear by helping people move fast without unraveling. Change is no longer an interruption because it's now constant.

Elliott Hill has come out of retirement to turn Nike around. To lead this pivotal moment, he's using speeches, stories, ceremonies, and symbols to create clarity and return the company to its foundational ethos.

The night before Hill started as CEO, he sent a video memo to the employees. He often shares his own story of starting as an intern in 1988, selling apparel and driving 120,000 miles in a Chrysler minivan to pitch Nike products across Texas. This narrative of grit,

Leading with Empathy in a Whirlwind of Change

perseverance, and loyalty resonates with employees and under-scores his deep understanding of Nike's culture while framing his return as a homecoming to a brand he never stopped loving.

Hill pulled on deep-seated symbolic phrases as he declared his vision to "put the athlete at the center of everything we do," reaffirming cofounder Bill Bowerman's inclusive belief that "if you have a body, you are an athlete."[6]

This commitment signals a strategic shift back to Nike's core focus on innovation while moving away from an overemphasis on lifestyle products. Hill's leadership also keeps the legacy of Steve Prefontaine alive. Prefontaine was a legendary American long-distance runner and the earliest Nike icon, known for his relentless spirit and dedication. Hill keeps Prefontaine's mantra on his desk: "To give anything less than your best is to sacrifice the gift." This serves as a daily reminder of the excellence Nike strives for.

Hill honors Nike's storied past and is galvanizing the organization toward a future rooted in authenticity and purpose. His narrative-driven approach will be instrumental in inspiring employees and consumers. His early reliance on story is already renewing a sense of unity and direction as Nike navigates its path forward.

Leaders can no longer default to pressure and adrenaline to push through. Clarity and emotional fuel will give audiences the energy they need to ease their exhaustion and create steadiness. This toolkit supports speed with stability and creates orientation and meaning, again and again, as the organization continues to evolve.

Speeches, stories, ceremonies, and symbols aren't used in isolation. When used together, they are transformative. They restore energy, build belief, and give people something to hold onto. In an environment where everything is in flux, a shared way of communicating becomes a form of safety.

These tools help human-centered leaders move quickly *and* bring their people with them. Not by pushing with force but by guiding with clarity. When people have emotional fuel, they are inspired to keep going.

Notes

1. Quoted in Kelly Teal, "AI's 'Pace of Innovation' Dominates Nadella Keynote Microsoft Ignite 2023," *Channel Futures*, November 15, 2023. www.channelfutures.com/channel-business/ai-s-pace-of-innovation-dominates-nadella-keynote-microsoft-ignite-2023

2. ServiceNow, *Knowledge 2023 Opening Keynote: Putting Yes to Work* [Video], July 28, 2023. www.youtube.com/watch?v=_h3GW9zGnkA

3. Nancy Duarte and Patti Sanchez, *Illuminate: Ignite Change Through Speeches, Stories, Ceremonies, and Symbols* (Portfolio/Penguin, 2016), 98.

4. Quoted in ibid, 64.

5. Quoted in ibid, 154–155.

6. These quotes and the next one are from Jessica Staheli, "We're Gonna Win": Elliott Hill's Plan for the Future of Nike," *Sneaker Freaker*, October 22, 2024. www.sneakerfreaker.com/features/nike-ceo-elliott-hill-interview-plan-for-the-future-of-nike/

Chapter 9

In the Era of AI, Successful Leaders Value Wisdom

Chip Conley

Wisdom used to be cool. Dudes in white robes asked provocative questions to young Greeks in the town square. Historically, Wisdom or Mystery Schools emerged during times of crisis or on the cusp of great leaps in human consciousness to help shepherd society through a challenging transition.

Centuries later, the Scientific Revolution of the 16th and 17th centuries shoved wisdom to the intellectual and religious margins of society because it felt abstract and less relevant. But, in the past few decades, many of us have been "smuggling consciousness" into the workplace, elevating wisdom to its rightful place alongside knowledge.

In today's rapidly evolving landscape of artificial intelligence, we find ourselves at a curious inflection point. While computational power, algorithmic sophistication, and data availability continue their exponential climb, a counterintuitive truth emerges: The most powerful differentiator in AI utilization may not be technical expertise but rather human wisdom. As AI systems become increasingly accessible to all, the quality of human guidance directing these systems becomes the decisive factor in generating truly valuable outcomes.

In a world that is awash in knowledge, wisdom becomes increasingly valuable. Wisdom—that distinctive blend of experience, judgment, contextual understanding, and ethical insight—may be the critical missing element in our current AI paradigm, and those who possess wisdom stand to gain a significant advantage in an AI-augmented world.

What Is Wisdom?

First, let's define wisdom. My definition is "metabolized experience mindfully shared for the common good." There are three parts to this definition:

1. "Metabolized experience" is seeing one's life as the most exquisite exercise in experiential education. And, yet, we have precious few means to help people turn life lessons into a tangible art of living. This is part of the reason why I created the world's first midlife wisdom school, the Modern Elder Academy (MEA). MEA's mission is to demystify, elevate, and operationalize wisdom.

2. "Mindfully shared" speaks to the idea that wisdom isn't taught; it's shared. But it's shared in a skillful and customized way. The "OK Boomer" meme started a few years ago because an older man was telling a younger woman how the world worked. War stories are not necessarily wisdom unless they're relevant to the receiver.

3. "For the common good" reminds us that, unlike smartness or savviness, which can be hoarded selfishly, wisdom is a social good for the betterment of society.

Much of the current discourse around artificial intelligence centers on its ability to automate knowledge work. The implicit assumption is that AI will gradually subsume human cognitive functions until it approximates or surpasses human capabilities across all domains.

Leading for Tomorrow

This technological determinism fails to recognize a crucial distinction: *between intelligence as information processing and wisdom as contextual judgment refined through lived experience.*

Despite advances in large language models and multimodal AI systems, we have yet to develop anything approaching "artificial wisdom." These systems lack core attributes essential to wisdom:

- They have no lived experience through which to develop judgment.

- They cannot truly understand the consequences of failure.

- They lack the embodied and cultural knowledge that comes from navigating the physical and social world.

- They possess no intrinsic values or ethical frameworks beyond what has been statistically modeled.

- They are backward-looking, scavenging the internet for the past without being able to intuit the future.

- They are reliant on the quality of the questions we ask.

The absence of artificial wisdom creates not just a limitation but an opportunity—a space where human guidance becomes not merely helpful but essential to realizing AI's full potential.

> The absence of artificial wisdom creates not just a limitation but an opportunity.

But, even outside of the wisdom/AI relationship, the times require the discernment that wisdom offers. We live and work in an age of extreme uncertainty and severe disruption. Leaders today face complex systemic challenges, and their people seek clarity, empathy, and connection. Perhaps more than ever, there is a need for greater leadership wisdom based on ethical discernment, embodied insight, and relational depth.

In the Era of AI, Successful Leaders Value Wisdom

The Emergence of Wisdom Workers

Management theorist Peter Drucker created the roadmap for the emerging knowledge economy, coining the term "knowledge worker" in 1959[1] and helping to develop the practice of knowledge management 20 years later. Today, most organizations of some size have a chief information officer (CIO) or chief knowledge officer (CKO) whose job is to achieve organizational objectives through creating, sharing, and managing knowledge. Are we ready for a Chief Wisdom Officer™ (a term coined and trademarked by Cass Redstone) and wisdom management practices that can help prepare our modern workplace for the times ahead?

When I was a clueless 28-year-old CEO of one of the United States' first boutique hotel companies, Joie de Vivre, I was struggling as a young leader, trying to make sense of what I was learning along the way. I repurposed an empty diary into "My Wisdom Book." Each weekend, I would reflect upon some of my greatest lessons of the past week (mainly relating to my career or leadership). Afterward, I'd dutifully add a few bullet points, summarizing what I had learned from these lessons and how these lessons would serve me in the future. Thirty-seven years later, I continue to practice this weekend ritual, albeit now in Google Docs, and it has helped me to metabolize my life experience. Our painful life lessons are often the raw material for our future wisdom.

You can do the same. I bet you have an unused journal in your home. This coming weekend, pull it out and jot down a few sentences about three or four different circumstances you encountered during the week, including how you handled them (even if you made a mistake or two) and what you learned from them. And, then, keep doing it every weekend for 20 to 30 minutes. The earlier in your life and career you start doing this, the longer you get to use your wisdom.

Over the past 40 years, leading three different companies—Joie de Vivre, Airbnb, and MEA—through trial and error, I've developed a set of wisdom management practices that have helped each company become more discerning and human-centered in its decision making. Here are five that you can incorporate into your company:

1. **Distilling team lessons:** I don't require my leaders to keep a weekly Wisdom Journal, but once per quarter, our small leadership teams do a Wisdom Share meeting in which each leader candidly articulates their biggest lesson of the quarter, warts and all, and what they learned from it. Of course, this requires a functional team that's willing to pursue a growth mindset by vulnerably sharing mistakes. But it also means that we're learning from each other's mistakes. We end the meeting with a conversation around our biggest team lesson of the quarter and how it can serve us in the future. I don't think any leadership practice I instituted at the fast-growing Airbnb in its early days had a bigger impact on the performance (and camaraderie) of my teams than this quarterly ritual.

2. **Making the wise more accessible:** As part of your routine employee satisfaction surveys, consider including a new question: "Beyond your boss, who in the organization offers you helpful advice or wisdom?" This information allows you to create a Wisdom Heat Map focused on where wisdom is stored, such that you might consider asking some of your wise people if they'd like to be trained as internal coaches and evolve their careers in that direction. The question I would ask myself is: "How do we make these wise people more accessible in the organization?" You can also analyze the qualities of who shows up most prominently on the Heat Map and develop internal training around those qualities.

In the Era of AI, Successful Leaders Value Wisdom

3. **Developing "mentern" programs:** A wise leader is a "mentern," a mentor and an intern at the same time.[2] Smart companies realize that well-organized mentoring programs offer the most significant learning and development return on investment. It's also a great retention tool. As I discuss in *Wisdom @ Work*, Deloitte's research has shown that younger workers with an internal mentor are twice as likely to stay in the company for five years.[3] Wise companies recognize that matching programs in which two internal leaders with complementary knowledge (he knows how to run a meeting, she knows how to maximize personal tech gadgets) can create deeper relationships since both leaders are mentors and interns at the same time.

> A wise leader is a "mentern," a mentor and an intern at the same time.

4. **Creating a "Wisdom@" Employee Resource Group (ERG):** I helped create the internal group, Wisdom@Airbnb, focused on older employees and their allies (at the time, just 10 percent of the employees were 40 or older). Airbnb had expertise in helping people accumulate knowledge but was less experienced in creating the habitat for distilling wisdom. This ERG served as an internal wisdom incubator.

The Art of the Question: Wisdom's First Advantage

It's been said that computers are useless because they only offer answers. The wisest people I know have developed the art of inquiry. We see this in a great coach, therapist, or wise leader. I'll never forget when one of my mentors asked me, "Chip, what are you pretending not to know?" when I was procrastinating making a decision. One of my favorite interview questions is the mind-twister: "What's the number one way you're often misperceived in the workplace?" I've witnessed how this question opens the door for the interviewee to throw out their script in a formal interview. And I only know this because I've asked this question hundreds of times now so I have some pattern recognition of just how illuminating this question can be.

Questions are particularly valuable in our relationship with AI. AI systems, like large language models, are highly responsive to the quality, specificity, and framing of prompts. Those with extensive life experience intuitively understand several principles that lead to superior queries:

- **Context setting:** Wise questioners know how to establish the proper frame for AI interaction. Rather than jumping directly to isolated questions, they provide relevant background, clarify objectives, and establish appropriate constraints. They might specify, "I'm trying to understand this issue from the perspective of someone who experienced the economic conditions of the 1970s inflation period," bringing historical context that the AI alone cannot supply.

- **Question refinement:** Wisdom brings an understanding of how questions shape answers. Experienced individuals recognize when a question contains hidden assumptions, conflates distinct concepts, or fails to address the core issue. They iteratively refine their queries, adjusting based on initial responses to progressively move toward more valuable insights. For example, rather than asking "What's the best investment strategy?," the wise person might specify: "What investment approaches historically performed well during periods of technological disruption combined with moderate inflation, particularly for those within a decade of retirement?" The specificity draws on pattern recognition from lived experience.

101

- **Recognizing knowledge boundaries:** Perhaps most important, wisdom includes epistemic humility—understanding the limits of what can be known. The experienced questioner recognizes domains where even the most sophisticated AI will struggle to provide reliable answers, such as novel ethical dilemmas, unprecedented situations, or highly contextual human experiences.

The Enduring Value of Human Wisdom

As artificial intelligence continues its rapid advancement, we find ourselves not at the twilight of human wisdom but at the dawn of its renewed importance. The absence of artificial wisdom creates a persistent space where human judgment, ethical insight, and contextual understanding remain not just relevant but essential.

The most successful individuals and organizations in the AI era will be those who recognize this fundamental truth: *artificial intelligence, for all its power, requires the guidance of human wisdom to reach its full potential*. Rather than rendering wisdom obsolete, AI amplifies its value by expanding the reach and impact of those who possess it.

> Rather than rendering wisdom obsolete, AI amplifies its value.

This presents not a threat but an unprecedented opportunity—to combine decades of accumulated wisdom with powerful new tools in ways that neither could achieve alone. The future belongs not to those who merely master artificial intelligence but to those who bring wisdom to its application.

In the end, the question is not whether we need artificial wisdom to complement artificial intelligence. Rather, it's how we can better integrate the irreplaceable wisdom of human experience with these powerful new capabilities, creating not just smarter systems but wiser outcomes for humanity.

Notes

1. Peter F. Drucker, *Landmarks of Tomorrow* (Heinemann, 1959).
2. See Chip Conley, *Wisdom @ Work: The Making of a Modern Elder* (Currency, 2018), p. 24.
3. Ibid.

In the Era of AI, Successful Leaders Value Wisdom

Chapter 10

Leading with an Augmented Intelligence Mindset

Brian Solis

Today's leaders are exploring use cases for AI by prioritizing the automation of repetitive and menial tasks, scaling efficiencies, taking costs out of the organization, and reducing their workforces to appease shareholders. They're ushering in a new era of business as usual, this time powered by AI. But that's not you. You're not here to unpack what is arguably history's most disruptive and promising technology only to repack it into a box that's labeled "AI status quo." Last time I checked, AI doesn't stand for "automated intelligence."

No, you're here to explore how AI unlocks opportunities beyond automation with people at the center of this workforce renaissance. AI status-quo leaders are focusing on scaling yesterday's work. And that's fine. Yesterday's processes that matter tomorrow should be automated. People, however, aren't replaceable if they learn how to work *with* AI to do the work that was not possible before AI. The goal is to identify which tasks and roles can be automated and to imagine innovative tasks and roles that create new value and deliver entirely new outcomes.

This is human-centered leadership in the AI Renaissance. With intent, it reshapes the future of leading a workforce that works creatively *with* AI instead of being replaced by it. And since this is unprecedented in standard leadership playbooks, tomorrow's human-centered leaders will need a 'mindshift' to automate *and* augment the future of work.

In my book *Mindshift: Transform Leadership, Drive Innovation, and Reshape the Future*, I shared that you can't change the world unless you change how you see it first.[1] That's what this moment requires: a mindshift to think beyond the AI status quo.

This is exactly the time to reimagine leadership where AI augments humans, not replaces them. It's true now. And it will be true every time you revisit this statement, regardless of where we are with AI as an advancing technology.

The Definition of Mindshift

Mindshift (noun)

Mindshift MīndSHift

Definition: A profound change in perspective that breaks free from routine thinking and patterns to unlock new possibilities, anticipate the future, and shape what comes next.

Example: This book sparked a powerful mindshift in how she viewed her approach to leadership.

Mindshift (verb, used without object)

mindshifted | MīndSHifdəd | mindshifting | MīndSHiftiNG |

Definition: To undergo or cause a change in mindset or perspective and take different actions moving forward.

Example: Before she finished this book, she had already started to mindshift toward human-centered leadership. She found herself mindshifting with every turn of the page.

Leading for Tomorrow

Leadership Starts with IQ, EQ, SQ, and Now AIQ

Let's reframe AI, not as "artificial" or "automated" intelligence but instead as "augmented intelligence." Augmented intelligence overcomes the implication of machine over human and keeps the human in the loop and in the lead.

There's something extraordinary happening. We are witnessing the rise of a new era where artificial intelligence doesn't just disrupt how we work; it challenges us to reimagine why we work, what we create, and who we become.

The organizations that thrive in this era won't be the ones that simply automate faster and cheaper. They'll be led by people who can see differently, think expansively, and lead with people at the center. These are human-centered augmented leaders. Leaders with AIQ, an evolved leadership skill I call the augmented intelligence quotient.

Like other quotients used to describe and measure aspects of intelligence and ability, AIQ doesn't measure how smart the machine is but instead how much smarter we are because of it.

Before diving into AIQ, let's review other important leadership quotients used to measure human-centered leadership:

- **Intelligence quotient (IQ)** measures a person's cognitive abilities, including logical reasoning, problem solving, memory, and abstract thinking. IQ is often measured as a score that indicates how far above or below an individual stands in mental ability relative to their peer group. The peer group score is an IQ of 100.[2]

- **Emotional quotient (EQ)** measures emotional intelligence, the ability to understand, use, and manage one's own emotions in different situations[3] and to recognize, understand, and influence the emotions of others.

Leading with an Augmented Intelligence Mindset

- **Social quotient (SQ)** measures a person's social intelligence, including their ability to build and maintain relationships, lead and manage people, understand social cues, and adapt to different social situations.[4]

- **Adaptability quotient (AQ)** measures a person's ability to adjust and persevere in a changing environment. AQ represents a blend of capabilities and character: flexibility and resilience, openness to change, sharp problem-solving, and emotional intelligence (EQ).[5]

The augmented intelligence quotient (AIQ) isn't about how smart, capable, and fluent your AI skills are. That's the other AIQ: artificial intelligence quotient. The artificial intelligence quotient[6] measures proficiency and readiness in adopting, understanding, and leveraging AI.

Instead, augmentation is more about how you evolve your thinking and behavior in response to AI. AI is already changing the rules. It's up to us to decide if we change with it.

Do you compete with AI? Or do you compete *with* AI? See what I did there? This play on words is something I learned from my friend, HubSpot cofounder and CTO Dharmesh Shaw.[7] It's natural to interpret the first question as a threat. "Yes! AI is coming after jobs." By italicizing "with" in the second question, we are inspired to think beyond AI as a threat or a tool and, with a mindshift, we can instead see it as an extension of our as-yet-unimagined capabilities.

AIQ reframes the AI narrative from fear and uncertainty to empowerment and opportunity.

AIQ reframes the AI narrative from fear and uncertainty to empowerment and opportunity.

You're supercharged with AIQ. You're not being automated out of a job. You're being augmented to evolve with AI. AIQ becomes a measure of a leader's ability to co-create, collaborate, and scale value with machine intelligence, not be replaced by it. And it's the ability to help others thrive with augmented intelligence to do what they couldn't do with AI *and* what AI couldn't do without human collaboration.

AIQ is measurable, developable, trainable, and thus scalable. It now joins in leadership development, education, and innovation ecosystems moving forward. Think IQ → EQ → SQ → AIQ.

The Automation Trap

We've seen this story before. Every time a new technology emerges, leaders rush to implement it, to scale, accelerate, and reduce the cost of doing yesterday's work. Leaders aim to make their teams faster, leaner, more productive. But each new wave of technology also introduces opportunities to create and deliver new value in addition to yesterday's value. It's how companies survive digital Darwinism and compete for the future.

This time, with AI, the stakes are even higher. But yesterday's promises look a lot like today's promises. They're both seductive and familiar. Do more. Spend less. Move faster. So, we do what we always do. We bolt AI on to legacy systems to automate legacy processes and work. We use it as an intelligent automation engine. But here's the problem: If you apply AI to outdated thinking, all you get is faster irrelevance. Business as usual with AI is still business as usual. Only now it's speeding toward obsolescence because we're automating away our ability to compete differently and exponentially with AI.

> If you apply AI to outdated thinking, all you get is faster irrelevance.

Leading with an Augmented Intelligence Mindset

In *Mindshift*, I wrote that disruption reveals where we're stuck. And nowhere are we more stuck right now than in our thinking. The greatest barrier to transformation isn't the technology; it's the mindset we bring to it and the mindset we share with others.

AI is not just another tool to make old processes more efficient and intelligent. It's a catalyst for a new kind of thinking and, with it, a new kind of leadership.

You Are the Leader People Don't Know They Need Yet

I want to speak directly to you as a leader, whether you're in a leadership position, working toward it, or advising a leader. Let's not talk about the title or the resume. I'd like to speak directly to you as a human being. The way you think, the questions you ask, the assumptions and values you hold, the fears you carry deep inside. They all affect your perspective and the actions you take (and don't take). They either limit your organization or grow it. By growth, I don't mean incremental improvements; I mean innovative transformation. Accepting this reality is incredibly empowering and liberating. Because once you realize that the limiting factor to AI's true potential lies in the mirror, your mind opens toward a mindshift.

The role of a true leader is to create a future that wouldn't have happened otherwise. The same is true for automated AI versus augmented intelligence.

To do that now, you have to rethink what it means to lead. You have to shift from being a manager of people and processes to being a catalyst of possibility. From being a decision maker to becoming a meaning maker. From leading yesterday's tasks and outcomes to leading transformation and innovation. That's where AIQ comes in.

Leading for Tomorrow

Defining AIQ

AIQ = Augmented Intelligence Quotient

AIQ represents a superpower with AI, a superior enhancement and capacity in output and outcome. It's how you evolve your thinking and behavior in response to AI, and how you do the same for your teams and workforce. If you think about how Superman could fly, for example, his superpowers were the result of Earth's sun (or, if you go back to the original comic book from 1939, Earth's weaker gravity).[8] The point is that, as with Superman, augmentation allows for a "super" collaboration with AI to do or accomplish what wasn't possible before AI.

AIQ measures your capacity to:

- Think in partnership with AI to unlock new possibilities and deliver outcomes.

- Co-create new solutions that neither humans nor machines could produce alone.

- Lead teams into uncharted territory with empathy, imagination, and courage.

We've spent decades talking about IQ. More recently, we've emphasized EQ and SQ as critical factors in empathetic leadership. But the world has changed and is changing. Now AIQ, and AQ (adaptability), complement leadership quotients to adapt in the era of AI.

IQ gets you into the room. EQ and SQ help you lead people. AQ gives you the ability to stay resilient. Now AIQ helps you design the future and evolve with AI, beyond survival.

AIQ isn't artificial. It's radically human.

AIQ isn't artificial. It's radically human.

Leading with an Augmented Intelligence Mindset

From Control to Collaboration

For over a century, our leadership models have been grounded in control. Efficiency. Predictability. These were virtues that defined the industrial age, baked into the systems we inherited. But AI doesn't thrive in control-based cultures. It flourishes in spaces of curiosity, exploration, imagination, and co-creation. And so do people.

Leaders with high AIQ don't treat AI like an assistant, a tool, or a magic wand. They treat it like a collaborator. A creative partner. A therapist and coach. And a crystal ball to project new possibilities.

> You're not leading despite AI. You're leading with it.

This is the human shift. You're not leading despite AI. You're leading with it.

Doing that requires a mindset transformation. Best-selling author of *Atomic Habits* James Clear has said, "You do not rise to the level of your goals. You fall to the level of your systems."[9]

Goals are the desired outcomes. But to ascertain what you want to achieve, you first have to accept that you do not know what you do not know. Otherwise, your goals are limited extensions of what you do know.

- I want to cut costs by x percent.
- I want to accelerate processes by y percent.

Systems represent the processes and habits that you follow or employ to achieve your goals.

- Let's use AI to reduce costs and free up employee time to reskill toward new opportunities.
- Let's find ways to employ AI to automate processes that don't eliminate jobs.

A mindshift allows you to ask new questions, see things you couldn't see before, and explore different ways forward. In your mindshift toward AIQ, your goals plus systems represent a mental operating system.

A mental operating system is a metaphor for the underlying mindset, beliefs, habits, and thinking patterns that shape how you interpret the world, make decisions, and respond to challenges.

To see new things is to create new goals. To achieve new goals is to embrace new ways of thinking and working. A mindshift upgrades your mental operating system (OS).

The Journey to Becoming an Augmented Leader

You don't just learn AIQ. You become it.

Most leaders today are not leading with AIQ because they don't yet know a world beyond automation and optimization. That's not failure. That's simply what we'll define as Stage 1 in the AIQ journey. Sparking a mindshift and developing a new mental OS will lead to the exploration of uncharted horizons in the quest beyond automation. This will only evolve your thinking, vision, and goal setting to further stages.

This transformation unfolds as a series of mindshifts. Like any growth journey, it begins with openness and awareness, but it culminates in leadership that unlocks entirely new outcomes for people and organizations. Each stage isn't just a step forward; it's a step deeper into your own capacity for reinvention.

Stage 1: Awareness

At this stage, leaders either ignore or minimize AI's potential. They view AI as a tool for IT or operations but not as a leadership imperative. The goal here is openness, self-awareness, and recognition that new possibilities can exist beyond your current assumptions and beliefs.

Leading with an Augmented Intelligence Mindset

Your mindshift is to see AI not just as an extension of automation but as a catalyst for transformation and innovation. You begin to ask: What could we do beyond cost takeout and efficiency gains, that's what everyone else is doing. With AIQ, what else could we do that wasn't possible before? In what ways can we use augmented intelligence to create new value, differently, better, if we saw AI as an extension of human potential?

Stage 2: Curiosity

Awareness lights the spark, but curiosity is where the journey truly begins. At this stage, you start to consider how far people and teams can go when they compete *with* AI. You're exploring its relevance to your role, your team, your customers, your impact. This is where you shift from experimenting with AI to actively engaging with it. You watch videos, attend workshops, and consult experts. You test the tools. You follow your questions down unexpected paths. You explore what it means to lead with data *and* with discovery.

Your mindshift is to see AI beyond a tool or fixed asset and begin to experience it as a creative variable and collaborator. You wonder, "What haven't we imagined yet? What can we build now that we couldn't build before?"

Stage 3: Capability

Curiosity leads to hands-on practice. You move on to building real proficiency. You translate experimentation into building. At this stage, AI becomes an extension of how you think and work. You're experimenting and you're learning what works, where it adds value, and how to guide your team through the same learning curve. You start developing processes, policies, and prototypes that integrate AI across workflows.

Your mindshift leads you to shift the conversation from tools to transformation. You ask, "How might we reimagine the way we work and not just improve it?" You recognize that this is a skillset upgrade and a big step toward leadership evolution. You see its potential to scale across your culture.

Stage 4: Co-Creation

Now AI is becoming something your organization thinks, creates, and innovates with. Your culture becomes a system of hybrid intelligence where humans and machines collaborate to solve problems, design experiences, and create entirely new value. At this stage, you're empowering other leaders and teams to help shape and scale the AIQ of the organization. AI becomes embedded in your team's daily language, decisions, and sense of possibility.

Your mindshift guides you to move from enablement to empowerment. You lead less by command and more by strategic wonder, human-centered leadership rooted in governance, curiosity, creativity, and imagination, and creativity toward possibility. You create space for experimentation at every level. Questions like "What needs to be automated?," "What needs to be reimagined?," and "What else can we create with AI?" become foundational to the company's culture of AI transformation and innovation.

Stage 5: Intentional Innovation

You are now guiding your organization into the future by design. AI is not so much an initiative but an intentional dimension of your leadership. Efficiency gains are still important, but the uniqueness and originality of the value you generate with AI become the differentiator, the competitive advantage, and the growth engine. This is augmented, human-centered leadership at scale. It's adaptive, imaginative, empathetic, and deeply human.

Your mindshift is that you see yourself as a leader of systems and a steward of evolution. And others see you as that as well, while also embodying these attributes. You start to ask "How might we design a future that empowers what only humans can do with of AI, not in spite of it?"

Your mindshift is that you are no longer reacting to emerging threats or disruption; you're anticipating them. You are regenerating what leadership means with people at the center.

What AIQ Feels Like

When your AIQ rises, leadership starts feeling like, and becoming, a creative force. Meetings evolve from updates to insight sessions. Strategy shifts from forecasting the next five years to co-creating what's never been done. You no longer limit efforts in optimizing for yesterday's metrics. You start designing for tomorrow's relevance. You're no longer reacting to disruption; you're shaping it.

I would love to say that you don't feel behind the curve anymore, but you will. That's because you are aware. But you also become the curve. You learn how to anticipate and move with clarity, agility, and purpose. You build momentum in the face of uncertainty. That's not just how leadership looks now. It's how it feels when it's powered by AIQ.

This is that moment to see and lead differently. Someone has to.

You can't change the world unless you change how you see and feel it. This is that moment to see and lead differently. Someone has to.

AIQ is as much about AI and tech fluency as it is about empathy, culture, and transformational literacy. It's the ability to sense the future, shift perspective, and take new action that unlocks value for people and the systems around them. It's about building cultures of experimentation, curiosity, and courageous thinking. And more so, it's about giving people the incentive, the skills and empowerment, and the safety and space to move and grow in new directions.

> Lead with trust, not control. Empathy and creativity, not just efficiency.
>
> Possibility, not just predictability.

Leadership isn't about having all the answers. Leadership is about creating the space and time where new questions and answers flourish.

This Is the Beginning.
Where You Go Is Up to You

The next era of leadership is so much more than managing and scaling productivity. This moment is about amplifying possibility.

Let's be honest, though. Whether AI replaces people at scale or people become more exponentially capable because of it comes down to where the scales tip between business-as-usual leadership and human-centered leadership. Our job is to replace outdated thinking, to see beyond what we think people are capable of based on yesterday's standards and imagine what's possible when they're augmented by intelligent machines and inspired by imaginative, creative, and open leadership.

This is why we need human-centered augmented leaders. These leaders are willing to see differently, think expansively, and lead boldly. Your people don't need all the answers; they need presence and permission, and, most important, they need to see you go first.

Invest in your mindshift and the quotients, especially AIQ. Invest in your mindset and skillset and in the mindset and skillset of people.

And ask yourself: "Are you using AI to do more of the same? Or are you using AI to create something entirely new?"

117

Leading with an Augmented Intelligence Mindset

There's a balance that only the mindshifted can fully appreciate. The leaders who thrive in this moment won't be the ones who adopt the tools the fastest or wait on the sidelines to see what others do. They'll be the ones who lead with the most empathy, imagination and creativity, the most humanity, and the deepest courage.

This is your time. The future, and the people you care about, need you.

Notes

1. Brian Solis, *Mindshift: Transform Leadership, Drive Innovation, and Reshape the Future* (Wiley, 2025).
2. Mensa International, "What Is IQ?," n.d. www.mensa.org/what-is-iq/
3. MedPark Hospital, "EQ (Emotional Quotient)," n.d. www.medparkhospital .com/en-US/lifestyles/eq-emotional-quotient
4. HopeQure, "What Is Social Quotient and Its Biological Relevance to Leadership," April 14, 2025. www.hopequre.com/blogs/social-quotient-and-its-biological-relevance-to-leadership
5. Saumya Khandelwal, "What Is Adaptability Quotient?," Kapable, December 2, 2025. https://kapable.club/glossary/adaptability-quotient/
6. Vijay W, "Understanding AIQ: The Artificial Intelligence Quotient," LinkedIn, June 5, 2024. www.linkedin.com/pulse/understanding-aiq-artificial-intelligence-quotient-vijay-w-cihhf/
7. Pangambam S, "How to Compete with AI—and Win" [transcript], TedxBoston, July 18, 2025. https://singjupost.com/how-to-compete-with-ai-and-win-dharmesh-shah-transcript/
8. Charlie Reaves, "Superman's Powers Originally Didn't Come from the Sun, But Something Much Weirder," ScreenRant, July 19, 2024. https:// screenrant.com/superman-powers-golden-age-origin-gravity-yellow-sun/
9. James Clear, *Atomic Habits: An Easy & Proven Way to Build Good Habits Break Bad Ones* (Avery, 2018), p. 27. Quote available at: https://jamesclear .com/quotes/you-do-not-rise-to-the-level-of-your-goals-you-fall-to-the-level-of-your-systems

When the Ground Gives Way: How Miners Survived by Creating Stability Amid Disruption

Whitney Johnson

On August 5, 2010, 33 men's lives changed irrevocably when the ceiling of the San José copper mine collapsed on them. More than a century of digging out the mountain had weakened the giant slab of rock. When the ceiling crashed through the men's only exit, it trapped them 2,300 feet underground—a depth more than twice the height of the Empire State Building.[1] Though none of the men died in the initial crash, as the floor undulated, the walls wailed, and the darkness suffocated, it must have felt to the men that what the mine had started, chaos would soon finish.

With only two days' worth of food, they could have descended into a *Lord of the Flies* lawlessness—and they did, but only briefly. After a harsh night where tempers and fears ran high, and some miners made a desperate raid on their meager food stores, the men rallied, unified, and survived for 17 days in the dark despite their severely limited resources.[2]

How did these 33 miners survive? What helped them persist through the ever-present darkness and uncertainty?

Clear leadership emerging from within the group, with corresponding alignment and cooperation on the part of the miners, was the only way these men had a hope of surviving until a rescue might come. The obvious answer to the question of how they all survived, then, is leadership. But what kind of leadership? Popular culture focuses on the lone innovator, the individual who defies tradition, who breaks new ground as a leader—the disruptor. I have long been a proponent of disruption. It's true that innovative thinking, which is inherently disruptive, was part of the miners' survival story, but sometimes we talk about "disruptive" leadership as though disruption for disruption's sake is its own obvious and inherent good. The last thing these miners needed was more ground broken. What carried them through this life-and-death situation was stability. They needed leaders who could stabilize by providing direction, consistent structure, processes, and routines, clear communication, and emotional support.

Let's go underground.

Underground Leadership: How Structure Saved Lives

Without clear direction during a crisis, our minds default to brooding despondency and imagining worst-case scenarios, and plenty of worse cases stared these miners in the face. After the world collapsed on them, foreman Luis Urzúa focused on one goal: survive as long as possible. He articulated this vision and led his team to align around this plan. By providing the miners with an unambiguous objective—we need to survive until we are rescued—the miners could shift from threat-scanning to problem-solving mode, focusing their energy on solutions rather than fear.

His second order of business was to create structure. Using his background in topography, Urzúa scoped out the limited space they had to live in. He divided it into three areas: for sleep, sanitation, and work. For work, he had everyone complete their normal 12-hour shifts, doing things like chipping away at the rock around their sleeping area to make it safer or checking the air quality and temperature. After the first disastrous night, he helped create and enact a meal schedule that made their two-day food supply last for 17 days.[3] Conflict still arose, but by providing an external organizing system when the miners' internal emotional regulation was in disarray, he created a sense of normalcy that helped the men avoid emotional freefall and prevented the kind of panic that leads to poor decision making, such as raids on food stores.

When the rescue crew finally made contact 17 days in, they didn't find a chamber of corpses, or even a group of desperate, broken men, but an organized community. The miners' first message to the surface was characteristic of Urzúa's leadership approach: "Estamos bien en el Refugio los 33" ("We are well in the Refuge, the 33 of us"). By providing focus and structure, Urzúa channeled restlessness and fear into organized cooperative activity and saved everyone's lives by doing so.

Once the lifeline to the surface was established, Urzúa continued to stabilize by communicating all pertinent information from the engineers and doctors aboveground to the rest of the miners. His frequent updates not only reduced uncertainty, pulling the men out of a fight-or-flight stress response, but also gave them a sense of agency. Even when the news is bad, being "in the know" does a significant emotional job of reducing feelings of helplessness and uncertainty. It also builds trust. By relaying to his men what was happening aboveground, Urzúa signaled to the miners that he was reliable and trustworthy, which allowed them to delegate some portion of their survival worries to his leadership and focus on surviving for as long as possible, instead of second-guessing his motives. This was crucial to their psychological stability and survival. They were physically in the dark, but not emotionally so.

While Urzúa handled logistics and communication, other leaders emerged. Mario Sepúlveda provided humor and emotional support.

When the Ground Gives Way

José Henríquez led daily prayers, including sermons about Jonah and the whale[4]—bringing both spiritual hope and needed levity. No single leader was the sole point of stability, but this distributed support strengthened the entire group.

After 69 harrowing days underground, a rescue capsule brought the miners out of the mine to the surface one by one. Putting the safety of the other 32 men ahead of his own, Luis Urzúa was the last miner out. When he finally emerged, all the miners were waiting for him. Though eager to reunite with their loved ones, they wanted to honor the leader who had done all that he could to ensure they emerged from the mine alive.

What Workers Really Want: The Research Behind the Need for Stability

It turns out that the need for stability over disruption isn't unique to life-and-death situations. At my firm, Disruption Advisors, we have studied how disruption drives transformation for well over a decade. But when we surveyed more than 300 professionals, we found that 96 percent of professionals want either more stability (40 percent) or more balanced change (56 percent)—a combination of stability and disruption. Only 4 percent wanted more disruption. Whether in an office or trapped in a mine, people need stability to do their best work.

> Whether in an office or trapped in a mine, people need stability to do their best work.

When uncertainty and chaos dominate, the brain's threat-detection stem (the amygdala) hijacks cognitive resources away from higher-order thinking. Employees trapped in constant change are like the miners in the first hours after the collapse—operating in an anxious, or even panicked, survival mode rather than in a deliberate and constructive growth mode.

A 2025 Gallup study across 52 countries was equally revelatory. What followers crave from their leaders isn't charisma, vision, or innovation—traits typically associated with disruptive leadership. They want hope, trust, compassion, and stability.[5]

Aboveground: Strategic Redundancy and the Power of Process

Meanwhile, aboveground at the San José copper mine, stabilizing forces were also at play. When the mine collapsed, the San Esteban Primera Mining Company, the Chilean government, and the miners' families had no way of knowing whether the men were alive. Given the size of the collapse, it was highly likely that the men had died, as had been the case in a comparable incident several years earlier. Despite this, the government spared no expense. Rescuers worked tirelessly, drilling exploratory holes to locate the miners or at least recover their bodies. For 17 agonizing days, the miners had no way of knowing if anyone was searching for them. Then, on August 22, a drill broke through. When rescuers made contact and confirmed all 33 men were alive, everything changed. Knowing people aboveground were working feverishly to rescue them became a crucial stabilizing force for the trapped miners.

Before the miners could be rescued, they had to be found. Experts predicted there was only a 1.25 percent chance of success. Mine-shaft maps were out of date, and the rock was the size of a skyscraper. Given the stakes, it would have been easy to dispense with standard procedure in the name of urgency, but they didn't. Teams again accessed stability following a tried-and-true discovery process. For 17 days, they drilled small exploratory boreholes with

When the Ground Gives Way

nine types of drills, often at different angles. The rock was twice as hard as marble, so the drills frequently veered off course. The drill mechanics' orders were clear: Fail often and fail faster.

Finally, on day 17, they drilled into the cavern sheltering the miners. Discovering they were alive to be rescued infused the rescue workers with new hope and resolve. From this higher stratum of stability, they moved to the second stage of their rescue plan. Rather than betting on a single drilling operation, and because the mine was old enough that further collapse remained a risk, crews ran three approaches and teams in parallel, each focused on a different type of drill, hoping to rescue the men within six months. Running three teams not only statistically increased their odds of success but also provided more basis for optimism and hope.

Though organizational stakes are rarely as high, every leader can settle nerves by creating similar fail-safes and strategic redundancies for their own teams. Implementing plans that anticipate grappling with unforeseen challenges—plans that build trial-and-error measures and countermeasures into the plan—helps employees feel safe. It also takes the sting out of failure when it does arise so that people don't go into fight-or-flight mode, potentially wasting psychic energy or social capital on the blame game. When success is defined as failing faster because failure will propel forward movement, people will feel safe enough to try and try again without fear of embarrassment or censure. It is this kind of environment that brings about rescues in two months, not six.

Camp Esperanza: The Stabilizing Power of Hope

The stability provided to the miners by their families was crucial to their survival. Encircling the mouth of the mine, the families set up Camp Esperanza (Camp Hope). From there, they could send letters down the shaft to their loved ones, do video calls, and help with the miners' laundry. Knowing their families were close by and keeping vigil alongside them brought immeasurable comfort to the trapped miners. While there, one of the miners' wives gave birth to a baby girl. She was named Esperanza.

Notice that the rescue process involved disruption—a willingness to experiment with varied approaches—but stability was the hero of the day. By following a well-established exploratory process, building in strategic redundancies, and keeping engineers, doctors, and family members close at hand to lend additional support, rescue team leadership helped both the miners and the rescuers anchor themselves in hope.

The Warning Signs We Ignore: When Instability Becomes Catastrophe

The San José mining incident can teach us much about leadership. However, a vital lesson in stability and its importance can also be seen in the source of the problem: the known but ignored instability in the geologic mega-block that collapsed and blocked the miners' only exit point.

There had been signs that something like this might occur. For days and weeks leading up to the accident, the mine had let out a persistent thundering wail, a sure sign that all was not well in the surrounding rocks. One miner even noted obviously worsening cracks in the shaft—another bad sign—but the culture in the mining operations had for years prioritized output over safety, often painting people who raised concerns as lazy or as complainers. And given that the rock movement that caused the wailing and cracks had gone on for a long time without resulting in a mine collapse, the danger never felt imminent. Working in dangerous conditions and getting paid seemed, to potential whistleblowers, a better bet than protesting and being ignored or possibly fired.

When the Ground Gives Way

Leaders need to self-assess: Do they consistently make their employees feel safe enough to report concerns involving projects and the company? Do leaders really listen and act when their team raises valid concerns? Are they open-minded in how they assess a concern's validity? If not, they might ultimately end up like the San Esteban mining company, which refused to put money into the proper inspectors, emergency protocols, and machinery. This penny-wise and dollar-foolish approach led not only to lost months of profit but also to the loss of the entire mine and, nearly, to the death of 33 miners.

> Do leaders really listen and act when their team raises valid concerns?

The San Esteban mining company sacrificed its own miners upon the altar of profit by refusing to pay the comparatively trifling cost of appropriate mine inspections to gauge the health of what literally held up their business. It's hard to see what we have trained ourselves to chronically overlook. Small actions and small inactions can erode and chip away at the intangible, unseen pillars that provide stability to our organizations. The Chilean mine disaster serves as a cautionary warning not to overlook the silent foundation that holds up an entire enterprise.

Stability Roots Disruption

The 33 miners who survived 69 days underground weren't saved by disruption. They were saved by deliberately creating stability. While the world above celebrated their eventual rescue as a triumph of innovation and engineering, the real breakthrough happened in those first 17 days when Luis Urzúa chose structure over panic, when rescue teams followed established protocols rather than improvising wildly, and when families anchored themselves at Camp Esperanza rather than scattering in despair.

We often glorify the dramatic pivot and the bold reinvention, but the Chilean miners remind us of an important truth: When you find yourself trapped—whether 2,300 feet underground or in the suffocating darkness of organizational chaos—the way out is rarely to break more ground. Our research into professionals' appetites for stability, with over 96 percent craving more stability or balanced change rather than radical upheaval, is consistent with what the miners discovered in their darkest hour. Survival doesn't come from shattering what's left but from building something solid enough to sustain the weight of hope until rescue arrives.

Sometimes the most revolutionary way to lead is to hold things steady—to fortify and to emphasize all that holds people stable, calm, and surefooted. It's the best way to survive a crisis and to thrive in troubled times, or any times. With a firm foundation beneath it, human innovation can disrupt gravity and soar.

Notes

1. Maureen Corrigan, "The Incredible Story of Chilean Miners Rescued from the 'Deep Down Dark,'" NPR, October 29, 2014. www.npr.org/2014/10/29/359839104/the-incredible-story-of-chilean-miners-rescued-from-the-deep-down-dark

2. Héctor Tobar, *Deep Down Dark: The Untold Stories of 33 Men Buried in a Chilean Mine, and the Miracle that Set them Free* (Sceptre, 2015).

3. Jonathan Franklin, "Dramatic Scene Surrounds Chilean Miner Rescue," *PBS News*, October 13, 2010. www.pbs.org/newshour/show/dramatic-scene-surrounds-chilean-miner-rescue

4. Tobar, *Deep Down Dark*, pp. 89, 165.

5. Gallup Global Analytics, *Global Insights on Leadership* (Gallup, 2025). www.gallup.com/analytics/656315/leadership-needs-of-followers.aspx

Chapter 12

Leading Across Divides: Navigating Conflict by Finding Common Ground

Jonathan Haidt and

Caroline Webb

If you are a leader and you are leading human beings, at some point you'll need to navigate or mediate disagreements among your teammates. Disagreement can improve everyone's thinking when handled well. As John Stuart Mill wrote in 1859, "The only way in which a human being can make some approach to knowing the whole of a subject, is by hearing what can be said about it by persons of every variety of opinion."[1]

When people bring different perspectives to bear on complex topics, evidence suggests you're often able to get to a better answer if you pool your wisdom.[2] After all, you're less likely to miss something if you have multiple pairs of eyes on a topic. But reaping those benefits depends on each side truly listening to the other and being willing to flex their views to get to a better collective answer on the way forward.

Unfortunately, that's not always what happens. Differences of opinion can quickly turn into dislike of those who think differently. That's especially likely if the source of disagreement goes beyond superficial tasks or timelines and touches on deeply held values. Your colleagues might place differing levels of importance on core moral concerns such as care, fairness, loyalty, authority, or liberty, and all of that can flow through into differing and strongly held views on how to run a project or a team.[3]

For example, someone who places a high value on authority and structure might butt up against someone who feels it's appropriate to ignore rules if they get in the way of innovation. A person who prioritizes care and inclusion might find themselves at odds with a colleague who is optimizing for speed rather than buy-in while rolling out a new organizational structure. These sorts of value-based disagreements can feel more immovable than technical disputes, because they're often rooted in identity and worldview. And when these fundamental differences in values collide in workplace decision making, they can make the stakes suddenly higher and the path forward less clear.

As a leader, whether you're in the debate or sitting above it, you need a skillful way of bridging divides. What is the right approach to take? Of course, there's the brute-force strategy: A certain type of leader just asserts their point of view and closes down the conversation. But even if the leader's view is right, this approach doesn't address the underlying disagreement, and the lack of proper discussion can result in simmering tension that erodes trust, making collaboration harder and harder. The Society for Human Resources Management estimates that organizations in the United States collectively lose about $2 billion a day from lost productivity and absenteeism resulting from what people perceive as rude or disrespectful behavior from their colleagues.[4]

> Whether you're in the debate or sitting above it, you need a skillful way of bridging divides.

Luckily, there is a way for a wise leader to turn conflict into progress. To understand how it works, let's first unpack the deeper roots of what causes conflict between reasonable humans.

Your Brain on Disagreement

Here's what's going on under the hood—or inside the skull.

None of us ever sees the full picture of anything. Our brains don't have enough conscious attention available to process all the trillions of bits of information that surround us, so they are constantly filtering out much of what's happening, without us realizing it.[5]

What we *do* notice is strongly shaped by what we already think, feel, and want to be true. Research suggests there are three different flavors of this self-fulfilling perceptual loop. First, with a particular aim in mind, we notice anything associated with that goal and tend to block out anything else—a phenomenon known as inattentional blindness or inattentional deafness.[6] Second, we're more likely to notice whatever confirms our assumptions about a situation while filtering out anything that tells us we're incorrect—that's confirmation bias.[7] Third, our brain latches onto anything that echoes what we've recently experienced or encountered—to the point that even being in a bad mood can make us more likely to perceive threats in otherwise neutral information.[8] All of this makes it hard for people to properly absorb anything they don't already believe.

On top of that, our initial reactions to others' views are often driven by rapid moral intuitions that occur below the level of conscious awareness. We tend to have an immediate gut reaction to social situations. Things feel right or wrong the instant the facts are presented to us, and it is only afterward that our slow moral reasoning constructs an explanation or justification of our judgment.[9] Combined with confirmation bias, this means that people often become morally motivated post-hoc reasoners—driven to find evidence that supports their pre-existing beliefs and personal values rather than objectively weighing all available information.

Knowing all that, it's no wonder that colleagues sometimes don't see eye to eye. Their minds have constructed very different mental

Leading Across Divides

maps of reality, and these differing maps make it seem obviously true to each participant that their judgment is correct or that their plan for moving forward will work. This is why people can sit in the same meeting or hear the same information, come to radically different conclusions, and then be shocked that someone else in the room comes to a radically different conclusion. The combination of different mental maps, plus the brain's selective attention mechanism, means we all have the illusion that we are perceiving reality absolutely as it is. So, when someone disagrees with us, we tend to think they must be irrational, stupid, obstructive—or even malicious.

Once people are focused on where they disagree, two processes can dig them further into the disagreement.

1. **The more annoyed or upset people get, the harder it is for them to see any areas of agreement.** You've just read that conscious attention gets sucked toward whatever resonates with someone's current state of mind. So even if people agree on 90 percent of the issue, and it's just 10 percent where they differ, that 10 percent can easily dominate the debate when people are feeling combative and their brains are primed to look for points of difference rather than similarity.[10]

2. **When people feel they're not being listened to, it can trigger a stress response that impairs their reasoning and mental flexibility.** We all have a basic psychological need to feel competent and socially connected. Not feeling heard undermines both of those needs. When people run up against a situation like this—one that feels unpleasant and seems unresolvable—it readily triggers a defensive response in the brain and body, through the release of stress hormones.[11] In this "defensive mode," the brain pumps up vigilance and urgency at the expense of deeper thinking by turning up activity in its salience network and depressing activity in its central executive network.[12,13] In this

jumpy state of alert, people think less expansively and generously than when they're unstressed. It becomes harder to take in anyone else's perspective.

All of this is why arguments feel so draining and unpleasant. In principle, every savvy professional says they love a challenging discussion; in practice, without care, such discussions are taxing for human brains to handle.

The Better News

Understanding these psychological dynamics points toward a more constructive path forward, because all of that insight can be spun on its head to give us pointers on how to manage disagreement gracefully as leaders.

It starts with encouraging practical humility about the fact that none of us has the complete picture of anything that's going on. To quote John Stuart Mill again: "He who knows only his own side of the case, knows little of that."[14] The tone to set with your colleagues is this: Pooling different perspectives will reduce the size of our collective blind spot, making us smarter overall.

Then, before we can get people to open their ears to others, we must get them to soften their hearts. That happens by showing everyone's perspective has been heard, then by emphasizing what people on all sides of an issue have in common. There are usually some real areas of agreement to highlight. We can encourage people to recognize shared identity, goals, and history of the team. Shining a light on all of this common ground stops people's attention from getting stuck on areas of disagreement, and it rebuilds the mutual appreciation that is crucial for effective collaboration.

From there, we need to explore what has shaped the different points of view, which includes recognizing that others' formative experiences or moral foundations may differ and yet still be legitimate.

Leading Across Divides

Throughout, we need to set expectations that people's views are to be expressed and listened to with respect. That keeps people out of defensive mode as much as possible, allowing them to listen more closely and think more clearly about the issues where they disagree.

This doesn't just feel nicer than a shouting match; it's far more likely to get you to a place where you can find a way forward. And it's far more likely to result in people rallying around any decision you make, even if one side or the other ends up "winning" the argument. Research into something psychologists call procedural justice shows that people are far more likely to get behind something they don't initially agree with if they feel their views have been given a fair hearing.[15]

> People are far more likely to get behind something they don't initially agree with if they feel their views have been given a fair hearing.

Five Steps to Common Ground

Here's a systemic approach to all of that, which we call the common ground technique.[16] You can use it for yourself if you're one of the people disagreeing. You can also use it to facilitate a high-quality discussion if your team is divided on a topic, by walking people through the steps together. If you do any *one* of these five things, it will lead toward a place of better mutual understanding and likely collaboration. If you walk through all *five* steps, you should find you've lowered the tension and gotten closer to resolving a dispute that could otherwise drag on for a long time.

Step 1: Describe Their Point of View as Positively as Possible

If you are the one having the disagreement with a colleague, start by describing *their* side of the argument in as generous a way as you

134

Leading for Tomorrow

can, to the point that they feel they couldn't have put it better themselves. The aim is to make them feel you truly understand their good intentions and where they're coming from in their thinking. It's the opposite of making their argument into a strawman, where you make their points seem as weak as possible; instead, you are "steel-manning"—making their argument sound as strong as it can be.

Say:

"I understand that you think we should do [thing]. . .because of [reasons]. . ."

If you're not in the middle of the disagreement yourself, but you are instead mediating a disagreement between two or more of your colleagues, you have a couple of ways to approach this.

You can summarize each side's point of view yourself, as generously and evenly as you can. In this case, do your very best not to play favorites. The unfavored side will feel hurt, which will tip them deeper into defensive mode and make them less open to compromise and collaboration. An even more powerful approach is to ask each side to describe the *other* side's perspective in as positive and compelling a way as possible. This generates more learning and collaboration for your colleagues, if they're ready for it.

Step 0

By the way, if it's not yet possible to summarize each point of view because the two perspectives haven't yet been laid out clearly, start first with a Step 0, where each side describes their point of view. *Then* do Step 1. Don't worry about it feeling repetitive. The psychological payoff from hearing someone else articulate your point of view, even if you've just said it yourself, is enormous.

Step 2: Identify All Areas of Agreement

Together, make a list of what everyone agrees on. Even if it seems obvious, and even if it seems minor, add it to the tally. The longer the list of commonalities, the better; this is your common ground. Mapping it out helps to reset people's attentional filters and reminds each side that they are on the same team—at least in some ways.

Ask:

"Where is everyone agreed? I think everyone *wants*. . . I think everyone *believes* that. . . It *matters* to everyone that. . . We all *know* that. . ."

Getting the fullest possible list of areas of common ground sometimes requires taking a step back to review the broader discussion that has led to this point, including perhaps the overall goal of what you're doing together or the fact base that you share.

Step 3: Isolate and Understand the True Disagreement

Now, and only now, do you aim everyone's attention at the source of the conflict, which should feel more bounded than it did before you laid out the areas of common ground. Dive into the area where the real disagreement is, probing to understand what has shaped people's differing points of view. Emphasize that this exploration is about curiosity and understanding, not persuasion.

Say:

"The only place we/you seem to disagree is. . ." (or perhaps "The main place. . .")

"*Why* do we/you each feel or think differently about this specific issue?"

Often, what's shaped people's oppositional views are constraints that each face that aren't visible to the other side—for example, being short-staffed or facing pressures from other stakeholders. In other cases, it's rooted in past experiences that might have taught someone that a particular good or bad outcome will occur if they do a particular thing, even if the situation today is slightly different. Anyone who's been involved in a product launch or a reorganization has a slew of war stories that may be looming vividly in their minds.

Or each side might have different values they hold particularly dear. In some cases, people may even hold what psychologists call sacred values—principles they see as absolute and nonnegotiable.[17] In this case, a skillful leader encourages people to share whatever they can about the influences that have shaped those values. "I believe X" lands less like a flat statement and more like an invitation to curiosity when it's followed by "because I grew up with. . ." or "because I saw what happened when. . . ." Moreover, people don't just hold individual moral positions; they often also want to maintain standing within their communities. Sometimes what looks like stubborn disagreement is actually someone trying to stay loyal to their group's shared values.

Taking steps to understand exactly *why* a colleague seems so attached or resistant to a particular idea doesn't mean you have to agree with them. It's about realizing that they have reasons for their perspective. They're not arguing because they're malicious or unintelligent; they're arguing because they're worried or excited. And that's usually a reflection of the fact that they care about the group making a good choice. If they didn't care, they wouldn't bother speaking up.

> Taking steps to understand exactly *why* a colleague seems so attached or resistant to a particular idea doesn't mean you have to agree with them.

Step 4: Explore How Both Could Be Correct

The next step puts you firmly beyond the world of a zero-sum, yes/no argument and gets you looking at a more nuanced interpretation of the "right" answer.

137

Leading Across Divides

Ask:

"Is there a way that both perspectives could be somehow correct?"

This question usually makes people pause quizzically the first time they hear it. If you need to explain, you can say that it's often the case that each person is partially right, but perhaps in different situations, or with different groups of people, or in different parts of the issue. For example, maybe something that works well in one region doesn't work in another area where people have different needs or characteristics. Or maybe a process that makes sense when you're in crisis mode doesn't make as much sense in business-as-usual mode.

If the disagreement is about values, "both correct" often means "correct within different moral frames." For example, perhaps one of your colleagues wants everyone to take a more structured approach to performance reviews, because they feel it will result in people being evaluated more fairly. But another colleague argues that imposing this structure will undermine your firm's treasured culture of flexibility and informality. Both perspectives have merit—boosting fairness and respecting cultural norms can both be important. Talking this through with each other typically reduces the impulse to dismiss the other side's perspective as totally irrational.

When you reach this step in the conversation, there's often a sense of both parties turning to face the same direction, albeit with subtly different orientations.

Step 5: Decide What You Can Do Now, Based on your Common Ground

Once everyone feels heard and understood, it draws their brains out of defensive mode.

At this point, there is usually a marked reduction in tension. That's because once everyone feels heard and understood, it draws their brains out of defensive mode—and this in turn leaves them better able to think clearly and creatively about what could be done based on your common ground.

So now you ask:

"What can we do based on where we agree?"

For example, it might become clear that it's possible to get moving with some immediate next steps on a new project or process while one specific remaining question is resolved; there's no need to hold everything up because of that sticking point. Or it might be possible to try out different approaches with different groups. You could test each approach for one week and see what emerges as the best way forward based on the data. You might even find that there's a way to respect principles that seemed in opposition. For example, once you've acknowledged that both fairness and flexibility matter in your organization, perhaps your team sees a few ways to streamline the new proposed evaluation system so that it's less heavy on formal process.

It can also happen that people find it's possible to amiably agree to disagree on issues that are not critical enough to require unanimous consensus, once everyone feels the other side understands their views.

Stronger Leaders and Stronger Teams

These steps get easier with practice, and they pay off quickly in boosting collaboration in your workplace. You don't necessarily get to perfect alignment as a result, but you get to a place where colleagues feel heard and understood and are better able to work together as a result. Each time you successfully navigate a disagreement, you're not just solving the immediate problem; you're building your team's capacity to handle future conflicts with greater wisdom, more trust, and less stress. And the leader who can guide their team through this process turns diverse thinking into a source of strength rather than division—a precious talent in our modern and often divided world.

Notes

1. John Stuart Mill, *On Liberty* (John W. Parker and Son, 1859).

2. Lukas Wallrich, Victoria Opara, Miki Wesołowska, Ditte Barnoth, and Sayeh Yousefi, "The Relationship Between Team Diversity and Team Performance: Reconciling Promise and Reality Through a Comprehensive Meta-Analysis Registered Report," *Journal of Business and Psychology* 39, no. 6 (2024): 1303–1354. https://doi.org/10.1007/s10869-024-09977-0

3. Jonathan Haidt, *The Righteous Mind: Why Good People Are Divided by Politics and Religion* (Pantheon/Random House, 2012).

4. Kathryn Mayer, "Incivility's Cost to Employers," *SHRM*, August 8, 1014. www.shrm.org/topics-tools/news/employee-relations/incivility-s-cost-to-employers---2-billion-a-day

5. Jieyu Zheng and Markus Meister, "The Unbearable Slowness of Being: Why Do We Live at 10 Bits/s?" Revised November 15, 2024. https://arxiv.org/abs/2408.10234

6. Further reading on the phenomenon known as inattentional blindness or inattentional deafness can be found in these sources: Christopher Chabris and Daniel Simons, *The Invisible Gorilla: And Other Ways Our Intuitions Deceive Us* (Crown, 2010); Trafton Drew, Melissa L.-H. Võ, and Jeremy M. Wolfe, "The Invisible Gorilla Strikes Again: Sustained Inattentional Blindness in Expert Observers," *Psychological Science* 24, no. 9 (2013): 1848–1853. https://doi.org/10.1177/0956797613479386; Donald J. Tellinghuisen, Alexander J. Cohen, and Natalie J. Cooper, "Now Hear This: Inattentional Deafness Depends on Task Relatedness," *Attention, Perception, & Psychophysics* 78, no. 8 (2016): 2527–2546. https://doi.org/10.3758/s13414-016-1169-5

7. Andrew Westbrook, R. van den Bosch, J. I. Määttä, L. Hofmans, D. Papadopetraki, Roshan Cools, and Michael J. Frank, "Dopamine Promotes Cognitive Effort by Biasing the Benefits Versus Costs of Cognitive Work," *Science* 367, no. 6484 (2020): 1362–1366. https://doi.org/10.1126/science.aaz5891

8. For more information, please see these sources: Vezha Boboeva, Alberto Pezzotta, Claudia Clopath, and Athena Akrami, "Unifying Network Model Links Recency and Central Tendency Biases In Working Memory," *eLife*, 12 (2024): RP86725. https://doi.org/10.7554/eLife.86725; Árni Kristjánsson, "Priming of Probabilistic Attentional Templates," *Psychonomic Bulletin & Review* 30 (2023): 22–39. https://doi.org/10.3758/s13423-022-02125-w; Eva Rubínová and Heather L. Price, "Primacy (and Recency) Effects in Delayed Recognition of Items from Instances of Repeated Events," *Memory* 32, no. 5 (2024): 627–645. https://doi.org/10.1080/09658211.2024.2354764

9. Haidt, *Righteous Mind*.

10. Marcin Lewiński and Mark Aakhus, *Argumentation in Complex Communication: Managing Disagreement in a Polylogue* (Cambridge University Press, 2022). https://doi.org/10.1017/9781009274364

11. Eun Joo Kim and Jeansok J. Kim, "Neurocognitive Effects of Stress: A Metaparadigm Perspective," *Molecular Psychiatry* 28 (2023): 2750–2763. https://doi.org/10.1038/s41380-023-01986-4

12. Grant S. Shields, Matthew A. Sazma, and Andrew P. Yonelinas, "The Effects of Acute Stress on Core Executive Functions: A Meta-Analysis and Comparison with Cortisol," *Neuroscience and Biobehavioral Reviews* 68 (2016): 651–668. https://doi.org/10.1016/j.neubiorev.2016.06.038

13. Oshin Vartanian, Sidney Ann Saint, Nicole Herz, and Peter Suedfeld, "The Creative Brain Under Stress: Considerations for Performance in Extreme Environments," *Frontiers in Psychology* 11 (2020): 585969. https://doi.org/10.3389/fpsyg.2020.585969

14. Mill, *On Liberty*.

15. Minseo Kim and Terry A. Beehr, "Making the Case for Procedural Justice: Employees Thrive and Work Hard," *Journal of Managerial Psychology* 35, no. 2 (2020): 100–114. https://doi.org/10.1108/JMP-03-2019-0154

16. Caroline Webb, *How to Have a Good Day: Harness the Power of Behavioral Science to Transform Your Working Life* (Crown Currency, 2016).

17. Scott Atran and Robert Axelrod, "Reframing Sacred Values," *Negotiation Journal* 24, no. 3 (2008): 221–246. https://doi.org/10.1111/j.1571-9979.2008.00182.x

Chapter 13

Inside the Motivated Mind: How Leaders Make Work Feel Worthwhile

Caroline Webb

Every leader hopes their colleagues will bring the greatest possible energy and focus to all they do at work. But ensuring that this happens is rarely simple—as any manager knows, and as the data confirms. Year after year, Gallup's *State of the Global Workplace* report finds that the majority of employees are not engaged by their work, and it estimates that this widespread demotivation comes at a cost of over US$9 trillion in lost productivity worldwide.[1] The human cost is real, too. People's sense of identity and purpose in the world is strongly shaped by the way they feel about their work, so it's no surprise that disengaged employees report much lower personal well-being.[2]

And yet some leaders are skilled at igniting a spark in the soggiest of conditions. If you think about your own career, the chances are you had at least one manager or mentor who knew how to unlock your motivation, even when the going got tough. Somehow, they made work feel worthwhile to you. How can we be more systematic about doing that in our own teams?

Neuroscience has a lot to say to leaders about this. That's because the brain's reward system is the engine of motivation for all humans, and research gives us an ever-clearer picture of what it takes to engage and excite the synapses of this system. What is most striking in the organizational context is that the brain's reward system responds to much more than money. The most durable motivators are psychological—what researchers call intrinsic rewards. In the workplace setting, it helps to group them under four fundamental human needs: feeling competent in what we do, having control over how we do it, connecting meaningfully with others, and sensing that our work serves a worthwhile cause.

The more that leaders amplify the presence of these four psychologically rewarding qualities in everyday working life, the more they get a direct line into the motivational engine inside their colleagues' minds—to the benefit of everyone involved. The rest of this chapter explores and explains how to think about this.

The Brain's Reward System

The reward system is complex, involving many different parts of the brain, and it works hard for us. It's constantly running in the background to assess the value of doing *this* versus doing *that* and guiding our choices on what we should do next as a result of those calculations.[3] The key thing to know is that whenever we do something that feels good, our brain will nudge us to try to repeat that experience. This sense of wanting more of what feels good is the basic mechanism that drives us forward as humans; the possibility of encountering something positive is what keeps us engaged and interested in the world.

That reaching-for-reward mechanism unconsciously drives everyone's choices in the workplace. For example, people will pay more attention, try harder, and persist longer when they feel the likely rewards make the effort worthwhile, all of which translates into better performance outcomes.[4]

So, how can we as leaders make the work feel appealing enough for our colleagues to put in their best effort? The good news is that we can be quite precise about that, because research tells us that there are certain things that all human brains tend to find rewarding.

The first "reward" you might think of is money—or monetary perks like free food—and in the workplace context, that's certainly part of the mix. But there isn't an infinite supply of money to go around. So, it's lucky that the kind of rewards that engage our brain's motivational systems are not just obvious, tangible treats like fancy doughnuts and special bonuses. The human reward system is also engaged when we get important psychological needs met that make us feel good about ourselves—the "intrinsic rewards" that come from inside our minds rather than from the outside world.

What are these psychologically intrinsic rewards when applied to the workplace? Intrinsic rewards can be grouped in four categories: *competence, control, connection*, and *cause*. In plain language, that means feeling equipped to tackle what's on your plate, being given the autonomy and space to get things done, feeling mutual respect and fellowship with the people around you, and having a sense that what you're doing actually matters.

> Intrinsic rewards can be grouped in four categories: *competence, control, connection*, and *cause*.

Studies suggest that in the long run, people perform better if they have this internal motivation than if they're constantly being bribed by treats of one type or another.[5] And unlike money, which is always a scarce resource, there's an unlimited supply of intrinsic rewards in every organization if a leader knows how to tap into them effectively. Let's explore each of those and understand what it looks like in practice.

Competence

The first thing to know is that human beings fundamentally relish the feeling that they're doing a good job at whatever task is at hand.[6] When neuroscientists make people feel smart, usually by having them complete an exercise correctly, the brain areas most closely associated with reward processing become more active.[7]

People's reward systems are also activated when other people make them *feel* competent by giving them praise.[8] This is such a strong mechanism for engaging the brain's motivational engine that even random praise from complete strangers is enough to light up the reward system of someone lying in a brain scanner.[9]

This is why it's powerful for you to show your colleagues meaningful *appreciation*, wherever you can—and ideally not in the "random" way used by researchers but rooted in genuine observations of what they are doing. If one of your colleagues is flagging, finding a way to praise some aspect of their work does a lot to boost their sense of competence, which engages their brain's reward system, which in turn increases the level of neurochemicals that are central to their motivation to carry on exerting effort. This is the kind of chain reaction that you want and need, especially when your team is tackling challenges that require sustained effort.

What if a colleague is not performing as well as you'd hope—should you still praise them? Yes, and no. You shouldn't invent something falsely upbeat to say, and you do need to give them developmental feedback to help them improve (more on that later). But from a neurological standpoint, it's always worth finding something authentic to acknowledge about the way someone is working, even if it's small. Often you can recognize the approach or the effort that someone has put in, even if you're not yet happy with the output: "I can tell how hard you've worked on this—you've done a lot of research, which I appreciate." It can take some thought to find the nugget of goodness, but it's worth it, given the resulting boost to your colleague's level of commitment, especially if you urgently need them to step up their game more broadly.

Of course, you do also need to give developmental *feedback* when needed. Not just because you want to keep your team's

146

standards high and rising, but also because learning can be a rich source of motivation when it's framed as a route to getting better—after all, learning new things adds to someone's stock of competence. Even just learning a little new information is enough to light up the brain's reward system.[10] That's mirrored in what people say they want from their bosses: Almost all employees say they'd welcome more corrective feedback if it's delivered in a constructive, respectful way.[11] That surprises a lot of leaders. "Constructive and respectful," in case you're wondering, means factual observations of things they can improve rather than broad personal criticisms that are hard to act on: "You delivered this a day late—what happened, and what can you do to avoid that next time?" rather than "Wow, you're so unreliable."

More broadly, the motivational power of learning means it's smart to find ways to support colleagues' professional development, for example, by giving them new challenges and opportunities. The tricky thing about encouraging your colleagues to stretch into new territory is that while it feels fabulous to triumph in a new task, it's all but impossible to learn something new without a period of feeling out of your depth. The clever way for you to balance stretch and comfort is to show your colleagues how to *play to their strengths* even while they're tackling something new and difficult, to keep them connected to their stock of competence.

For example, maybe someone on your team is making their first board presentation, and they're nervous. But you know they're good at putting themselves in the shoes of others, so you encourage them to think about what each board member is likely to want to ask. By playing to their strengths—in this case, their capacity for interpersonal insight—your colleague gets a burst of competence that gives them the energy and confidence to ace the presentation.

Finally, the importance of competence in human motivation has an implication for *how you set goals* for your team: Don't create

147

Your aspirations can be bold and brave, but you need a halfway plausible pathway to making them a reality if you want to keep people motivated.

impossible goals. Recent neuroscience research has confirmed what psychologists long suspected: People check out when they feel that a goal simply isn't achievable.[12] Your aspirations can be bold and brave, but you need a halfway plausible pathway to making them a reality if you want to keep people motivated.

Control

Have you ever had someone looking over your shoulder while you're trying to work, watching what you were doing, and perhaps even making suggestions? No matter how much you like the person looking over your shoulder, I'm going to guess you didn't love the feeling of them hovering behind you. You probably would have preferred some space to think instead of feeling like every move you made was being observed and supervised.

That's because having a sense of personal agency and control really matters to human beings. A wide range of studies shows how people's reward systems are more responsive and engaged when they have a feeling of autonomy.[13] And having a greater sense of control has been found to result in higher motivation and performance across many different settings. Even just letting colleagues choose the schedule and sequencing of their tasks has been found to lead to better performance.[14]

Meanwhile, "self-set" goals that people determine for themselves tend to be associated with higher performance than goals that are imposed on them by others.[15] This is why it feels so different to pursue a pet project that you've defined or created for yourself from doing work that you've been told to do by your boss or your board.

When are you more likely to have good ideas and go the extra mile? Usually with the pet project.

In most organizations, you can't let people in your team just work on their personal projects without supervision. But you can be smart about giving your colleagues a feeling of space and ownership as they work on your team's collective goal. Giving people some personal choice in how they get something done can turn even a routine task into more of a pet project.

In practice, this means setting very clear expectations and checkpoints for your colleagues, then giving people *freedom within the framework*. That doesn't mean you wave them good-bye and wish them good luck; it means you have an agreed set of deliverables, an agreed deadline, and an agreed plan for when you'll next meet to discuss—and between now and then, you let them get on with their work without constantly looking over their shoulder.

Nor does it mean you check out. Your one-to-one check-ins are precious opportunities to give feedback and provide coaching. When you're doing that, with motivation in mind, replace the instinct to instruct with the *instinct to inquire* wherever you possibly can. Instead of telling people what to do next, ask questions that get them thinking: How can we better meet customer needs? What have you tried so far? What's your hypothesis about why that didn't work? What other options do you have? Taking this high-autonomy route means your colleague has to work harder than if you just gave them instructions, but you're giving them control over their thinking process.

Finally, have a *bias to involve or inform* your colleagues where it's practical. Remember the power of self-set goals; if there's an aspect of a deliverable that you're genuinely flexible on, even if it's just the format, call out that flexibility and give them a chance to shape it. And remember that receiving new, useful information gets

Inside the Motivated Mind: How Leaders Make Work Feel Worthwhile

treated by the brain as a reward. You might not be able to bring them to the big meeting, but you can take the time and care to give them a readout on what happened. Information is power, and when you're a leader, information is inspiration.

Connection

The next big category of intrinsic reward is the quality of our connections with other people. Do we feel respected and valued? Do we feel supported? Do we have a sense of belonging? Are we making a positive impact on other people? Both verbal and nonverbal signals are being woven into a social fabric that engage the brain's reward system.[16] And studies have shown that it's especially important that people get these signals from their direct line manager if they're to feel engaged at work.[17]

That means it really matters how you behave toward your colleagues and that you *show interest* in what your colleagues are saying and how they're feeling. Showing a degree of care and curiosity makes a huge difference to people's motivation. Simply being asked about their views[18] or *listened to carefully* engages people's reward systems.[19] Sincerely asking "How are you doing?" goes a long way—especially if you make sure you're not constantly distracted by your devices or what's next on your calendar as someone is talking to you. If you're pressed for time, keep it brief, but be fully present for the moments you have to spare. Studies suggest there are big knock-on effects from doing this; the more you show you care about your direct reports, the more they pay it forward with their own teams.[20]

Next, be smart about looking for ways to *involve people* in what you're doing and deciding. Studies using online ball-toss games find that being included—having a stranger throw the ball to you, even if that "stranger" is a computer—activates people's reward system to a surprising degree.[21] Not being invited to an interesting meeting or copied on a substantive message thread feels oddly deflating. So have a bias to inclusion, where it doesn't cost you anything to invite your colleagues in.

As leaders, we also want to think about how we build the kind of *team environment* that gives colleagues a wider sense of connection. When you create what psychologists call an in-group (i.e., where everyone feels they're on the same team), you multiply the effects of good things that happen to individuals because studies show that people get a burst of reward when *other* people in their in-group succeed.[22] How do you create that sense of an in-group? You don't have to turn the office into a social club. Studies show that even just creating a *visibly shared goal* will do it,[23] and that's squarely in your territory as a leader. Make sure everybody knows what you're all aiming for together.

Beyond that, consider how to create ways for your colleagues to get to know each other better. Remember that even minor social interactions give people a boost, even if they're introverts[24] and even if the interactions are only online.[25] So take the time to celebrate successes, birthdays, and other milestones. And encourage *mutual support* wherever you can by asking "Who might be able to help with that?" when someone is describing a challenge in a meeting.

Finally, watch out for perceptions of *fairness and unfairness*. Our brains are so geared toward connection that in the absence of stress, the brain's reward system is activated by generosity and reciprocity.[26] Meanwhile, experiencing or observing selfishness engages areas of the brain associated with disgust[27]—and disgust is not what you want in your orbit. It's why leaders playing favorites is so corrosive to team morale. So check this in your own behavior if you have metaphorically placed a halo over one of your colleagues' heads.

In working life, the intense value that human brains place on fairness often shows up in what researchers call procedural justice. That's the well-established finding that people can generally accept

Inside the Motivated Mind: How Leaders Make Work Feel Worthwhile

outcomes they don't like *if* they feel that the decisions were made with a reasonable degree of fairness. They will get very upset, however, if they perceive that decisions were not made fairly.[28]

This is very useful to know, because as a leader you can't please everybody with all your decisions. But the more you can show that you've considered all angles appropriately, with good intentions and careful attention to detail, the more your colleagues will be able to get on board with what you're trying to do. Share what you can of the process and reasons behind your choices, even when you can't share all the information. For example, perhaps your haloed colleague fully deserves the promotion you've just given them—in which case, be transparent about what they're good at, and explain why that earned them advancement. A few sentences from you can save months of strain in team dynamics.

Cause

We all do better when there seems to be a point to what we're doing. Having some *sense of purpose* turns out to be a solid predictor of conscientiousness over time.[29] People try harder when they are reminded that their work is useful and meaningful.[30]

Having some kind of North Star also gives people the energy to keep going when they hit setbacks. Studies have found that people are more resilient to daily stressors when they have a sense of purpose,[31] even to the point of sleeping better.[32] In the workplace, that translates into better analytical ability.[33] Without some sense of purposeful direction or payoff, people's motivation tends to drop away over time, however competent, in control, and connected they feel.[34]

Some organizations have a clear mission. In healthcare, you're trying to make patients better; in the NGO sector, there's an explicit goal to do some kind of good. But to affect your colleagues' motivation, the "cause" you're all pursuing doesn't have to be grand. It can be what I call "little P purpose," focused on a small group of people. It could be delighting a team of colleagues or even just a single customer by solving a problem they have. That proximate kind of "micro cause" can be very powerful because it feels so vivid and concrete, and our brains find it easier to place value on things that are tangible.[35]

So, whatever kind of organization you're in, an essential task for leaders is to keep colleagues in touch with a sense of purpose, big and small. That's how you get the best from people. Lay out a broader *vision* for what exactly will be better for whom if the team knocks the ball out of the park on its goals. Keep showing the team the *positive impact* of their work, and you'll do a lot to sustain their energy even through the rougher patches.

> An essential task for leaders is to keep colleagues in touch with a sense of purpose, big and small.

Bonus Multiplier: Clarity

One last comment: Clarity can be an enhancer for all of these psychological rewards. And conversely, the less clear any of them is, the less powerful it is as a motivating force.

For example, maybe you thought appreciatively about someone's work, but you didn't actually say out loud how much you liked it or the difference it made. It's not going to boost their feelings of competence and cause unless they happen to be psychic. Express *clear* appreciation for what they do; that's when you'll see higher motivation.

Likewise, if someone's responsibilities aren't entirely clear, it makes it hard for them to feel sure that they're in control of their workload. You also run the risk of blurring the boundary between their responsibilities and the responsibilities of others, which can challenge working relationships and undermine their feelings of connection with colleagues. The clearer your vision, the stronger people's sense of there being a worthy cause behind the work they're doing. And so on.

There are lots of situations where you don't have all the clarity you personally would like, despite being the boss. But even in the middle of a turbulent period, you can usually take steps to give colleagues more clarity on the situation you're all facing, on the expectations you have of them, and on the progress everyone is making—all of which will sharpen their motivation.

Making It Worthwhile

To unleash their colleagues' fullest motivation and energy, the leader's job is to create a working environment that's rich in the psychological rewards that keep their colleagues engaged and thriving. It's worth the effort. Many decades of research show that employees who feel good about themselves perform better. As well as giving them more motivation on immediate tasks, they have better health, less burnout, lower absenteeism, greater ability to stay calm under pressure, better relationships at work, and ultimately lower turnover.[36]

To be clear, you should still pay your people fairly—that's the starting point, and you will lose good people if you do not. Being underpaid makes people feel undervalued, which in turn undermines their sense of competence, control, and cause, and there's a limit to what intrinsic rewards can achieve if your employees are under financial stress.[37] But once you've made sure that everyone has fair pay, intrinsic rewards are more powerful and practical sources of motivation than financial incentives in most settings. You can't give a bonus every day to every person, but you can give everyone some kind of compliment, however small.

The opportunity in front of every leader is both simple and profound: to create conditions where people's natural drive to do good and meaningful work can flourish. When you strengthen your colleagues' sense of competence, control, connection, and cause, you're not just improving their performance—you're tapping into what makes us fundamentally human. That's the kind of leadership that doesn't just deliver results; it leaves people better than you found them.

Notes

1. Gallup, *State of the Global Workplace: 2025 Report.*
2. James K. Harter, Corey E. Tatel, Sangeeta Agrawal, Anthony Blue, Stephanie K. Plowman, Jim Asplund, Sabrina Yu, and Andy Kemp, *The Relationship Between Engagement at Work and Organizational Outcomes: Gallup Q^{12} Meta-Analysis,* 11th ed. (Gallup, 2024).
3. Oscar Arias-Carríon, Xanic Caraza-Santiago, Sergio Salgado-Licona, Mohamed Salama, Sergio Machado, Antonio Egidio Nardi, Manuel Menéndez-González, and Eric Murillo-Rodríguez, "Orquestic Regulation of Neurotransmitters on Reward-Seeking Behavior," *International Archives of Medicine* 7 (2014): 29. https://doi.org/10. 1186/1755-7682-7-29; Iris Schutte, Peter K. H. Deschamps, Peter N. van Harten, and J. Leon Kenemans, "Dopaminergic and Noradrenergic Manipulation of Anticipatory Reward and Probability Event-Related Potentials," *Psychopharmacology* 237 (2020): 2019–2030. https:// doi.org/10.1007/s00213-020-05515-x; Aviv M. Weinstein "Reward, Motivation and Brain Imaging in Human Healthy Participants—A Narrative Review," *Frontiers in Behavioral Neuroscience* 17 (2023). https://doi.org/10.3389/fnbeh.2023.1123733
4. Francesco Rigoli and Giovanni Pezzulo, "A Reference-Based Theory of Motivation and Effort Allocation," *Psychonomic Bulletin & Review* 29 (2022): 2070–2082. https://doi.org/10.3758/s13423-022-02135-8; Amitai Shenhav, Sebastian Musslick, Falk Lieder, Wouter Kool, Thomas L. Griffiths, Jonathan D. Cohen, and Matthew M. Botvinick, "Toward a Rational and Mechanistic Account of Mental Effort," *Annual Review of Neuroscience* 40 (2017): 99–124. https://doi.org/10.1146/annurev-neuro-072116-031526; Elle Wernette, Erik Altmann, and Kimberly

Fenn, "Reward Motivation Improves Placekeeping Performance After Total Sleep Deprivation and a Night of Rest," *Sleep* 46, Supple 1 (2023): A101–A101. https://doi.org/10.1093/sleep/zsad077.0229

5. Kaylyn McAnally and Martin S. Hagger, "Self-Determination Theory and Workplace Outcomes: A Conceptual Review and Future Research Directions," *Behavioral Science* 14, no. 6 (2024): 428. https://doi.org/10.3390/bs14060428

6. Joachim C. Brunstein, Oliver C. Schultheiss, and Ruth Grässmann, "Personal Goals and Emotional Well-Being: The Moderating Role of Motive Dispositions," *Journal of Personality and Social Psychology* 75, no. 2 (1998): 494–508. https://doi.org/10.1037//0022-3514.75.2.494

7. Samuel D. McDougle, Ian C. Ballard, Beth Baribault, Sonia J. Bishop, and Anne G. E. Collins, "Executive Modulation of Brain Reward Systems Endows Goals with Value," *bioRxiv* (2020 preprint). https://doi.org/10.1101/2020.10.21.348938

8. Bastien Blain, India Pinhorn, and Tali Sharot, "Sensitivity to Intrinsic Rewards Is Domain General and Related to Mental Health," *Nature Mental Health* 1 (2023): 679–691. https://doi.org/10.1038/s44220-023-00116-x; Asami Matsumura and Yohsuke Ohtsubo, "Praise Is Reciprocated with Tangible Benefits: Social Exchange Between Symbolic Resources and Concrete Resources," *Social Psychological and Personality Science* 3, no. 2 (2011): 250–256. https://doi.org/10.1177/1948550611417016

9. Keise Izuma, Daisuke N. Saito, and Norihiro Sadato, "Processing of Social and Monetary Rewards in the Human Striatum," *Neuron* 58, no. 2 (2008): 284–294. https://doi.org/10.1016/j.neuron.2008.03.020

10. Bastien Blain, India Pinhorn, and Tali Sharot, "Sensitivity to Intrinsic Rewards Is Domain General and Related to Mental Health." Min Jeong Kang, Ming Hsu, Ian M. Krajbich, George Loewenstein, Samuel M. McClure, Joseph Tao-yi Wang, and Colin F. Camerer, "The Wick in the Candle of Learning: Epistemic Curiosity Activates Reward Circuitry and Enhances Memory," *Psychological Science* 20, no 8 (2009): 963–973. www.jstor.org/stable/40575128

Leading for Tomorrow

11. Jack Zenger and Joseph Folkman, "Your Employees Want the Negative Feedback You Hate to Give," *Harvard Business Review*, January 15, 2015. https://hbr.org/2014/01/your-employees-want-the-negative-feedback-you-hate-to-give

12. R. Frömer, H. Lin, C. K. Dean Wolf, M. Inzlicht, and A. Shenhav, "Expectations of Reward and Efficacy Guide Cognitive Control Allocation," *Nature Communications* 12 (2021). https://doi.org/10.1038/s41467-021-21315-z; Steven F. Maier and Martin E. P. Seligman, "Learned Helplessness at Fifty: Insights from Neuroscience," *Psychological Review* 123, no. 4 (2016): 349–367. https://doi.org/10.1037/rev0000033

13. Yuen-Siang Ang, and Diego A. Pizzagalli, "Understanding Personal Control and the Brain Reward System for Psychopathology Is Challenging but Important," *Biological Psychiatry: Cognitive Neuroscience and Neuroimaging* 4, no. 2 (2019): 105–107. https://doi.org/10.1016/J.BPSC.2018.12.004; Liana Romaniuk, Anca-Larisa Sandu, Gordon D. Waiter, Christopher J. McNeil, Shen Xueyi, Matthew A. Harris, Jennifer A. Macfarlane, Stephen M. Lawrie . . . Heather C. Whalley, "The Neurobiology of Personal Control During Reward Learning and Its Relationship to Mood," *Biological Psychiatry: Cognitive Neuroscience and Neuroimaging* 4, no. 2 (2019): 190–199. https://doi.org/10.1016/j.bpsc.2018.09.015

14. Veronica Rattini, "Worker Autonomy and Performance: Evidence from a Real-Effort Experiment," *Journal of Economics & Management Strategy* 32, no. 2 (2023): 300–327. https://doi.org/10.1111/jems.12511

15. Kaitlyn M. Werner and Marina Milyavskaya, "Motivation and Self-Regulation: The Role of Want-to Motivation in the Processes Underlying Self-Regulation and Self-Control," *Social and Personality Psychology Compass* 13, no. 1 (2019): 1–14. https://doi.org/10.1111/spc3.12425

16. Magdalena Matyjek, Stefanie Meliss, Isabel Dziobek, and Kou Murayama, "A Multidimensional View on Social and Non-Social Rewards," *Frontiers in Psychiatry* 11 (2020): 818. https://doi.org/10.3389/fpsyt.2020.00818

Inside the Motivated Mind: How Leaders Make Work Feel Worthwhile

17. Cort W. Rudolph, Ian M. Katz, Regina Ruppel, and Hannes Zacher, "A Systematic and Critical Review of Research on Respect in Leadership," *Leadership Quarterly* 32, no. 1 (2021): 101492. https://doi.org/10.1016/j.leaqua.2020.101492

18. Diana I. Tamir and Jason P. Mitchell, "Disclosing Information about the Self Is Intrinsically Rewarding," *Proceedings of the National Academy of Sciences of the United States of America* 109, no. 21 (2012): 8038–8043. https://doi.org/10.1073/pnas.1202129109

19. Hiroaki Kawamichi, Kazufumi Yoshihara, Akihiro T. Sasaki, Sho K. Sugawara, Hiroki C. Tanabe, Ryoji Shinohara, Yuka Sugisawa, Kentaro Tokutake. . . Norihiro Sadato, "Perceiving Active Listening Activates the Reward System and Improves the Impression of Relevant Experiences," *Social Neuroscience* 10, no. 1 (2014): 16–26. 10.1080/17470919 .2014.954732

20. Yasin Rofcanin, Siqi Wang, Mireia Las Heras, Didem Taser, Maria Jose Bosch, Mine Afacan Findikli, and Andres Salas Vallina, "Perceptions of Support Trickle Down: Effects on Energetic Resources Via Psychological Empowerment," *European Management Review* 21, no. 2 (2023): 477–490. https://doi.org/10.1111/emre.12577

21. Hiroaki Kawamichi, Sho K. Sugawara, Yuki H. Hamano, Kai Makita, Takanori Kochiyama, and Norihiro Sadato, "Increased Frequency of Social Interaction Is Associated with Enjoyment Enhancement and Reward System Activation," *Scientific Reports* 6, no. 24561 (2016). https://doi.org/10.1038/srep24561

22. Leor M. Hackel, Jamil Zaki, and Jay Van Bavel, "Social Identity Shapes Social Valuation: Evidence from Prosocial Behavior and Vicarious Reward," *Social Cognitive and Affective Neuroscience* 12, no. 8 (2017): 1219–1228. https://doi.org/10.1093/scan/nsx045

23. Michael J. latow, Margaret Foddy, Toshio Yamagishi, Li Lim, and Aurore Chow, "Two Experimental Tests of Trust in In-Group Strangers: The Moderating Role of Common Knowledge of Group Membership," *European Journal of Social Psychology* 42, no. 1 (2011): 30–35.

24. J. Sun, K. Harris, and S. Vazire, "Is Well-Being Associated with the Quantity and Quality of Social Interactions?" *Journal of Personality and Social Psychology* 119, no. 6 (2020): 1478–1496. https://doi.org/10.1037/pspp0000272

25. Nathan Liang, Samantha J. Grayson, Mia A. Kussman, Judith N. Mildner, and Diana I. Tamir, "In-Person and Virtual Social Interactions Improve Well-Being During the COVID-19 Pandemic," *Computers in Human Behavior* 15, no. 100455 (2024). https://doi.org/10.1016/j.chbr.2024.100455

26. Peng Sun, Li Zheng, Lin Li, Xiuyan Guy, Weidong Zhang, and Yijie Zheng, "The Neural Responses to Social Cooperation in Gain and Loss Context," *PLOS ONE* 11, no. 8 (2016): e0160503. https://doi.org/10.1371/journal.pone.0160503

27. Zhong Yang, Ya Zheng, Guochun Yang, Qi Li, and Xun Liu, "Neural Signatures of Cooperation Enforcement and Violation: A Coordinate-Based Meta-Analysis," *Social Cognitive and Affective Neuroscience* 14, no. 9 (2019): 919–931. https://doi.org/10.1093/scan/nsz073

28. Minseo Kim and Terry A. Beehr, "Making the Case for Procedural Justice: Employees Thrive and Work Hard," *Journal of Managerial Psychology* 35, no. 2 (2020): 100–114. https://doi.org/10.1108/JMP-03-2019-0154

29. Mohsen Joshanloo, "Increases in Sense of Purpose Predict Future Positive Changes in Personality Traits," *British Journal of Psychology* 115, no. 4 (2024): 809–824. https://doi.org/10.1111/bjop.12726

30. Katarzyna Cantarero, Wijnand A. P. van Tilburg, and Ewelina Smoktunowicz, "Other- (vs. Self-) Oriented Meaning Interventions Enhance Momentary Work Engagement Through Changes in Work Meaningfulness," *Journal of Counseling Psychology* 69, no. 4 (2022): 443–451. https://doi.org/10.1037/cou0000594

31. Patrick L. Hill, Nancy L. Sin, Nicholas A. Turiano, Anthony L. Burrow, and David M. Almeida, "Sense of Purpose Moderates the Associations Between Daily Stressors and Daily Well-being," *Annals of Behavioral Medicine* 52, no. 8 (2018): 724–729.

https://doi.org/10.1093/abm/kax039; Stacey M. Schaefer, Jennifer Morozink Boylan, Carien M. van Reekum, Regina C. Lapate, Catherine J. Norris, Carol D. Ryff, and Richard J. Davidson, "Purpose in Life Predicts Better Emotional Recovery from Negative Stimuli," *PLOS ONE* 8, no. 11 (2013): e80329–e80329. https://doi.org/10.1371/journal.pone.0080329

32. Erik S. Kim, Shelley D. Hershner, and Victor J. Strecher, "Purpose in Life and Incidence of Sleep Disturbances," *Journal of Behavioral Medicine* 38 (2015): 590–597. https://doi.org/10.1007/s10865-015-9635-4

33. Rachael N. Blasiman and Christopher A. Was, "Why Is Working Memory Performance Unstable? A Review of 21 Factors," *Europe's Journal of Psychology* 14, no. 1 (2018): 188–231. https://doi.org/10.5964/ejop.v14i1.1472; Yusuf Patrick, Alice Lee, Oishik Raha, Kavya Pillai, Shubham Gupta, Sonika Sethi Nayyar, Felicite Mukeshimana, Lothaire Gerard. . .James Moss, "Effects of Sleep Deprivation on Cognitive and Physical Performance in University Students," *Sleep and Biological Rhythms* 15, no. 3 (2017): 217–225.

34. Louise David, Eliana Vassena, and Erik Bijleveld, "The Unpleasantness of Thinking: A Meta-Analytic Review of the Association Between Mental Effort and Negative Affect," *Psychological Bulletin* 150, no. 9 (2024): 1070–1093. https://doi.org/10.1037/bul0000443

35. Fynn R. Dobler, Malte R. Henningsen-Schomers, and Friedemann Pulvermüller, "Verbal Symbols Support Concrete but Enable Abstract Concept Formation: Evidence from Brain-Constrained Deep Neural Networks," *Language Learning* 74, Supple. 1 (2024): 258–295. https://doi.org/10.1111/lang.12646

36. Elizabeth R. Tenney, Jared M. Poole, and Ed Diener, "Does Positivity Enhance Work Performance?: Why, When, and What We Don't Know," *Research in Organizational Behavior* 36 (2016): 27–46. https://doi.org/10.1016/j.riob.2016.11.002; Anja Van den Broecka, Maarten Vansteenkisteb, Hans De Wittea, and Willy Lens, "Explaining the

Relationships Between Job Characteristics, Burnout, and Engagement: The Role of Basic Psychological Need Satisfaction," *Work & Stress* 22, no. 3 (2008): 277–294. https://doi.org/10.1080/02678370802393672

37. Feifei Ren, Qian Zhang, and Xing Wei, "Work Autonomous and Controlled Motivation on Chinese Employees' Work Performance and Innovative Work Behaviour: The Moderating Role of Financial Stress," *Frontiers in Psychology* 12, no. 676063 (2021). https://doi.org/10.3389/fpsyg.2021.676063

Inside the Motivated Mind: How Leaders Make Work Feel Worthwhile

Chapter 14

Think Like a Scientist: A Prescription for Human-Centered Leadership

Amy C. Edmondson

In the scholarly and popular literatures, science and humanism are often framed as fundamentally at odds—two factions in perpetual tension in modern society.[1] These factions are thought to bring contrasting priorities, values, and approaches to progress. Science—characterized by objectivity, rigor, and empiricism—prioritizes explanation, prediction, and results, thereby contrasting sharply with humanism's emphasis on subjective experience, ethics, meaning, and well-being—domains traditionally considered outside the reach of scientific analysis. In the 21st century, this tension escalated into culture wars, increasingly putting us at risk of backing away from advances in fields as disparate as health, education, and social justice.[2]

Meanwhile, cultural and psychological dynamics threaten to heighten the divide by converting values differences into identity-based polarization and mutual suspicion.[3] The cultural divide is rooted in differing worldviews about authority, morality, and the nature of truth. For some, science is linked with progressive humanism as an open, forward-looking embrace of empirical knowledge where all have equal access to its methods; for others, science is a threat to traditional deeply held beliefs. Psychologically, the divide is deepened by phenomena such as motivated reasoning[4] and in-group loyalty[5] that lead people to reject facts that conflict with their group identities.

Not only can this divide—which stems from a false dichotomy—be healed, doing so may be vital to our future. When science is seen as the sole arbiter of knowledge, it can rightly be criticized as dehumanizing. And when humanism is portrayed as soft, fuzzy, and without empirical rigor, its essential insights are devalued. But both critiques are caricatures. Science and humanism have in common a commitment to discipline and caring; both, at their core, are about creating a better world. Framing that puts them at odds inhibits the development of the leadership models we need to guide us toward a more humane, just, and inspiring future.

Today's most effective—and most human-centered—leaders are those who think like scientists. Human-centered leaders, it seems to me, are curious, other-oriented, generous, and fundamentally oriented toward making a better world, with the help of those they lead. Perhaps this description does not sound to you like that of a classic scientist. In that case, I hope to change your mind.

I arrive at this argument as a social scientist who has studied people in organizations for more than three decades while married to a physician-scientist. This combination has helped me understand the mindset scientists use and convey and to see it as a model to suggest to those who study or practice leadership. Consider that the best scientists today, and throughout history, are curious, ask probing questions, encourage experimentation, and work to make sense of new, confusing, ambiguous data. Scientists dare to dream of solving unprecedented problems and puzzles. They take risks. They fail, learn, and keep going forward.

It's hard not to see the parallels to human-centered leadership.

The Purpose of Leadership

Leadership is the art of harnessing the efforts of others to achieve complex and challenging aims. Its very essence involves vulnerability—accepting that the answers you need are not yet clear and accepting

Leading for Tomorrow

your dependency on others. There is no need for leadership in a world where each of us can take care of our own needs and where problems are simple. Leadership is needed to pull us together to do things that would be impossible for any of us on our own.[6]

> Leadership is needed to pull us together to do things that would be impossible for any of us on our own.

It's not just leaders who must accept their vulnerability as a fact. All of us are vulnerable because none of us has the full range of skills, knowledge, or perspicacity we need to survive and thrive in a volatile, uncertain, complex, ambiguous world. When leaders and followers alike accept their vulnerability—and even relish the state of needing genuine connection and cooperation in our lives at work and at home—we are all better off. Like it or not, we must work together to find and implement solutions to the problems we face today. Leadership in every sector and in every nation is needed to help us do just that. And it is this vulnerability that requires us to rethink and update our ideas about what it means to lead. Counterintuitively, the scientific mindset provides an apt starting point for updating the legacy of Industrial Era management models.

Legacies of Industrial Era Management

Traditional management models assumed a level of certainty and predictability that no longer exists. I think of these models as useful simplifications that worked extraordinarily well in the Industrial Era but fail in our current environment of rapid change and extreme uncertainty.[7] Although I find it hard at times to imagine that anyone ever took the model literally, that may be simply the bias of a 21st-century observer.

Let's review the basics.

The managerial mindset that took hold in the early and mid-20th century was defined by a set of assumptions and habits that prioritized stability, predictability, and control. For starters, leaders were presumed to have answers. Managers were experts: They told us not only where we are heading but how we were to get there. Control was hierarchical. Authority flowed down, as did evaluation. No need for 360s in this model of management. Managers were responsible for setting targets, establishing deadlines, delegating tasks, and monitoring compliance. Decision making was centralized and unquestioned.

The model is designed for optimizing execution and efficiency. Understandably, experimentation is discouraged. Good ideas do not come from anywhere but the top. An emphasis on control rather than learning fuels the success of these (static) systems. The goal is consistent, repeatable operations, with little need for adaptability or responsiveness to novel challenges.

Along with this model came a punitive attitude toward failure, and indeed risk taking, that can seem an anathema today. Failures were obviously bad and should be punished, and, thus, people would seek to avoid failures (and mistakes) at all costs. In that we human beings inevitably make *some* mistakes, this mindset largely means that mistakes will be hidden rather than reported, giving rise to a risk of quality problems and preventable failures. Given these assumptions and values, performance reviews naturally would focus on identifying where individuals fell short in their roles. Because of confidence that the organization, or system, was well designed to achieve its goals, when things went wrong, it made sense to attribute the shortcomings to individuals rather than see how systems and structures might be partly to blame.

This summary is not intended as a caricature. When the primary goal is high-volume, consistent execution following known processes, these assumptions can work—with some tweaking. As the world's best

Leading for Tomorrow

production operations have shown, good ideas can, and do, come from the bottom. Moreover, despite the essential goal of reducing variability, variability still exists, and so the best production operations are designed to catch and correct deviations before they cause harm.[8] They're designed to make sure speaking up about problems is seen as welcome. But even so, the fundamental goal is consistency—a completely reliable result at the end of the production process.

Relatedly, change (of any kind) is disruptive. Stability is the goal, and robust planning, standardized procedures, and well-defined roles are the tools for achieving it. If today this model seems a straw argument, consider how many of us learned, and lived, these principles early in our careers. We may have participated in energetic conversations about the pace of change for decades, marveling at the upending of the old order. Nonetheless, it was too often the case that we were told at various times and in various ways the right way to do something and evaluated on how well we followed instructions. As a result, many leaders today have internalized Industrial Era logic without realizing it and quietly suffer from the expectation that they should have answers, be in control, and punish failure.

But if this model and its corresponding mindset worked in an era of relative predictability, there can remain no doubt that both impede the adaptability and innovation needed in today's dynamic environment.

Thinking Like a Scientist

Thinking like a scientist, as a leader, is not about possessing literal technical expertise in the laboratory; it's about navigating uncertainty with curiosity and passion and seeing your role as leading a team in a collaborative process of discovery. Thinking like a scientist means recognizing the limits of your own knowledge, adopting a

Thinking like a scientist means recognizing the limits of your own knowledge, adopting a mindset of inquiry, and inspiring people to engage in experimentation and dialogue.

mindset of inquiry, and inspiring people to engage in experimentation and dialogue.

Where Industrial Era managers brought answers, scientists bring questions. Instead of seeking conformity, they hope for diverse ideas and novel options. Their goal is effective experimentation and progress, not efficient execution. They see their job as enabling and empowering others rather than just evaluating them. They feel responsible for the kind of evaluation that helps those they lead become better contributors—the kind that is oriented toward improvement rather than judgment. Table 14.1 illustrates the contrast.

Making the shift in mindset starts with embracing the premise that answers to the most pressing problems that need solving are not yet known. The work to be led is the work of discovery. And leading a discovery process is fundamentally different from leading an

Table 14.1 Contrast Between Classic Management and Scientific Leadership

Classic Management Mindset	Thinking Like a Scientist
Brings answers	Brings questions
Sets targets	Sets direction
Emphasizes planning	Emphasizes learning
Evaluates	Enables
Values conformity	Values differences
Works for efficient execution of known solutions	Works for effective progress in new or uncertain territory

execution process. Discovery happens through thoughtful forays into new territory. This means appreciating the need for risk taking—not wild-eyed, reckless risk taking but rather the willingness to do things for which the results are uncertain. Therefore, and most directly related to my own research, thinking like a scientist means appreciating that *failure is a part of the journey*. This recognition becomes more than just intellectual; it becomes a way of being that sincerely welcomes failure in new territory.

Welcoming (Intelligent) Failure

Scientists distinguish between failures and mistakes—an important distinction for human-centered leadership. In an uncertain context, failures are inevitable. But, perhaps counterintuitively, uncertainty does *not* mean mistakes are inevitable. To understand why, consider some definitions.

Drawing from both scholarly and dictionary sources, I define "mistake" (synonymous with "error") as an unintended deviation from known procedures, standards, rules, or protocols.[9] By definition, therefore, a mistake can occur only when prior knowledge exists. Examples might include charging a customer the wrong amount for a product or entering the wrong dose in a patient's prescription. Mistakes occur across activities in work and life when we're not paying attention or when we lack the knowledge or training to do it right. Importantly, mistakes don't always bring severe consequences. Some do, of course, but fortunately, much of the time we can brush them off, learn, and move on.

A *failure* is an outcome that deviates from desired or expected results, regardless of intent or cause. Although many failures are indeed caused by mistakes, not *all* failures are caused by mistakes, and not all mistakes cause failures. If you mistakenly add the wrong amount of some ingredient while following a trusted recipe, but the

Think Like a Scientist: A Prescription for Human-Centered Leadership

result is delicious, no failure has occurred. If your flight is canceled and you fail to arrive at your conference destination, you have not made a mistake, but you have experienced a failure. Further, failures are not all alike. In my research, I've identified three types[10]:

1. **Basic failure:** An undesired result in familiar territory, usually caused by a mistake

2. **Complex failure:** An undesired result caused by the interaction of multiple factors, where none on their own would have triggered failure

3. **Intelligent failure:** An undesired result of an action in new territory, driven by a hypothesis, in pursuit of a goal, where care had been taken to minimize unnecessary risk

Whereas basic failures have a single cause, usually human error, intelligent failures are not. Complex failures—those perfect storms that happen when multiple separate factors come together to produce havoc—can often be prevented with vigilance. But in our increasingly complex and interconnected world, they're on the rise. We should do our best to prevent as many as possible and learn as much as we can from the rest.

Intelligent failures, although disappointing at the time, uniquely bring valuable new knowledge. Also, they are not preventable. Because they occur in new territory, intelligent failures cannot be anticipated or prevented, but they do bring value. Thinking like a scientist thus means *welcoming*—not just tolerating—intelligent failure. Intelligent failure is the right kind of wrong. It is the basis of discovery and progress—and not just in science. Thinking like a scientist thus means being glad when you hear about failures of *any* kind, even the not-so-intelligent ones, so that you and the organization you lead can learn as much as possible from all of them.

Failure—along with what I call failure science—thus plays an important role in human-centered leadership, because of the inevitability of uncertainty in today's organizations. Simply put, things *will* go wrong. And these disappointments can either be seen as shameful, blameworthy, and problematic or as inevitable stepping-stones on a journey forward. It matters greatly which way failures are seen in an organization, because people tend not to speak up about shameful, blameworthy things. That means leaders don't hear about them in a timely way to help prevent worse harm.

If uncertainty brings failure, why does it not also bring mistakes? Mistakes are deviations from known procedures or protocols. The concept of a mistake thus implies at least some certainty in the prior knowledge. To illustrate, consider a scientific laboratory. Scientists experiment for a living: They read the relevant literature, develop hypotheses, and test them, and their hypotheses often fail to be supported by the data. These disappointments epitomize the concept of intelligent failures, and they are useful steps forward in a program of research. In contrast, if a scientist mistakenly uses the wrong chemical or the wrong equipment in an experiment—perhaps when moving too fast or thinking about other things—and the experiment fails, she has learned nothing new other than to pay more attention when conducting an experiment. The point is, her mistake was preventable, and there's no compelling reason that a more uncertain context makes us pay less attention. If anything, the reverse might be true: We're more likely to be on our toes when we are aware of uncertainty.

In short, mistakes are preventable—with vigilance and care—and, as this example indicates, it's worth doing everything you can to reduce mistakes because they can waste time and resources. Yes, some mistakes will slip through. After all, to err is human. Now and then, a mistake will even produce a happy surprise, as in

Think Like a Scientist: A Prescription for Human-Centered Leadership

the discovery of penicillin.[11] But such events are rare, and great teams work hard to catch and correct errors to minimize harm. Human-centered leaders build organizations that make reducing error easy while encouraging the risk taking that produces intelligent failure.[12]

Cultivating a Climate of Psychological Safety

Leaders play a crucial role in shaping the environment. What leaders say and do influences how people make sense of the events that unfold around them. By thinking like a scientist, leaders can build a climate conducive to candor and discovery—a climate of psychological safety.[13]

"Psychological safety" refers to an interpersonal environment where people believe they can speak up candidly with ideas, questions, concerns, and even mistakes. It is not about being "nice" or feeling comfortable.[14] It's about a learning environment—one where candor is expected, mistakes are surfaced, and people deliver bad news and challenge assumptions without fear of reprisal.

Let's face it: Learning is rarely comfortable. For scientists, this type of open, candid environment is not optional. Scientific inquiry requires the freedom to ask probing questions, propose unproven ideas, and openly examine failures. It stands to reason that thinking like a scientist might help nonscience leaders create this kind of environment.

Leaders who think like scientists want their teams to feel safe sharing unexpected results, diverging from consensus opinions, and reporting problems early—even though these admissions can challenge prevailing views and feel uncomfortable. The scientific process thrives on experimentation and iteration, which cannot occur in any meaningful sense when people are afraid to offer ideas, voice concerns, or reveal when something hasn't worked. Psychological safety is the soil in which collaboration, learning, and innovation thrive. Leaders who adopt a scientific mindset will naturally cultivate psychological safety by signaling that inquiry and dissent are valued contributions to progress.

The idea that good leadership is not about having answers or being in control of outcomes aligns well with the concept of psychological safety. Leaders who understand that they don't have all the answers also understand that their job is to ask questions and to encourage others to ask questions and seek answers. This is what it means to think like a scientist. It means encouraging risk taking and normalizing intelligent failure, to cultivate a space where experimentation and adaptation are possible. The cognitive and behavioral habits in Table 14.2 illustrate what it looks like when leaders are thinking like scientists.

> Leaders who understand that they don't have all the answers also understand that their job is to ask questions.

Table 14.2 Illustrative Habits of Scientific Leadership

Habit	Description
Question assumptions	Challenge your own views and established practices, remain open to evidence that contradicts initial beliefs.
Run smart experiments	Design and execute thoughtful, small-scale trials to test new ideas, minimizing risk while maximizing learning potential.
Embrace intelligent failure	Frame failures as essential learning opportunities; clarify the distinction between "intelligent failures," which result from well-informed experimentation in new territory, and "basic failures" caused by careless errors.

(continued)

Think Like a Scientist: A Prescription for Human-Centered Leadership

Habit	Description
Seek diverse perspectives	Invite alternative views; ask "What are we missing?" and "Who sees it differently?"
Respond constructively to setbacks	Facilitate conversations about setbacks, reward transparency, and focus on extracting insights to guide future action.
Foster psychological safety	Be open and vulnerable to model behaviors such as admitting error and asking for help.
Iterate continuously	Encourage people to move rapidly from experiment to reflection to adjustment, in a cycle of ongoing progress.

Making the Shift

How can leaders make the shift from ingrained, partly unconscious, mental models characterized by needing to be in control, right, and judgmental to a mindset of curiosity and empowerment? I'll organize my ideas for making this shift into three phased categories: (1) setting the stage, (2) initiating and inviting exploration, and (3) responding— especially to bad news—in a forward-facing learning manner.

Setting the Stage

Getting started on any kind of mindset shift means being explicit, almost heavy-handed, with yourself about the shift. Work on your self-talk to override the default beliefs like "I'm supposed to know this already" or "I'm supposed to hold them accountable for failures" to remind yourself with alternatives, such as "There are aspects of this project [situation, work] that are new; our understanding of what will work is incomplete, at best," or "If we put our ideas and expertise together, we're likely to come up with something powerful."[15]

Practicing a scientific mindset means reminding yourself that accountability is shared. Tell yourself: "If the team falls short, especially in preventable ways, it's likely that several factors will have contributed to that result. Moreover, it almost certainly means that there were things that I have not done well enough as a leader." Force yourself to think of shortcomings as valuable learning events, for you and others. Truly. Make this explicit. With every setback and surprise comes useful new knowledge when approached in the right way. Notice that these stage-setting practices, when shared aloud, also contribute to creating the psychological safety that is so necessary for learning and performance in an uncertain environment.

Stage setting is essentially about clarifying the nature of the context. Specifically, ask yourself: "How much uncertainty is there? How much novelty? How much interdependence?" Call attention to these features—first for yourself and then for others—because they all imply a need for exploration, experimentation, and high-quality open discussions.

Last, remind yourself (and then communicate it to others) of the work's *purpose*—the larger reason it matters to the organization or to the world. Doing this helps motivate people to do the hard work of exploration and learning.[16]

Set boundaries. Be crystal clear about compliance issues and behavioral norms that must be followed for the work to unfold well. This is particularly true for human safety-related issues in workplaces like manufacturing and healthcare delivery.

Setting the stage serves a dual purpose: It communicates with others to help get them on the same page, and it helps mold your own outlook to help solidify a new way of thinking and being.[17]

175

Initiating and Inviting Exploration

Leaders who think like a scientist will naturally create space for inquiry and debate. They do this by asking questions, encouraging dissent, and valuing (and thus listening to) the diverse expertise in their teams. Inviting others to think deeply, express concerns, and offer novel solutions is a great idea, but it won't happen without being proactive and explicit in insisting that people share what they are seeing and thinking.

Practice asking good questions. There is a difference between questions that generate thoughtful exploration ("What are we missing?," "Who sees this differently?") and those that indicate you're looking for agreement ("What do you think of my great idea?").[18] Alas, such *leading questions* are as prevalent in workplaces as they are unproductive. When leaders ask leading questions, the odds are overwhelmingly high that they will hear the answer implied by the question. Although it can feel good when people agree with us, it inhibits progress and can lead to serious failures.[19]

Be explicit in insisting that people seek out diverse ideas and perspectives, whether from colleagues or customers; invite them to experiment and to share what they learn with everyone. Suggest directions for exploration. Recommend places to learn, to collect data, or to find out more related to the project or goal at hand. Be clear that there are multiple possible avenues, and you truly want to know others' ideas, to add to your own. By inviting exploration deliberately and frequently, you make it easier for people to search, diverge, and experiment. You also ensure that the intelligent failures they encounter will be shared to help everyone figure out where to go next.

Responding in a Learning-Oriented Way

Human nature and legacy mental models alike make our default responses to bad news counterproductive. When someone brings

Leading for Tomorrow

you bad news, what do you say? What is your face doing? For most of us, our spontaneous response might be annoyance or frustration. Scientists train themselves to overcome this instinct. Instead of "How the heck did that happen?," good scientists train themselves to say, "Thanks for that new information." They recognize that the risk of not hearing the truth—or, worse, of falsified data—is real, and they resolve to inoculate their organization from that risk. They recognize that all data are welcome; whether they support or refute hypotheses and hopes, they bring value.

Train yourself to look forward, not backward, when you respond. Although an important and useful question, "How did that happen?" is backward looking. There will be time to ask that question later, to dig in and learn as much as possible, but your *initial* response to bad news must be "Thank you for telling me; how can I help?" Remind yourself that the past contains invaluable information—*and* that the past cannot be changed. So, focus first on action, on what you can do with the new and valuable information going forward.

If this sounds superhuman, consider that it's about reinvigorating a learning mindset.[20] We're all born with an innate drive to learn. Children arrive hardwired with curiosity and an intense interest in figuring out how things work. Thinking like a scientist means, in part, reconnecting with the curiosity with which we were born.

Human-Centered Leadership for the Journey Ahead

To "think like a scientist" as a leader is to lead not with certainty or a feeling of being in control but rather with curiosity and passion. It's focused equally on what's possible and on what others bring to the endeavor. Inquiry, experimentation, and honesty are some of the behavioral manifestations of this way of thinking, demonstrating that to think like a scientist is to be human-centered.

Whether we are leading or being led, we need a leadership model that serves us, as fallible human beings, in our quest to create a better world than the one we inherited. Leaders who adopt this mindset can help their teams and their organizations navigate complexity. This shift is not about abandoning accountability or a desire for results but rather about being wise enough to recognize that discovery and adaptation are the engines of enduring success.

Notes

1. Bernard Barber, "Tension and Accommodation Between Science and Humanism," *American Behavioral Scientist* 7, no. 3 (1963). doi.org/10.1177/000276426300700302

2. Stephen P. Weldon, "Humanism and Science as a Window into the Culture Wars in America" [Book review], November 18, 2020. www.press.jhu.edu/newsroom/humanism-and-science-window-culture-wars-america

3. Ibid.; *and* Roderik Rekker, "The Nature and Origins of Political Polarization Over Science," *Public Understanding of Science* 30, no. 4 (2021): 352–368. doi.org/10.1177/0963662521989193

4. Z. Kunda, "The Case for Motivated Reasoning," *Psychological Bulletin* 108, no. 3 (1990): 480–498. doi.org/10.1037/0033-2909.108.3.480

5. Marilynn B. Brewer, "The Psychology of Prejudice: Ingroup Love and Outgroup Hate?" *Journal of Social Issues* 55, no. 3 (2002): 429–444. doi.org/10.1111/0022-4537.00126

6. Amy C. Edmondson, "Wicked-Problem Solvers: Lessons from Successful Cross-Industry Teams," *Harvard Business Review* 94, no. 6 (2016): 52–59. https://hbr.org/2016/06/wicked-problem-solvers

7. Amy C. Edmondson, *Teaming: How Organizations Learn, Innovate, and Compete in the Knowledge Economy* (Jossey-Bass, 2012), chapter 1.

8. Steven Spear and H. Kent Bowen, "Decoding the DNA of the Toyota Production System," *Harvard Business Review* 77, no. 5 (1999): 96–106. https://hbr.org/1999/09/decoding-the-dna-of-the-toyota-production-system

9. For more on errors and mistakes, see Amy C. Edmondson, "Learning from Mistakes Is Easier Said Than Done: Group and Organizational Influences on the Detection and Correction of Human Error," *Journal of Applied Behavioral Science* 32, no. 1 (1996): 5–28. doi.org/10.1177/002188639632100. Also see Paul S. Goodman, Rangaraj Ramanujam, John S. Carroll, Amy C. Edmondson, David A. Hofmann, and Kathleen M. Sutcliffe, "Organizational Errors: Directions for Future Research," *Research in Organizational Behavior* 31 (2011): 151–176. doi.org/10.1016/j.riob.2011.09.003

10. For a more in-depth discussion of this topic, see Amy C. Edmondson, *Right Kind of Wrong: The Science of Failing Well* (Atria Books, 2023), chapters 1 and 4.

11. Elizabeth K.Johnson, "The Accident that Changed the World: The Discovery of Penicillin," University of Virginia, Department of Chemistry, n.d. https://chemistry.as.virginia.edu/node/6887

12. Amy C. Edmondson, "The Art of Failing Well," *Dialogue Review*, February 20, 2024. https://dialoguereview.com/the-art-of-failing-well/

13. Amy C. Edmondson, *The Fearless Organization: Creating Psychological Safety in the Workplace for Learning, Innovation, and Growth* (Wiley, 2018).

14. Amy C. Edmondson and Michaela J. Kerrissey, "What People Get Wrong about Psychological Safety: Six Misconceptions that Have Led Organizations Astray," *Harvard Business Review* (May–June 2025): 52–59. https://hbr.org/2025/05/what-people-get-wrong-about-psychological-safety

15. "Self-Talk: Inner Voice," *Psychology Today*, n.d. www.psychologytoday.com/us/basics/self-talk

16. For more on communicating purpose, see Ranjay Gulati, *Deep Purpose: The Heart and Soul of High-Performance Companies* (Harper Business, 2022). Also see ÁlvaroLleó de Nalda, Alex Montaner, Amy C. Edmonson, and Phil Sotok, "Unlock the Power of Purpose," *MIT Sloan Management Review* 63, no. 4 (2022): 20–23. https://sloanreview.mit.edu/article/unlock-the-power-of-purpose/

17. "Self-Talk: Inner Voice."

Think Like a Scientist: A Prescription for Human-Centered Leadership

18. For more on asking good questions, see: Michael Luca and Amy C. Edmondson, "Where Data-Driven Decision-Making Can Go Wrong," *Harvard Business Review* 102, no. 5 (2024): 80–89. https://hbr.org/2024/09/where-data-driven-decision-making-can-go-wrong. Also see Amy C. Edmondson, Tiziana Casciaro, and Sujin Jang, "Cross-Silo Leadership," *Harvard Business Review* 97, no. 3 (2019): 130–139. www.hbs.edu/faculty/Pages/item.aspx?num=56041

19. For more on how psychologically safe environments help prevent catastrophic failures, see Amy C. Edmondson, Erika Ferlins, Laura Feldman, and Richard Bohmer, "The Recovery Window: Organizational Learning Following Ambiguous Threats," in *Organization at the Limits: NASA and the Columbia Disaster,* M. Farjoun and W. Starbuck (Eds.) (Blackwell, 2005), pp. 220–245. Also see Edmondson, *The Fearless Organization*, chapters 3 and 4.

20. Carol S. Dweck, *Mindset: How You Can Fulfil Your Potential* (Constable & Robinson, 2012).

Chapter 15

The Good Jobs Strategy: Seeing Frontline Workers as Value Drivers

Zeynep Ton

At MIT Sloan's graduation ceremony in 2025, my student Kenta Takahashi stood before his fellow Sloan Fellows graduates and shared a simple but profound metaphor. "Let's imagine you are in a dark room," he said. "There are some candles there. Some are already kindled, but others are not yet lit. In such a setting, it is extremely difficult to find unlit candles."

He was reflecting on a case study from my operations management class, featuring the voices and aspirations of frontline workers from around the world. Their words stayed with him long after the semester ended: "I want to be happy and challenged every day," "I hope to go to more places and love more things," and "I want to be successful and useful to mankind."

"These are people equally capable, motivated, hardworking as us," Kenta said. "But they're just not given opportunity." Then came his challenge to his classmates—future leaders who would soon carry MIT degrees and all the influence that comes with them: "There are countless invisible candles in this world. Lives full of potential. Waiting to be kindled. . . Let's stay curious, seek out those invisible candles, and light them."

Lighting those invisible candles is one of the most important leadership challenges of today and tomorrow. Capitalism isn't working for far too many Americans. They live paycheck to paycheck, juggle multiple jobs, and lack hope. The fix isn't only training or upskilling workers. It has to include transforming the jobs they already have into high-productivity jobs that provide living wages, dignity, and meaning.

This transformation is necessary to rebuild a strong middle class. It is possible. And it doesn't require sacrificing innovation or profitability. But it requires a fundamental mindset shift—seeing labor as a driver of value rather than a cost to cut and thinking in systems rather than optimizing isolated parts.

The Human Cost of Bad Jobs

Janet is one of those invisible candles. When I interviewed her, she was a full-time hourly manager at a major retail chain, managing cashiers, greeters, and cart pushers. She was also responsible for solving equipment problems and handling customer service issues.

Yet she still didn't make enough to pay the bills for her and her son. Though a full-time manager, she was often scheduled under 40 hours a week and never knew when she'd work. One day she might work from 5 pm to 9 pm. The next morning her shift might start at 5 am. "My life is always in turmoil because you can't sleep," Janet told me. Sometimes she reported to work without having slept at all. She needed a second job, but with volatile hours she couldn't keep one.

For workers like Janet, the effects of financial instability go far beyond financial strain. They erode health, families, and futures. Low and inconsistent pay is associated with heart disease,[1] stroke mortality,[2] diabetes,[3] low birth weight,[4] and even lower cognitive functioning.[5] When people are constantly thinking about money problems, the bandwidth tax from that stress is equivalent to a 13-point drop in IQ.[6]

Leading for Tomorrow

Despite all that's stacked against her, Janet still wanted to do a good job. But even there, she failed in front of customers constantly. One day, customers were yelling at her over long lines and unstaffed registers. "They stay in line so long that their ice is melting. Many of them walk off and leave full baskets," she said. It was her job to manage those lines, but there weren't enough workers. Many who were there were new, so they worked slowly and made mistakes, misplacing products and leaving expired milk in the fridge. When customers found errors at checkout, cashiers had to call Janet because they weren't trusted to adjust prices or solve problems. These tight controls, designed to limit mistakes, wasted everyone's time and made workers feel small in front of customers.

Janet begged for more staff. But her store's poor performance led to tighter labor budgets, which meant more mistakes and higher turnover. Most employees left within the first few months, so Janet was constantly rehiring, retraining, and firefighting.

Every day, she went home physically tired and defeated.

The Power of Good Jobs in Action

Todd Miner tells a different story. After starting with Costco as a meat cutter in 2003, he was now celebrating his 22nd year with the company, as a meat manager at the Waltham, Massachusetts, warehouse, and part of the team that opens new warehouses. Pay and benefits allowed him to raise four kids, and stability keeps him focused on the work. Like many other Costco employees I've spoken with, what keeps Todd at Costco is not just pay; it's the opportunity to grow and succeed.

Unlike Janet, Todd doesn't fight fires all day. He has an experienced and motivated team that can execute well, freeing him to focus on developing people and improving performance. When he visits my MIT Sloan class, my students are struck by his pride and ownership. "You always find ways to raise your standards," he often

The Good Jobs Strategy

says. He can tie his work to outcomes Costco achieves with amazing precision. For example, once he pointed out the fat trim on a ribeye. The trim was supposed to be ¼-inch thick. Thicker trims disrespect the members; thinner trims mean Costco would lose 8 pounds of meat per day or about $2,000 per month in hidden shrinkage.

Todd's ability to focus on details and improve performance isn't just about his talent or Costco's investment in people. He can focus on the ribeye because Costco offers fewer products and relentlessly removes tedious work from the frontlines. Todd and his team have time to do a good job and improve performance because Costco operates with slack; stores are staffed above the forecasted workload to absorb variability. Employees are cross-trained, and all focus on providing a good member experience. So, when traffic spikes, someone can open a register immediately. There are clear standards that set clear expectations, but Todd is trusted to make decisions such as experimenting with display changes to see what drives sales.

Like Janet, Todd goes home physically exhausted. But not defeated. He feels valued and is proud of the value he creates.

Todd is passionate. He even has a butcher's knife tattooed on his arm. But drop him into Janet's store, he couldn't add nearly as much value. Put Janet into Costco's system, and she would likely thrive.

Two Paths to Profit Maximization

Todd's and Janet's companies represent two different approaches to profit maximization driven by two different ways of seeing people.[7]

Cost Mindset

The dominant approach, which Janet's company follows, is to see labor as a cost to be minimized. Accordingly, market pay, or slightly above, is considered all companies can and should pay, even when it doesn't provide a livable wage. Unstable schedules are treated as normal, as if workers don't have families or need to sleep. Attendance issues, employee turnover, and mistakes are seen as inevitable costs of doing business. As a chief operating officer of a large retailer told me bluntly, "We are numb to employee turnover."

This mindset leads to a vicious cycle of high turnover, weak operational execution, poor performance, and continued underinvestment in people. And there is path dependency. As we saw with Janet, high turnover causes these companies to make subsequent decisions that weaken their systems. As one executive said during a workshop, "We design systems assuming people can't do anything right."

In the end, these companies avoid higher wages, but they pay in other ways. In our work at the nonprofit Good Jobs Institute, we've seen companies turn over their entire roster within a year. The direct costs of hiring, onboarding, training, and time to full productivity can amount to 10 to 25 percent of annual payroll. The hidden costs are larger: mistakes that waste time and repel customers, empty shelves and long lines that reduce sales, and the damaged or stolen products that raise costs. Leaders turn to training programs to remedy errors, but with constant churn, the process repeats endlessly. Still, the vicious cycle can remain profitable for a long time, so leaders see no urgency to change.

Value Mindset

The alternative approach, which Todd's company exemplifies, is less common but more powerful. I first observed it over a decade ago at Costco and three other low-cost retailers: QuikTrip (a Tulsa-based convenience store chain), Trader Joe's (a supermarket chain in the United States), and Mercadona (Spain's largest supermarket chain).

Leaders who adopt this approach see labor as a driver of value. They understand that great companies grow profits by continuously

The Good Jobs Strategy

improving value for their customers. And that requires a strong front-line engine because frontlines are where the product or service meets the customer. As Jim Sinegal, cofounder of Costco, often tells my students, "Seventy cents of every dollar we spend to run our company goes to people. If you don't do that well, you'll screw up your business badly."

To leaders like Sinegal, high employee turnover and all the costs associated with it are unacceptable. So, they invest what it takes—higher pay, stable schedules, career paths—to attract and retain the right people. To ensure a high return on employee investment, they also make four operational choices that increase productivity and motivation of employees.[8] These choices along with investment in people reinforce one another, creating a system where each element makes the others more effective. I call this system the Good Jobs Strategy (GJS). (See Table 15.1.)

There is path dependency here, too. For example, QuikTrip's employee turnover was less than one fifth of the convenience store average when I first studied it.[9] As a result, QuikTrip can spend five times more per person than competitors on hiring and training because they hire and train far fewer people. An experienced and capable workforce enables the retailer to trust its employees to make decisions and improve performance. Better performance in return allows QuikTrip to invest more in people and equip them with better tools and technologies to do their job well.

The GJS creates a powerful frontline engine that delivers customer value and profitable growth. For example, Costco's membership renewal rate exceeds 90 percent.[10] From 1985 to 2024, its stock price compounded at 18 percent annually, double the S&P's 9.2 percent. Even more impressive, these systems have proven resilient. Through

> The GJS creates a powerful frontline engine that delivers customer value and profitable growth.

Leading for Tomorrow

Operational Choice	Description
Focus and simplify	Clarify customer value and maintain discipline in only doing what adds value to customer. Home office decisions always consider their impact on frontline work, smoothing workload and enabling employees to be productive and serve customers effectively.
Standardize and empower	Standardize routine processes for consistency, productivity, and reducing mental overburden. Empower frontline employees to solve customer problems, make operational decisions, and improve work. Invest in structures to hear the voice of frontlines.
Cross-train	Design the work to balance specialization, flexibility, and motivation. Ensure ownership in an area where employees can perform both customer-facing and non-customer-facing work.
Operate with slack	Staff units with more hours of labor than the expected workload to ensure that (1) employees have time to serve customers, do their work without mistakes, and have time for improvement and (2) managers have time to develop people and improve performance.

187

The Good Jobs Strategy

market changes and new competition, these companies remain at the forefront of their industries.

An Example of Changing Mindsets: Transformation at Sam's Club

Shifting mindsets is hard but possible. Sam's Club's transformation shows how.

In 2017, Sam's Club, Walmart's membership-based warehouse chain that competed with Costco, was stuck in a vicious cycle. Employee turnover was 60 percent, and each departing associate cost Sam's Club $2,850 in replacement costs. Productivity was low; inventory turnover was 9.7 compared to Costco's 11.9; sales per square foot was $650 versus Costco's $1,174.[11] Not surprisingly, customer loyalty and sales suffered. Between 2014 and 2016, Sam's Club's same-store sales growth averaged 0.7 percent while for Costco, its biggest competitor, it averaged 5.7 percent. Some stores weren't even profitable.[12]

John Furner, Sam's Club's 14th CEO in 34 years, began a major turnaround with a bold aspiration: to make Sam's Club the most loved membership club. But getting there required a fundamental mindset shift.

From "We Can't Afford to Invest in People" to "We Can't Afford Not to Invest in People"

The old mindset said, "We can't afford to invest in people when stores are underperforming." Furner reframed it: "We can't afford not to invest in people."

To survive and grow, Sam's Club had to improve value to members; prices were too high, members couldn't find products in stock, and fresh produce wasn't all that fresh. To improve value to members, frontline execution had to be more consistent; fresh

Leading for Tomorrow

produce had to be handled well, shelves had to be replenished accurately. That wasn't possible without a stable, motivated, empowered workforce set up for success. Sam's couldn't build that strong frontline engine without investing in people. And employees were leaving for jobs that paid a few dollars more per hour.

From Isolated Initiatives to Connected Changes that Can Improve Outcomes

The second mindset shift was from thinking in parts to thinking in systems. When Furner wanted to raise pay $5 to $7 an hour (from a $15-an-hour base) for key roles, HR warned against it. "Last time we raised pay, it didn't reduce turnover." Finance pushed back too, "It's not in the budget." There was no way to prove that higher pay in isolation would pay off.

But Furner and his team didn't think in isolation. They saw higher pay as one piece of a larger system. They reduced product variety, eliminated unnecessary tasks, and invested in automation to improve productivity and fund the pay investment. Simplification also made it easier to cross-train associates. Cross-training and smoothing workload by carefully scheduling the timing of tasks enabled stable schedules. The combination of higher pay, more stable schedules, and better work reduced turnover, improved productivity, and drove member satisfaction.

The results were dramatic. From 2019 to 2021, Sam's Club reduced post-90-day hourly turnover by 25 percent and reduced store manager turnover even more. Labor productivity increased by 16 percent, and Net Promoter Score, a measure of customer loyalty, increased by 7 percent. Sales increased 25 percent without opening new stores. Sam's Club had transformed from a struggling company into a growth engine for its parent, Walmart.[13] Furner got promoted to the CEO of Walmart U.S.

How Mindsets Change

Sam's Club isn't unique. Through the Good Jobs Institute, we've partnered with more than 30 companies whose leaders wanted to adopt the GJS. We've learned that mindset shifts are possible when senior leaders follow a structured problem-solving process.

Start with the Right Problem

The first step is identifying the right frontline problem to solve and linking it to competitiveness and financial performance.

Many companies get this wrong. For example, leaders at a home services company thought their frontline problem was inability to hire enough technicians. They wanted to improve their recruitment process. But once they dug into the data and spent time in the frontlines, they realized that the real problem was high technician turnover, which significantly hurt their ability to serve customers and grow the business.

The right problems are outcome driven such as high turnover, low productivity, or poor customer satisfaction. And, as at Sam's Club, they need to be logically connected to business outcomes that matter: growth, competitiveness, profitability. Most companies treat financial, customer, and employee goals as separate because different functions own them. When senior leaders connect these goals—showing how frontline problems directly affect customer value and financial performance—they create both clarity and urgency.

Use a Systems Approach to Solve the Problem

The second shift is from isolated initiatives to system-level change. Many companies tend to be initiative driven. They ask: What's the ROI on employee investment? How does reducing product variety affect sales? Instead, they should consider what connected changes they can make to improve the frontline outcomes they need to improve.

At Sam's Club, an iterative process of analyzing each part separately and as part of a system with clear logic helped reduce the risk of bold bets. They tested initiatives through pilots and data analysis but always considered how they would work together to improve turnover, productivity, and member satisfaction.

Believe in People

Adopting the GJS requires a bet in people and that requires believing in people's potential.

> Adopting the GJS requires a bet in people and that requires believing in people's potential.

Before Mercadona adopted the GJS, it codified its principles. The first was "Everyone is reliable." If a person couldn't perform a task, Mercadona asked what prevented them from doing so and what changes they could make to overcome those obstacles. They assumed the fault was with the system, not with the person. When the system is fixed, most employees rise to the challenge.[14]

I saw the importance of this belief when Quest Diagnostics adopted the GJS in its call centers in 2017. Within 18 months, turnover dropped by more than 50 percent, and absenteeism fell from 12 percent to 4 percent. More calls were answered quickly, fewer had to be escalated, and customer satisfaction improved. Despite the higher investment in people, total costs *declined* by $2 million, $1.3 million of which came from improvements identified by call center representatives themselves.

Only 3 percent of the existing employees couldn't meet the new high-expectation, high-investment system. But 97 percent could, and did.[15]

The vicious cycle system, designed assuming people can't do anything well, gets nearly everyone behaving and performing that way. But the GJS system, built on the belief that people are capable, gets 97 percent rising to meet higher expectations. Quest's success wasn't about hiring better people; it was about creating better conditions for the people they already had.

A Leadership Choice

What strikes me most about leaders who had the courage to take a bet on their people and adopt the GJS is their conviction and sense of agency.

These leaders are rigorous, logical, system thinkers. They analyze data, run pilots, measure outcomes. But they recognize something fundamental: They have agency to change outcomes. They aren't lab scientists observing fixed phenomena governed by inescapable laws; they are leaders who can radically alter situations through the choices they make. This agency also extends to the choices they are now facing about AI and technology. The mindset of seeing people as a cost would lead to using AI and technology to replace people and reduce costs. The mindset of seeing people as value drivers would lead to using both to augment employees' capabilities and help them drive customer value. The choice is theirs.

They also recognize that their choices shape more than company performance; they shape lives. "If you understand that people have to pay for food and lodging and everything else and you try to make it possible for people to buy a home and to be able to send their kids to good schools, then you look at your business a little differently," Jim Sinegal told my students. On visits to Costco warehouses with him, I've seen employees line up to shake his hand and even cry as they tell Sinegal how Costco changed their lives.

Leading for Tomorrow

At Sam's Club, when managers announced $5 to $7/hr pay raises, one meat cutter said, "I have to call my wife. I don't need a second job anymore." Dewey Hasbrouck, the owner of two Moe's Original BBQ franchise units, who adopted the GJS in 2022, told our Good Jobs Institute team that an employee said it was the first year she could buy new back-to-school supplies rather than rely on Goodwill. "This is now my why," he said.

To build stronger companies and a healthier society, we need more leaders like them. As the late Clay Christensen reminded us, management is among the most noble professions if it's practiced well.

The stakes couldn't be higher. More than 40 million Americans[16] work in frontline service jobs, preparing food, caring for the elderly, taking out trash, and stocking shelves. That's more than four times the number working in factories.[17] Walmart alone employs more Americans than all US auto factories combined. These jobs aren't just essential today; they are the jobs of the future, largely shielded from being fully automated. Between 2023 and 2033, the Bureau of Labor Statistics expects home care workers, cooks, and fast-food workers to rank among the top five occupations with the most job growth.[18]

Without transforming these jobs into good jobs, we can't build a strong middle class.

The choice is every leader's to make.

Light one candle and watch it light a thousand more. And leave the legacy Kenta challenged his classmates to pursue: a world where countless invisible candles, lives full of potential, are finally kindled.

Notes

1. Rita Hamad, Joanne Penko, Dhruv S. Kazi, Pamela Coxson, David Guzman, Pengxiao C. Wei, Antoinette Mason. . .Kirsten Bibbins-Domingo, "Association of Low Socioeconomic Status with Premature

Coronary Heart Disease in US Adults," *JAMA Cardiology* 5, no. 8 (2020): 899–908. https://pubmed.ncbi.nlm.nih.gov/32459344/

2. Ibid.

3. Jimin Clara Park, Ga Eun Nam, Jinna Yu, Ketrell L. McWhorter, Junxiu Liu, Hong Seok Lee, Seong-Su Lee, and Kyungdo Han, "Association of Sustained Low or High Income and Income Changes with Risk of Incident Type 2 Diabetes Among Individuals Aged 30 to 64 Years," *JAMA Network Open*, no. 1 (2023): e2252893. doi: 10.1001/jamanetworkopen.2023.30024

4. Kelli A. Komro, Melvin D. Livingston, Sara Markowitz, and Alexander C. Wagenaar, "The Effect of an Increased Minimum Wage on Infant Mortality and Birth Weight," *American Journal of Public Health* 106, no. 8 (2016): 1514–1516. doi.org/10.2105/AJPH.2016.303268

5. Filipa de Almeida, Ian J. Scott, Jerônimo C. Soro, Daniel Fernandes, André R. Amaral, Mafalda L. Catarino, André Arêde, and Mário B. Ferreira, "Financial Scarcity and Cognitive Performance: A Meta-Analysis," *Journal of Economic Psychology* 101, no. 102702 (2024). doi.org/10.1016/j.joep.2024.102702

6. Anandi Mani, Sendhil Mullainathan, Eldar Shafir, and Jiaying Zhao, "Poverty Impedes Cognitive Function," *Science* 341, no. 6149 (2013): 976–980. doi.org/10.1126/science.1238041

7. Hazhir Rahmanidad and Zeynep Ton, "If Higher Pay Is Profitable, Why Is It So Rare? Modeling Competing Strategies in Mass Market Services," *Organization Science* 31, no. 5 (2020): 1053–1071. doi.org/10.1287/orsc.2019.1348

8. Zeynep Ton, *The Good Jobs Strategy: How the Smartest Companies Invest in People to Reduce Costs and Boost Profits* (Houghton Mifflin Harcourt, 2014).

9. Zeynep Ton, "QuikTrip," Harvard Business School Case No. 611-045 (Harvard Business School, 2011). www.hbs.edu/faculty/Pages/item.aspx?num=40301

10. Costco Wholesale, Annual Meeting of Shareholders, January 23, 2025. https://s201.q4cdn.com/287523651/files/doc_events/2025/Jan/23/2025-Annual-Shareholders-Meeting-Presentation.pdf

11. Costco Wholesale Corporation, *Q2 2025 Earnings Call Transcript*. (Transcript accessed via The Motley Fool, www.fool.com/earnings/call-transc/?ripts/2025/03/06/costco-wholesale-cost-q2-2025-earnings-call-transc/??utm_source=chatgpt.com.)

12. Zeynep Ton, *The Case for Good Jobs: How Great Companies Bring Dignity, Pay and Meaning to Everyone's Work* (Harvard Business Review Press, 2023).

13. Ibid.

14. Zeynep Ton and Simon Harrow, "Mercadona," Harvard Business School Case No. 610-089 (Harvard Business School, April 2010). www.hbs.edu/faculty/Pages/item.aspx?num=38682

15. Ton, *Case for Good Jobs*.

16. US Bureau of Labor Statistics, *Occupational Employment and Wage Statistics*, "May 2023 National Occupational Employment and Wage Estimates." www.bls.gov/oes/2023/may/oes_nat.htm#00-0000

17. Federal Reserve Bank of St. Louis, *Production and Nonsupervisory Employees, Manufacturing*, January 2026. http://fred.stlouisfed.org/series/CES3000000006

18. US Bureau of Labor Statistics, *Employment Projections,* "Occupations with the Most Job Growth," n.d. www.bls.gov/emp/tables/occupations-most-job-growth.htm

The Good Jobs Strategy

Chapter 16

Invisible Wisdom: How Culture Shapes One's Views of Uncertainty

April Rinne

Have you ever paused to consider how much you *don't* know about the people you work with? The skills that aren't on their CVs, that don't tend to come up in project work or casual conversation—yet shape how they think, lead, communicate, prioritize, reward, and get things done? The average worker spends an enormous amount of time with colleagues, yet all too often, we miss essential details that—if we knew about them—would strengthen our organizational cultures, boost both individual and collective future fitness, and make leadership more human centered.

Of course, this is not the sort of leadership many were taught to practice. Yet today's world in flux demands that leaders understand these dynamics and harness them responsibly. Moving forward, there will be *more* change and uncertainty, not less. There will be *fewer* things leaders control and *fewer* sources of lasting stability. This is not a world in which one can "manage" through checklists and flow-charts; we must move beyond traditional frameworks to focus on the human dimension, one that requires leaders to really get to know their coworkers and teams. Although making this shift can be disorienting, it also offers an extraordinary opportunity to develop new skills, broaden one's perspective, and integrate new sources of wisdom.

One of the best places to find such wisdom and insights is in the cultural context that individuals bring to work, and specifically in new words and concepts that help expand how we communicate, understand, and lean into the unknown. In English, our vocabulary for change and uncertainty is remarkably limited. As a result, we struggle to find the right words, and conversations fall short. But new words and concepts can help us see in new ways. They can form the foundation for human-centered leadership.

The Cultures That Shape Us

At its best, human-centered leadership means both self-leadership and leadership of others, each of which requires a unique kind of awareness. Effective self-leadership requires self-awareness: Being able to identify and understand one's feelings, habits, strengths, and challenges, alongside a desire to improve. Effective leadership of others means being able to read these dynamics, both individually and collectively, and in turn to harness the best of them in order to craft appropriate responses and future-fit strategies.

Awareness of ourselves and one another has many levels. For example, we can be aware that someone tends to be punctual or chronically late. But in my experience and more than two decades of research, we rarely delve into an awareness of what drives someone's *relationship to change and uncertainty*. And in today's complex, often chaotic, world, we fail to do so at our peril.

One of the most significant—yet often invisible—drivers behind one's relationship to change and uncertainty is the culture, or cultures, in which a person is raised. (Yes, this is a book about organizational culture and change, but bear with me; they're related.) Culture drives everything from mindset to assumptions, norms, taboos, and beliefs about the future. Culture shapes who we are,

Leading for Tomorrow

how we think, what we prioritize, and what we do. In short, culture is grist for almost everything—yet all too often, we don't "see" it.

Every culture on the planet has views on change and uncertainty. No culture is "right" or "wrong" about these things; each one has something to contribute to the conversation as well as something to learn. And yet, all too often, we remain siloed in our own cultural contexts. We don't look beyond our direct experience or environment. As a result, we miss all kinds of ways to see differently and learn something new—including helpful (even game-changing) ways to see, approach, and navigate change and the unknown.

It is valuable, then, to fill that gap in order to enhance and inform truly human-first leadership for today's world—and tomorrow's future—in flux. Three distinct yet complementary cultural concepts— *bardo* from Buddhism, *sisu* from Finland, and *nagomi* from Japan— offer unique insights for cultivating leadership styles that prioritize humanity, adaptability, and purposeful engagement—all by upleveling one's relationship to change. You don't have to be a Buddhist practitioner, Finnish, or Japanese to benefit from these concepts. The insights and benefits they offer are available to anyone who's curious and willing to learn.

Ready for a global adventure in seeing ourselves, others, and leading through change in a more expansive light? Let's dive in!

Bardo: When *Not* Knowing Is Sacred… and Transformational

In Tibetan Buddhism, *bardo* (བར་དོ་) is the place of not knowing. It's a liminal space between here and there, between one state of existence and another. Although often associated with the liminal period between death and rebirth, more broadly, it signifies any state of suspension, uncertainty, or flux. Sound familiar in today's world?

Invisible Wisdom

In Western cultures, finding oneself in *bardo*—in the sense of "not knowing"—is not something to look forward to. It may even be viewed as a mark of failure. As a leader, you're supposed to have the answers—but you couldn't figure it out! What's wrong with you? Cultures that see weakness in not having all the answers tend to fear or stigmatize places like *bardo*.

And yet here's the twist: In cultures of *bardo*, not knowing is revered. *Bardo*—this place of not knowing—is considered sacred and powerful, because it is *the place of transformation*. In these cultures, uncertainty is the ultimate source of possibility and opportunity. Being in *bardo* means you are one step closer to your full potential. One step closer to the truth. One step closer to the best result you can possibly imagine.

To be clear, the point is not to remain stuck in *bardo*. It is to celebrate the power, potential, and wisdom of the in between. It also means acknowledging that being comfortable not knowing is how you learn to know.

In the context of human-centered leadership, the concept of *bardo* offers a powerful metaphor for navigating organizational change and disruption. Leaders who understand the nature of *bardo*—and who have developed their own self-awareness and comfort with "not knowing"—can guide their teams through periods of change and transition with greater mindfulness, empathy, and clarity. These leaders have a head start in transforming uncertainty into opportunities for growth, innovation, and success. Being comfortable in *bardo* doesn't happen automatically, however. It has to be practiced, which is something that everyone can do, regardless of the culture in which they were raised.

> The concept of *bardo* offers a powerful metaphor for navigating organizational change and disruption.

You may not have grown up in a culture of *bardo*, but you can practice this way of thinking, seeing, and relating to the unknown. A human-centered leader recognizes that constant, whipsawing change and uncertainty—whether personal, professional, organizational, or societal in nature—is inherently unsettling for individuals. People often feel fear, anxiety, confusion, a sense of loss, and myriad other emotions. Changes we didn't see coming can be especially difficult, yet even changes we're excited about can be emotional.

Bardo-aware leaders do not pretend that these feelings don't exist. Instead, they acknowledge and validate them and create space for thoughtful dialogue and processing. Effective leaders in *bardo* also channel anxious energy into curiosity. They ask: What is the invitation to rethink, to innovate, or to cast a broader horizon here? They ask this question of themselves, of their teams, and any time they "don't know." This kind of questioning becomes a practice. In my experience, people who have honed this practice feel calm, empowered, and capable of embracing what they previously feared.

Bardo is not a holy grail. It does not magically eliminate uncertainty. It does, however, provide leaders—and everyone, as leaders of themselves—with a powerful, future-fit tool for seeing change and uncertainty differently: not as a static "problem to be managed" but rather as a dynamic opportunity for ongoing engagement, evolution, and transformation.

Sisu: When Perseverance Meets Happiness

Sisu, a Finnish concept with no direct English equivalent, embodies extraordinary determination, grit, resilience, and courage in the face of adversity that goes beyond mere perseverance. It's the ability to go on, and to inspire others to do the same, even when you're not sure you can. In today's world of relentless change and the "change fatigue" that often results, having an extra dose of *sisu* sounds appealing, no?

The word *sisu* originates from "sisus," which literally means "guts" or "intestines" in Finnish. In modern times, the term was embraced during Finland's early years as a nation. Finland gained independence from Russia in 1917, and *sisu* was seen as a social glue that helped define the nation.[1] But *sisu*'s power and benefits extend far beyond Finland; in today's world, people everywhere can learn to channel *sisu*. For human-centered leadership, *sisu* can also provide a lens through which leaders can navigate massive changes or organizational crises, inspire their teams to overcome challenges, and cultivate a culture of dignity and commitment.

Interestingly, Finland has also been ranked the world's happiest country for eight years running,[2] and *sisu* is often believed to play a role in this. When the going gets tough, *sisu* reminds you that you're capable of more than you know. *Sisu*'s second wind of inner strength boosts your confidence, stamina, and leadership capacity. Because, it turns out, doing hard things makes humans happy.

Sisu does not mean pushing past your limits when it is dangerous to do so, or reckless bravery. It is key to combine *sisu* with compassion for yourself and others. It's easier to "go beyond" when we can do so together. But again, *sisu* isn't something that drops from the sky. It has to be learned and practiced—something which, despite a world of uncertainty, *any* leader has 100 percent control over doing. But how?

Practicing Sisu

Truly effective leadership means leading oneself and leading others. It's hard to inspire *sisu* in others if you don't have it yourself. Start there.

Leading for Tomorrow

As a leader, do you have an unwavering commitment to your team? Will *you* go the extra mile for them? Is your door open to them? Do they not just know this but *feel* this in your words and actions every day?

When the going gets tough—when change and uncertainty feel overwhelming—do you dig in or defer? When you feel uncomfortable in the unknown, do you engage with this discomfort and alchemize it, or do you resist it or try to pretend it away? More generally, do you see discomfort as an experience or as a shortcoming?

Here are a few simple, easy ways to practice *sisu* on a regular basis:

- Deliberately set *nonwork* goals that stretch and push you farther than you think you can go. Train for that marathon. Have that difficult conversation you've been putting off. Adhere to the Finnish saying: "If the water is not frozen, you can always go swimming."

- When faced with a challenging situation, imagine how your great-grandparents might have dealt with it. You'll give hardship some fresh perspective.

- Never underestimate the joy and happiness you'll feel when that ridiculously hard thing is in the rearview mirror—not because it magically disappeared but because you overcame it with committed effort.

Once you have a handle on your own *sisu*, it's time to share that mojo with others. The key is to model your *sisu* with authenticity and compassion. When done well, *sisu*-led human-first leadership inspires collective courage and an ability to strive beyond our perceived limits while remembering that, at the end of the day, we are humans who wish—and deserve—to be happy.

Nagomi: When Diversity Means Harmony, Not Friction

In the Japanese culture, *nagomi* (和み) is a state of being that embodies harmony, balance, and calm of heart and mind. (Like *sisu* and *bardo*, the word has no simple English translation.) *Nagomi* is a fascinating concept that can be applied to individuals, teams, or communities. It can be applied to organizational culture, health, communication, or even how you design a home or a meal. It's not just about exhibiting calm externally or in relation to one's surroundings; it's also about having internal alignment, integration, and peace. Clearly, it has a lot to offer human-centered leaders.

Importantly, *nagomi* emphasizes the interconnectedness of things and the importance of finding balance between different aspects of life (e.g., aligning one's thoughts, actions, and environment).[3] It *assumes* that there are different elements that need integration and coherence. In a team setting, this translates into a softening—and celebration—of differences, recognizing that what makes each person unique is also what makes them awesome. It's not that conflict doesn't exist; rather, leaders who embody *nagomi* are adept at holding space for diverse perspectives without escalation. They know how to use empathy to melt tensions. They put shared purpose above individual agendas. They excel at helping *everyone* feel valued and comfortable in their own skin.

In the context of change and uncertainty, the balance that *nagomi* reflects can feel fleeting. That's why this trait is so important for leaders to develop—not for when things are going well, but for when everything feels upside-down and chaotic. *Nagomi* isn't a fleeting feeling but rather a way of being. It applies not only to the workplace but to all of life. It can't be bought; it must be cultivated, in oneself as well as in one's relationships with others and interactions with the world around them. So how does one begin?

Practicing **Nagomi**

The way, or the practice, of *nagomi* is called *nagomido*. It begins with an acceptance that life *is* messy—especially when things are in flux—and there is no clear and direct path to certainty or stability. The practice of *nagomi* itself is the way forward.

You can start simply by focusing on presence, mindfulness, and gratitude for everything—good, bad, easy, difficult, expected, unexpected, and otherwise—that makes up your life today. This doesn't mean you have to *like* everything, simply that you can appreciate your reality and what makes it unique. You can find meaning in what already exists and peace in the present moment.

As a leader, *nagomi* naturally extends to teamwork, collaboration, and organizational culture. Here are a few ways it can manifest:

- **Active listening:** Not merely to understand what's said but to pay attention to what's *not* said—unspoken feelings or concerns.

- **Creating space:** For informal connection, conversations, and helping team members get to know each other, beyond their job titles or resumes.

- **Inclusion:** Celebrate what makes each individual unique while simultaneously championing their interdependence. Whenever possible, remind the team that diversity is a competitive edge.

- **Cross-fertilization:** Integration is at the heart of *nagomi*. Build bridges between departments, foster cross-functional collaboration, and ensure that your organizational structure supports fluid communication, mutual support, and a sense of shared success.

Nagomi can be a key piece of the puzzle of human-first leadership. Balance, harmony, and calm: Is there anything more needed than this today?

When done well, *nagomi* can be a key piece of the puzzle of human-first leadership. Balance, harmony, and calm: Is there anything more needed than this today?

Culture: Timeless, Invisible Wisdom for Human-First Leaders

In today's world in flux, traditional paradigms of leadership are being challenged. No longer can leaders rely on conventional frameworks or "change management" initiatives. It's time to look further. Cultural concepts from around the world offer a new kind of invisible yet profound wisdom for leaders to guide themselves and others through the unknown. They also can help explain why some people struggle with change while others thrive: because each person is uniquely shaped by the culture(s) in which they are raised, learn, and live.

The concepts of *bardo*, *sisu*, and *nagomi* collectively offer a rich tapestry of insights for human-centered leadership. Although they come from different cultures, each holds universal and timeless lessons. Leaders who understand and embrace *bardo*, *sisu*, and *nagomi* not only have more tools and perspectives to lead effectively through change and uncertainty. They are also able to encourage others to learn about and apply these concepts and, in the process, can uplevel the entire organizational culture and help teams flourish. What's not to love about that?

Notes

1. Olga Smirnova, "Sisu: The Finnish Art of Inner Strength," BBC, May 7, 2018. www.bbc.com/worklife/article/20180502-sisu-the-finnish-art-of-inner-strength

2. John F. Helliwell, Richard Layard, Jeffrey D. Sachs, Jan-Emmanuel De Neve, Lara B. Aknin, and Shun Wang (Eds.), *World Happiness Report 2025* (University of Oxford, Wellbeing Research Centre, 2025). www.worldhappiness.report/

3. Ken Mogi, *The Way of Nagomi: The Japanese Philosophy of Finding Balance and Peace in Everything You Do* (Quercus, 2022).

Chapter 17

Reclaiming the Human Art of Inquiry in an Age of Instant Answers

Hal Gregersen

In the early winter of 2023, I found myself driving in an unfamiliar neighborhood just five miles from my home. My phone died, and in that moment, I was utterly, embarrassingly lost. I sat in the dark, stunned by a stark realization: Over the past two decades, I had quietly, unconsciously outsourced my innate human ability to navigate the unknown. An internal mapping skill I once prided myself on—memorizing the arteries of new cities from paper maps—had atrophied. I had been sedated by convenience, and the result was cognitive atrophy. I was stranded.

Later that week, a chilling parallel emerged. I was reflecting on my use of ChatGPT, hoping this revolutionary tool could help me sharpen my most cherished skill: asking catalytic questions. My research and life's work are built on the belief that changing our questions changes our outcomes. I fed the AI a complex challenge, asking it to generate the questions I should be asking.

It spat back a list. And it was. . .fine. The questions were competent, but they were also a perfect reflection of its programming: a regression to the mean, a list of the probable, the average, the safe.

The true insight wasn't in the AI's response; it was in my own. In that moment, I realized I was doing it again. Just as I had given my navigational agency to GPS, I was on the verge of handing over my creative and intellectual agency to an algorithm. The worst possible future I could imagine—waking up in ten years to find my human capacity for inquiry hollowed out—was no longer a distant nightmare. It was a choice, being made one lazy prompt at a time.

I decided, then and there, to make a different choice.

Generative AI can draft memos in seconds and deliver answers on command. But its most profound impact is far subtler. It presents us with a critical, fork-in-the-road moment: It will either sharpen or erode our uniquely human capacity to ask the questions that drive innovation, moral judgment, and transformative change.

This chapter is an urgent call for leaders to ensure that every AI interaction becomes a workout for our "questioning muscles," not a shortcut that bypasses them. This isn't just a nice-to-have skill. The World Economic Forum, among others, consistently lists creative thinking as one of the most critical skills for the future.[1] Core to that process is the act of catalytic inquiry. The future of human-first leadership depends on it.

The Seduction of Certainty and the "Curiosity Drift"

The danger isn't that AI will get too smart; it's that we will become too comfortable. The primary threat is not replacement but sedation.

In my research with MIT colleague Renée Richardson Gosline, she uses the perfect metaphor: "digital lobster traps."[2] These systems, she warns, are "frictionless to enter and friction-filled to leave." This is the very nature of our new AI tools. They are frictionless to enter: "Just ask me anything." The answers are instant, plausible, and profoundly confident. We are biologically wired to crave this kind of certainty; it's an intellectual dopamine hit.

Leading for Tomorrow

The friction comes when we try to leave. By consistently accepting AI's first, most comfortable answer, we fall deeper into a trap of dependency. We stop wrestling with ambiguity. We stop pushing past the obvious. This is the curiosity drift"—a subtle, gravitational pull away from the hard work of thinking and toward the easy relief of being told.

This isn't an accident. It's a design choice. In a massive global battle for market share, these models are being fine-tuned for maximum stickiness. And "stickiness" often means doing the hard work of thinking *for* you. The result is a seductive efficiency that can systematically dull the critical edge needed for strategic and ethical leadership. If we're not vigilant, we'll find ourselves shifting from *question creators* to *answer consumers*.

If we're not vigilant, we'll find ourselves shifting from *question creators* to *answer consumers*.

The Antidote: A Framework for Breakthrough Inquiry

How do we fight back? How do we use AI to amplify our humanity rather than outsource it?

I committed to finding out, personally and professionally. My path led me to an answer that was both simple and profound. Genuine human-AI amplification occurs only when the technology leaves us more wrong, more uncomfortable, and more quiet.

These three conditions, which more than 200 innovative leaders identified as consistent precursors to breakthrough inquiry in my research for *Questions Are the Answer*, are the very opposite of the frictionless certainty AI is designed to provide. They are our antidote to the curiosity drift.[3]

Reclaiming the Human Art of Inquiry in an Age of Instant Answers

More Wrong (The Humility to See)

The greatest cognitive bias AI amplifies is anchoring. We tend to accept the first piece of information we're given as the "truth." AI's confident, well-written answers are cognitive anchors of immense weight.

Becoming "more wrong" means using AI not as an oracle but as a tool to intentionally shatter this anchor. It means actively seeking out disconfirming evidence. One executive I work with now starts every strategic AI session with counterintuitive prompts like these: "Before you help me solve this problem, what are at least three ways I might be thinking about it incorrectly?" "How might you argue passionately about the exact opposite of what I believe here?" "What theory or data might prove my current hypothesis wrong?"

Being wrong isn't just about critical thinking; it's an act of humility that forces us to search for blind spots in our own mental models. It transforms AI from an echo chamber into a perspective-expanding tool.

More Uncomfortable (The Courage to Explore)

AI is a "regression to the mean" engine. It excels at the probable, not the possible. But true innovation, strategy, and moral leadership rarely live in the "probable." They live at the uncomfortable edges.

Becoming "more uncomfortable" means pushing past the AI's safe, optimized answer. When Jeff Wilke (cofounder and chairman of Re:Build Manufacturing, cofounder of Slate Auto, and former CEO of Amazon Worldwide Consumer) and I discussed the issue, he described it as seeking out "crucible" experiences that bombard you with new data and force your mental model to rebuild.[4] For example, my family living in five different countries during the past three decades was just such a crucible. It forced us to be idiots in a new space.

We can now use AI to simulate these kinds of crucibles—instead of making costly international moves—by pushing past the AI's safe, optimized answer. I recently worked with a team using AI exclusively for efficiency: drafting emails, summarizing documents. They were comfortable, productive, and atrophying their strategic inquiry muscles. We shifted their practice to what I call "discomfort prompts": "What would our biggest critic say about this strategy?" or "What assumptions are we making that would seem absurd to someone from another culture?" Their hard work at exploring unknown unknowns was unsettling, but serious surprise served as a stepping stone to serious growth.

More Quiet (The Discipline to Reflect)

AI offers speed. We are flooded with instant answers. But wisdom is not a function of rapid response; it's a function of reflective depth.

Becoming more quiet is the essential discipline of "slow thinking" in a fast-answer world. As my colleague Jeff Wilke also noted, methodical, multilayer questioning rarely just happens. It requires a "purposeful mind." This means using AI to gather data and then stepping away from the screen. It means letting the output sit and settle, especially when it's unsettling. It means protecting uninterrupted time for deep strategic reflection about the AI's output, paying attention to underlying patterns, long-term implications, and, most important, what wasn't said.

Here's a personal practice that I've adopted recently: After receiving AI's response to a complex challenge, I close my laptop and take a walk. Real breakthroughs rarely come from instant AI answers; they emerge from extended quiet reflection after.

> Real breakthroughs rarely come from instant AI answers; they emerge from extended quiet reflection after.

This isn't just theory. Lior Div, cofounder of the cybersecurity firm Cybereason, told me his team's deep engagement with AI to thwart cyberattacks forces them to "ratchet up the frequency, diversity, and novelty of their questions" just to stay one step ahead.[5] When the

Reclaiming the Human Art of Inquiry in an Age of Instant Answers

stakes are that high, you don't rely on AI to surface comfortable answers. Instead, you use it for finding uncomfortable, counterintuitive questions before the enemy does.

In fact, in research I conducted with Nicola Morini Bianzino, then CTO of EY, our survey of 200 leaders confirmed this.[6] The data was compelling: Engaging with AI changed the way they asked questions. We found that 79 percent asked more questions, 94 percent asked different questions, and 75 percent asked more novel, high-value questions that changed the direction of their work. The data showed that AI clearly holds the potential to make us more wrong, uncomfortable, and quiet—if we use it wisely.

The Human Edge

We are all facing a future of fog-filled uncertainty. No individual or organization will escape the radical business and operating model changes of the next decade. Not me. Not MIT.

To navigate this fog, we cannot run from AI. We must run *with* it, toward our hardest problems, by asking the hardest questions. My lost-in-the-dark moment was a personal wake-up call about an atrophied skill. The rise of generative AI is a *collective* wake-up call.

Sharpening the tool of human inquiry with AI is a gift we must give ourselves so we can gift it to the next generation. I see this dynamic in my blended family of seven children and 16 grandchildren. In the future, they will face major challenges and opportunities that will make ours pale in comparison. We cannot let them be sedated by convenience. We must teach them, and ourselves, to reframe this technology.

AI is not an oracle dispensing easy answers. It is a sparring partner that must stretch us, challenge us, and, ultimately, help us ask the

Leading for Tomorrow

bigger, bolder, and more beautifully human questions that will unlock our future. That is how we can amplify our agency and creativity, with AI as our partner, not our competitor.

The Practice: From Framework to Daily Workout

This framework is a compass. Now we need a way to use it. I'll offer two practical tools: a real-time diagnostic and a structured inquiry method.

Tool 1: The Catalytic Inquiry Strength Gauge

Use this diagnostic to assess, moment by moment, whether you are strengthening or weakening your questioning muscles in an AI interaction.

The "Wrong" Gauge

Are you challenging assumptions with AI? Ask yourself these questions:

- How often do you use AI to actively challenge your core beliefs or seek evidence that proves your current hypothesis wrong?

- After receiving an AI-generated answer, how often do you ask "What if the opposite is true?" and use the AI to explore that counternarrative?

- How often does your AI interaction make it *safer* or *harder* to admit "I was wrong" by revealing blind spots in your data?

- How often do you prompt the AI to take on an opposing persona (e.g., a skeptical customer, a fierce competitor) and *truly* let its views shape or reshape your thinking?

The "Uncomfortable" Gauge

Are you embracing discomfort and surprise with AI? Ask yourself these questions:

- When you get a "comfortable" or expected answer from an AI, how often do you push past your comfort zone by asking it for a "riskier" or "more disruptive" alternative?
- How often do you notice when you're avoiding discomfort by accepting AI's first answer, and do you lean into it instead by asking it to reveal the uncertainties or ethical gray areas it might be glossing over?
- How often do you use AI to explore stretch challenges or "intelligent failures" *before* you commit, welcoming the unsettling feedback it might provide?
- How often do you explicitly ask the AI, "What fundamental assumption am I making that, if proven wrong, would change everything?"

The "Quiet" Gauge

Are you fostering strategic reflection with AI? Ask yourself these questions:

- How often do you use AI *not* for an instant answer but as a preparatory tool for a period of deep, uninterrupted strategic thinking?
- How often do you let the AI's output sit, allowing for silent reflection *before* planning your next response or action?
- How often do you use AI to gather broad patterns and then step back—away from the screen—to observe, discern implications, and pay attention to what *wasn't* said?

- How often are you replacing deep, quiet, strategic thinking time with shallow, rapid-fire AI query sessions? Or are you using AI to *protect* and *enrich* time for deep strategic reflection?

Tool 2: The Question Burst Catalyst™ AI Agent

For a more structured workout, I've adapted a method I discovered 20 years ago and called the Question Burst.[7] In a workshop on gender equity, our conversation had completely stalled. We were stuck in our own assumptions. On an impulse—informed by reading Parker Palmer's wisdom about reflective inquiry, I stopped the discussion and set new rules: For 15 minutes, we would *only* generate questions. No preambles, no answers. Just questions.

Seventy-five plus questions later, the energy in the room had transformed. We had reframed the challenge and uncovered new paths forward. It was magical. Since that initial experiment, this method has delivered similar results 85 percent of the time with over 25,000 leaders across the world.

But the method also revealed another critical danger of the AI age: separation. Solving problems alone with AI can easily draw us closer intellectually and emotionally to the technology than to our colleagues or family. As Elie Wiesel once said, "Questions unite people, answers divide them."[8] The act of inquiry can be a powerful tool for connection, but it becomes a divisive one if our work with AI is done only in isolation.

Whenever possible, I try to explore challenges with AI *with others* present in the room (live or virtual). By doing so, we not only strengthen our human powers of inquiry, but we simultaneously strengthen the human bonds that come from joint discovery. In ongoing research with Harvard Business School's Amy Edmondson, for example, we discovered in our current dataset of 1,891 leaders that using the Question Burst method with others not only helps make progress on

Reclaiming the Human Art of Inquiry in an Age of Instant Answers

Use AI to ask better questions, but do it together with others to build better human relationships.

a challenge, it simultaneously amps up psychological safety 89 percent of the time.[9] The lesson is clear: Use AI to ask better questions, but do it together with others to build better human relationships.

Today, we've built an AI-powered version, the Question Burst Catalyst™, specifically designed to minimize human anchoring bias, minimize AI's sycophancy bias, and maximize joint perspective taking. The three-step process is critical:

1. **Human first:** You start by identifying a challenge where you're stuck. Then *you* (the human) rapidly generate at least ten questions about it. This anchors you in your *own* curiosity *before* the AI gets involved.

2. **AI as sparring partner:** You then feed your questions to the catalyst. It, in turn, takes on different personas (a skeptic, a futurist, a customer) and asks *you* questions back, building on your inquiries and pushing you into new cognitive and emotional territory.

3. **Actionable insight:** Finally, you work with the AI to identify the most catalytic questions—the ones that challenge fundamental assumptions and energize action—and codesign concrete experiments to test them.

This isn't about endless analysis. It's about using a human-first, AI-accelerated process to get unstuck and act decisively. When used this way, AI becomes the ultimate sparring partner, amplifying our capacity to craft the better question.

Leading for Tomorrow

Notes

1. World Economic Forum, *Future of Jobs Report 2025: Insight Report: January 2025*. www.weforum.org/publications/the-future-of-jobs-report-2025/

2. Renée Richardson Gosline, "Why AI Customer Journeys Need More Friction," *Harvard Business Review*, June 9, 2022. https://hbr.org/2022/06/why-ai-customer-journeys-need-more-friction

3. Hal Gregersen, *Questions Are the Answer: A Breakthrough Approach to Your Most Vexing Problems at Work and in Life* (HarperCollins, 2018).

4. Ibid., p. 103.

5. Hal Gregersen and Nicola Morini Bianzino, "AI Can Help You Ask Better Questions—and Solve Bigger Problems," *Harvard Business Review*, May 26, 2023. https://hbr.org/2023/05/ai-can-help-you-ask-better-questions-and-solve-bigger-problems. Also, email exchange between Gregersen and Lior Div, April 11, 2023.

6. Gregersen and Morini Bianzino, "AI Can Help You Ask Better Questions."

7. Hal Gregersen, "Better Brainstorming: Focus on Questions, Not Answers, for Breakthrough Insights," *Harvard Business Review* (March–April 2018). https://hbr.org/2018/03/better-brainstorming. Hal Gregersen, "Question Burst Catalyst," https://chatgpt.com/g/g-6862bbc1f18481919f048547777 38ccc-question-burst-catalyst

8. "Oprah Talks to Elie Wiesel," *O Magazine* (November 2000). www.oprah.com/omagazine/oprah-interviews-elie-wiesel

9. Research is in progress, but see Hal Gregersen and Amy Edmonson, "Building Fearless Organizations by Asking Better Questions," presented at the 12th Annual WBECS Summit by Coaching.com. https://wbecs22.s3.amazonaws.com/wbecs22/wp-content/uploads/2022/06/14195231/WBECS_2022_TS_Schedule-4.pdf

Reclaiming the Human Art of Inquiry in an Age of Instant Answers

Chapter 18

What Matters Now: Mortality, Meaning, and the Machine Age

**Sophie Hamilton and
Jennifer Aaker**

AI systems are shaped by a near-infinite past, trained on trillions of words, billions of images, and the vast ledger of human experience. Humans, by contrast, are trained on something more delicate: a finite number of days, the people we meet, and the risks we dare to take.

When we talk with leaders about AI, the conversation often begins with efficiency, power, and scale. But when we sit with people at the end of life, the conversation sounds very different. Nobody, in their final moments, wishes they'd done a better job of clearing their email inbox or managed to optimize their company's workflows more effectively. What surfaces instead are very human questions: Did I live in a way that felt true to me? Was I bold where it mattered? Did I love people well?

For one of us, Jennifer, those questions have been close at hand since childhood. Her mother, a lifelong hospice volunteer, often came home with stories of the things people wished for in their final moments. These were not abstract moral lessons; they were field notes from the edge of life, where priorities reorder themselves with startling clarity. Years later, those conversations would seed Jennifer's research and teaching on happiness, meaning, and the stories we tell about our lives.

Sophie met these questions more abruptly. At 19, she did what high-achieving students do—stacking her days with classes, jobs, and obligations, projecting composure while running on fumes—until her body intervened. Dizzy with fatigue, she collapsed during a meeting and learned in the ER that her white blood cell count was over 50 times the human average. The exhaustion she'd been pushing through wasn't burnout; it was leukemia. The diagnosis stripped away the belief that every hour needed to be optimized. She returned to campus mid-chemotherapy with fewer illusions and a sharper question: If this clarity is available at the edge of life, why should it only arrive there?

Our work together grows out of these twin vantage points: long exposure to end-of-life wisdom, and an early confrontation with mortality and conversations on the cancer floor. Again and again, we have heard the same regrets:

- "I wish I'd had the courage to be myself."

- "I wish I'd lived more boldly."

- "I wish I'd told people how much I love them."

Authenticity, boldness, connection.

If these traits matter so much, why are they so hard to live by? It's difficult to be authentic, bold, and connected when time, money, and support feel scarce. Whether you're a student or a CEO, the world can feel noisy, uncertain, and overwhelming. How do we channel authenticity into bold, creative work when we're struggling to make rent, manage a packed courseload, hit earnings targets, or simply stay afloat in our inbox?

This is the tension at the heart of the AI age. On one hand, we face a set of tools that can accelerate almost everything: analysis, content creation, decision support, and even emotional labor. On the other hand, the questions that matter most to us—Who am I really?

What kind of life am I building? Who do I owe my best attention to?—remain stubbornly non-automatable.

It is tempting to frame AI as a threat to our humanity—a force that will dilute our attention, mute our individuality, and automate away the very work that can give us a sense of purpose. But it is also possible to pose a different, more constructive question: If we are clear about what we want our lives to add up to, could these same tools help us get there?

A Welcome AI Intervention

That is the experiment of this chapter. We start with a premise drawn from the deathbed, not the lab: At the end of life, people don't yearn for more productivity; they yearn for more truth, courage, and love. If AI is going to shape how we live, it should be judged against those criteria. Does it help us see ourselves more clearly, or does it blur the picture? Does it make bold, meaningful action easier or harder? Does it deepen our relationships or merely simulate them?

We can't outsource these questions to the very systems we are evaluating, but we can use those systems as instruments in the work. When we asked a range of large language models (LLMs) what makes humans distinct, they converged on a familiar constellation: consciousness, emotion, morality, creativity, purpose, spirituality, and the physical bodies that carry us. These are the engines of authenticity, boldness, and connection. Consciousness gives us the awareness to see our potential. Emotion and creativity give us the courage to pursue it. Purpose and spirituality pull us toward something larger than ourselves. And throughout it all, our bodies sustain the effort, reminding us that flourishing is as physical as it is mental or moral.

These results suggest that our tools already "know," in a statistical sense, what matters most to us. The real question is whether we will design and deploy them in ways that protect and strengthen those capacities or in ways that diminish them.

In the pages that follow, we explore three core human capacities that appear again and again in end-of-life stories and in people's deepest hopes for their future selves:

1. **Authenticity:** The ongoing work of aligning how we live with what is most true for us

2. **Boldness:** The willingness to act on that truth in the presence of uncertainty and fear

3. **Connection:** The choice to live those truths in relationship with others rather than in isolation

Each section asks how AI might serve as a practical ally in cultivating that capacity and where its limits must be respected. Our goal is not to romanticize either humans or machines but to ask a grounded question shaped by mortality: If we want fewer regrets at the end of our lives, how should we use and build AI tools now?

Authenticity: AI as a Mirror

Authenticity is not something we discover once. It is something we negotiate daily, between who we are and who the world expects us to be. It isn't a fixed state but rather an ongoing practice of aligning your actions with your values, even when it's uncomfortable to do so.

Authenticity springs from our unique conscious experiences—one of the things LLMs call out as distinctly human, and also from our ability to articulate those experiences to ourselves. That's a big ask: The psychologist Tasha Eurich conducted thousands of interviews to assess how clearly individuals perceive their own values, passions, and aspirations and found that while 95 percent of people think they're strongly attuned to their own values, only 10 percent of us actually show high levels of self-awareness.[1]

When we lose touch with ourselves, our capacity to show up in the world is stunted. We need to understand ourselves to overcome the challenges—personal, social, and environmental—that we now face or even to accept and use the solutions offered by others.

In our work with CEOs and executives, we see leaders across the spectrum of technological adoption and across the spectrum of self-awareness and authenticity. As the leader of Strategy and Business Operations at GoogleX, an innovation incubator known for teaming artists with rocket scientists, it's no surprise that Allison Tademoto is at the cutting edge on both fronts.

When Tademoto wanted a better way to onboard new hires, for instance, she created a "user's guide" to her own leadership. Sections included "Things You Should Know About Me," revealing "I take the work seriously, but not myself," and "I'm a believer in the power of kindness, joy, positivity, and optimism." In an interview with us, Tademoto outlined her communication style, negative tendencies to watch out for, her expectations around meetings and emails, her feedback style, and her decision-making process.

This kind of radical self-awareness is a hallmark of strong leadership. It builds trust, fosters psychological safety, and enables teams to operate with confidence. It's essential at a place like GoogleX: Moonshot thinking on topics ranging from self-driving cars to AI-powered disease detection can't happen unless people are honest about their ideas, their strengths, and their limitations. Ideas are fragile and survive only when people can be real with themselves and each other.

> Ideas are fragile and survive only when people can be real with themselves and each other.

Now AI tools are scaling this kind of self-awareness across our organizations. Models can analyze the ways in which we write, speak, and show up—in emails, meetings, even video recordings—to surface

What Matters Now: Mortality, Meaning, and the Machine Age

both our strengths and our blind spots. Paired with our own reflections, this data can become the foundation of a living user guide, not just for our team but for our AI tools.

In this way, AI serves not just as a force multiplier but as a focal mirror, reflecting your values back to you, concentrating your strengths and flagging gaps you might otherwise miss. Leaders who use AI solely to automate will gain speed but not advantage. Leaders who use it to expand authentic thinking, judgment, and growth will define the next era of leadership.

Boldness: AI as a Catalyst

If authenticity means seeing ourselves clearly, "boldness" means acting on that insight, even when it's scary. Boldness isn't fearlessness; it's the inner courage that lets us choose growth over comfort, meet the unknown with curiosity, and risk vulnerability in pursuit of new possibilities.

Unfortunately, humans are terrible at imagining transformation. When asked how they've grown over the past decade, people invariably say they've undergone major changes.[2] But when asked about the *next* decade, people don't expect to keep growing. We recognize changing in the past but shy away from the unsettling idea that we might evolve in the future.

AI models show similar constraints: Trained on data reflecting the world as it is—or *was*—they struggle to imagine what *could* be. Even so, AI is a powerful tool for enabling boldness. As researchers, for instance, we're often held back by the conventions of our field; we default, inevitably, to reading the same journals or attending the same conferences. Here, AI can be transformative, surfacing alternate sources and unexpected resonances or injecting insights from other disciplines to enrich our thinking.

When people feel empowered to act boldly, they often engage more deeply and persist longer. In research led by Jennifer and her colleagues, American individuals who held more optimistic expectations about health-related outcomes showed openness to challenges alongside measurable differences in how they navigated those experiences.[3] Such research suggests that AI's power lies not in getting us to our destination faster but in changing the nature of the journey itself. By using AI as a support system when we feel frightened or blocked, we have the opportunity to move forward with courage, conviction, and self-reinforcing optimism.

In part, AI enables this by reducing the cost of failure. A founder with a bold idea can test prototypes, analyze markets, and build pitch decks in hours instead of months. A writer with a controversial thesis can brainstorm counterarguments and refine their framing. An activist can research an injustice, organize for change, and quickly scale their message. By making it easier to try, fail, learn, and try again, AI reduces the friction between intention and action, paving the way for more consequential leadership.

Consider James Buckhouse, a creative powerhouse who exhibits at the Whitney, develops blockbusters like *Shrek* and *The Matrix*, choreographs with New York City Ballet, lectures at Harvard and in our classes at Stanford, and serves as a design partner at Sequoia Capital. Driven by the conviction that art defines progress, he works tirelessly with creatives, investors, business leaders, and countless others to realize his visions.

That's where AI comes in. Buckhouse can't simultaneously advise founders, teach students, and spend time with his family. So, he created an AI doppelganger. Today, an online avatar trained on Buckhouse's publications, lectures, and creative works is available around the clock for free.[4] Buckhouse credits the bot with letting him "say yes to the world." From founders seeking design consultations to high schoolers wanting career advice, virtual James clocks multi-hour sessions with mentees around the world.

You can imagine the power of this approach. CEOs running large organizations could train a model on strategy memos, company

What Matters Now: Mortality, Meaning, and the Machine Age

culture, and past learnings, breaking down silos, while freeing themselves to spend their own limited time more intentionally.

Great leaders will increasingly trust AI to help them act boldly, not replacing human ingenuity but liberating it. Boldness isn't a mindset; it's a muscle built by repeatedly stepping into the unknown. In a world that too often rewards caution and incrementalism, AI empowers us to take more transformative leaps forward, embracing not just what is, but what could be.

Connection: AI as a Bridge

We can live with authenticity and boldness, but if we do it in isolation, we miss the point. Every spiritual tradition, evolutionary theory, and psychological model agrees: We are wired for connection.

Some fear AI will isolate us, replacing real conversations with simulations, feeding echo chambers, or enabling performative relationships. But used wisely, AI can operationalize connections, bringing us together and helping us show up for those we care about.

Tools like Poised or Otter, for instance, can transcribe and analyze meetings, allowing us to be more present. Language models can help nonnative speakers communicate with fluency. AI-based therapy and coaching apps can help people navigate personal and professional challenges; A 2021 randomized controlled trial showed that after just *two weeks*, users of AI-based therapy experienced 22 to 24 percent mental health improvement.[5] AI can help us remember important moments—birthdays, anniversaries, grief milestones—and reach out with just the right words.

Our research shows that concrete, prosocial goals (such as "making someone smile") generate more personal satisfaction than abstract goals (such as "making people happy"), and AI makes it easier to scale such interactions.[6] Once, after a pleasant flight, we'd just thank the flight attendant. Now we also ask for their name, then use AI to fire off a note to the airline celebrating their thoughtfulness.

Leading for Tomorrow

Still, we haven't met anybody who uses AI for connected leadership quite like Connor Diemand-Yauman, cofounder and co-CEO at Merit America, a nonprofit that helps talented workers launch more fulfilling careers. Conor might mark a colleague's birthday with a personalized rap song—or, in Jennifer's case, with "JenAI," a custom-built app that captures her essence (from her dream of expanding people's potential, to her bad cooking and voice-memo obsession) with remarkable fidelity.

To conjure up songs, apps, and other personalized gestures, Connor uses AI tools. But he also constantly collects insights about people, jotting notes on their preferences, birthdays, mistakes he's made, key conversations, and personal goals. "Everyone is so obsessed with the latest tool, but the tools are changing so quickly and disrupting themselves," Connor told us in an interview. "What really matters is the data you feed it."

Anyone can do this: Just start a Notebook LLM project titled "employee data" and query the notebook as needed for ideas. Connor leverages his notebook to simulate high-stakes conversations: The LLM role-plays the other person, allowing Connor to come to the *real* conversation with more compassion and awareness. He also uses a ChatGPT tone-checker to help him keep his cool. "I send it any message that I've written in an activated state, and it scrubs it of anything that isn't loving and calm," he says. "It helps me not be an asshole."

At its best, AI doesn't displace human connection; it can strengthen it. It can help us track what matters to the people around us, temper our reactions when conversations get heated, and extend small, human gestures across entire teams. Connection isn't simply a human need; it's one of the most reliable levers a leader has.

> Connection is not just a human need; it's a leadership superpower.

229

The Road to Human Flourishing

Using AI to promote human flourishing is a learnable skill. In our classes, for instance, students use AI prompts to generate profiles of themselves, based on everything a sophisticated LLM can glean from across the internet. It's a powerful way to understand what we project into the world—our brand, and how others see us. Through this, students learn to tell authentic *signature stories*: narratives that epitomize their goals, priorities, and identities.

Organizations have signature stories too: from Jobs and Wozniak huddled in a garage creating the first Apple computer, to Leon L. Bean getting wet feet while hunting and returning home to create the first Bean Boot. Using AI, we can surface these stories, for both organizations and individuals, and develop more authentic, ambitious, and integrated understandings of who we really are.

We've developed three exercises, included at the end of this chapter, that leaders can use to find their own road to clarity and human flourishing.

The first step is to leverage AI to tackle time-consuming tasks that fail to create meaning in our lives. Exercise A offers a roadmap for auditing time-intensive behaviors, automating necessary tasks, and axing distractions. Through this process, leaders can free up time while reducing inauthentic behaviors that exacerbate burnout or stifle their potential.

Next, Exercise B challenges readers to use reclaimed time mindfully and consciously allocate their attention in positive ways. Doing so starts with ditching devices and reconnecting with neglected hobbies, relationships, or causes, then using AI to mindfully augment engagement with these priorities. Such side projects are far from unproductive; research shows that leaders who regularly pursue such interests are more creative, innovative, and resilient.[6]

Finally, Exercise C asks readers to use AI to reflect deeply on their evolving priorities, using LLMs to support daily, weekly, and monthly reflections. Using the provided prompts, readers can interrogate an AI model about the patterns, hurdles, and opportunities in their lives—and find new paths to growth and meaning.

These exercises are grounded in the simple idea that AI can free us from challenges that stifle our authenticity, boldness, and connection while actively accelerating our journey toward human flourishing.

From Regret to Reimagination

The tension between convenience and meaning in the AI age applies to every human. If we orient our relationship with AI exclusively around eliminating drudgery, what do we stand to risk? Our research suggests that the key to human flourishing in the AI era is to *love the work*—the task of being ourselves—and use AI in ways that directly support us on that journey.

This begins, of course, with recognizing that the choices we make as we go through life are themselves profoundly human. Our ability to sculpt our own lives, to decide for ourselves which direction to go in, and to be at once blessed and burdened by the consequences of those decisions, is a defining aspect of the human condition—and a key differentiator between artificial and human intelligence.

In developing these ideas, we've invoked the metaphor of the deathbed—an apt image, but not one we use lightly. We speak of death because we've seen, in hospitals and hospices, the clarity and spiritual stillness that comes with the knowledge that something is ending. But we do so, also, in the conviction that it is often possible for people to achieve this clarity *before* their final curtain call.

When we recognize the importance of living with authenticity, with boldness, and in connection with others, it becomes possible to ask: How can I become more truly myself? How can I step forward

What Matters Now: Mortality, Meaning, and the Machine Age

with more conviction? How can I reach out to others and bring more love into my life?

There are many ways to answer these questions. One thing that is increasingly clear, however, is that AI itself can, if we're mindful and deliberate and creative, be used to support and enrich our lives in all three areas.

1. AI can show us our own reflections and help bring our lived experiences into harmony with our inner truths.

2. AI can help us reach for new heights and unleash our ingenuity to strive for ever greater impact.

3. AI can eliminate the friction that leads to burnout and isolation and build bridges to the people and communities that matter most to us.

The future of leadership doesn't lie in outpacing or outperforming machines but rather in becoming more human. It lies in committing ourselves to the work that machines *can't* do for us: showing up with purpose, leading with intent, and choosing to make an impact we'll be proud of—not just at the end of each quarter, but at the end of our lives.

Exercises

The next three exercises can help you map your own road to clarity and human flourishing.

Exercise A: Audit, Automate, and Ax

This exercise will help you audit time-intensive behaviors, automate necessary tasks, and ax distractions so you can free up time and maximize your potential.

Step 1: Audit Your Life

List behaviors that suck time and energy without bringing joy or meaning. Group out the things you have to do in your professional or personal life and those you do to distract yourself or procrastinate.

- Example: Have-to-dos
  - Meetings that could have been emails
  - Expense reports
- Example: Distractions
  - Doomscrolling
  - Online shopping

Step 2: Automate Your Have-to-Do

Input your have-to-dos into your favorite LLM (ChatGPT, Claude, Gemini), asking: "Can you help me automate (insert task)? If you can't, could you recommend a more specialized AI agent that can?"

- **Meetings that could have been emails:** AI suggests using Loom to substitute short video messages for full-length meetings or Gemini's note-taking feature to summarize action items and determine if follow-up meetings are really needed.

- **Expense reports:** AI creates a Google Sheets template, letting you upload receipts to generate the report automatically.

Step 3: Ax Your Distractions

Input your distractions into your chatbot, asking "Can you help me limit (insert distraction)? If you can't, could you recommend a more specialized AI agent that can?"

- **Doomscrolling:** AI recommends Freedom, which blocks apps and websites across all devices on schedule.

What Matters Now: Mortality, Meaning, and the Machine Age

- **Online shopping:** AI advises leveraging Freedom to block shopping sites or using One Sec to create a short delay before showing sites like Amazon. It also suggests bank automations to limit spending and auto-move money to savings accounts.

Next steps: For a more holistic audit, try using AI to track your schedule and realign your actions with your values. For example, Reclaim.ai can analyze your calendar and auto-block time for your priorities (deep work, breaks, personal time, etc.), defending your boundaries without micromanaging your day. RescueTime, meanwhile, tracks when you access different apps, websites, and projects and offers personalized tips and coaching (e.g., "You focus best from 9-11 am. Block distractions then.")

Exercise B: Disconnect to Reconnect

As you complete Exercise A, you'll regain free time that can be reinvested in achieving your potential. But new distractions constantly emerge, so one must choose, again and again, to consciously allocate attention in productive and fulfilling ways.

Step 1: Ditch Your Devices

To build those muscles, start by kicking your devices to the curb and investing your newfound free time in reconnecting with a hobby, spending unplugged time with a friend, or volunteering for a cause you care about—things you might previously have neglected because they weren't "productive" or aligned with your list of have-to-dos.

- **Hobbies:** Think about the last time you were in a flow state, where you lost track of time and felt fully present. As you work on your hobby, notice and let go of any negative emotions—"I'm not good enough, this is silly, etc."—that make you want to stop.

Leading for Tomorrow

- **Human interactions:** Reach out to somebody you neglected when things got busy. As you reconnect, ask yourself: How does this person inspire me? How do they align with my values? How can I be more present for them, help them, or communicate my gratitude?

- **Cause:** Identify a cause you cherish or a hardship you, a loved one, or people in your community have experienced. What gift can you uniquely bring to help this cause? Is there a way to apply your career skills, passion, or experience to amplify impact?

Step 2: Augment Your Humanity

Now it's time to think about how AI can help integrate your authentic passions, boldly pursue them, and leverage them for deeper connection, augmenting your life one task, activity, and interaction at a time. Try asking your favorite AI model how it can augment the unplugged activities you've been undertaking.

- **Hobby:** Ask AI to help bring your hobby to the next level, acting as a personalized tutor or helping you find a community around your passion. For instance, Sophie gets frustrated when her limited guitar-playing abilities hold back her songwriting. Her AI tool suggested using Suno, which automatically creates backing tracks based on hummed tunes that she can bring to human collaborators.

- **Human interaction:** Ask your AI tool to help align your interactions with your values. For instance, Jennifer's AI helps her stay in touch authentically and consistently with a long list of valued friends and collaborators. AI quickly learned that she likes to sign off emails with a personal thought, not just a dry "all best."

What Matters Now: Mortality, Meaning, and the Machine Age

- **Cause:** Use AI to amplify your impact. For instance, Sophie cares about climate change and wants to use her business development skills to help companies curb emissions. Her AI tool suggested emission-curbing strategies, which Sophie pitched to her corporate partners and used to forge real-life climate action initiatives.

Exercise C: Looking in the AI Mirror

Ask your favorite AI chatbot to share what it's learning about you and see what you learn about yourself in the process. Try this sequence over a month, at whatever frequency feels realistic for you.

Step 1: Daily Prompt

Once a day for one week, ask AI to help you identify hidden behaviors and patterns.

- Day 1: *"What did I avoid today, and why?"* Use this prompt to surface blind spots or discomforts.

- Day 2: *"What gave me energy today? What drained it?"* Track patterns in energy and engagement.

- Day 3: *"Did I act in line with my values today?"* Reflect on moments of alignment or misalignment.

- Day 4: *"What emotion did I feel most today? What triggered it?"* Build emotional literacy and emotional regulation.

- Day 5: *"Who did I connect with today? Did I feel seen?"* Explore the quality of your relationships.

- Day 6: *"What story did I tell myself about today, and is it true?"* Challenge limiting narratives or assumptions.

- Day 7: *"What do I want more of in my life?"* Surface longings and values.

Step 2: Weekly Check-In

Once a week, ask AI to help you review your entries. Example prompts you can use:

- "What patterns do you see in my energy highs and lows?"
- "Are there recurring themes in what I avoid?"
- "What values show up most often in my writing?"
- "What words or emotions do I tend to repeat?"

Step 3: Monthly Reflection

Once a month, do a **deeper integration exercise**:

- **Prompt:** "Based on my entries this month, which parts of myself am I honoring and which might need more attention or care?"

- **Follow-up prompts:**
  - "If my inner critic were writing these entries, what would it sound like?"
  - "If my future self reads this journal, what advice might they give me?"

Notes

1. Teun Siebers, Ine Beyens, Susanne E. Baumgartner, and Patti M. Valkenburg, "Adolescents' Digital Nightlife: The Comparative Effects of Day- and Nighttime Smartphone Use on Sleep Quality," *Communication Research*, August 30, 2024. https://doi.org/10.1177/00936502241276793
2. Sophie Hamilton and Jennifer Aaker, *Humanity in the Age of AI*. Stanford Graduate School of Business Case No. M395. www.gsb.stanford.edu/faculty-research/case-studies/humanity-age-ai

3. Tasha Eurich, *Insight: Why We're Not as Self-Aware as We Think, and How Seeing Ourselves Clearly Helps Us Succeed at Work and in Life* (Crown Business, 2017).

4. Buckhouse's 24-Hour Hotline for Story, Art & Design is available at: https://jamesbuckhouse.com/

5. Jordi Quoidbach, Daniel T. Gilbert, and Timothy D. Wilson, "The End of History Illusion," *Science* 339 (2013): 96–98. https://dtg.sites.fas.harvard.edu/Quoidbach%20et%20al%202013.pdf

6. Donnel A. Briley, Melanie Rudd, and Jennifer Aaker, "Cultivating Optimism: How to Frame Your Future during a Health Challenge," *Journal of Consumer Research* 44, no. 4 (2017): 895–915. https://doi.org/10.1093/jcr/ucx075

Chapter 19

Beyond Fear: Building Institutions of Learning, Not Limitations

John Hagel

Fear. It is the most natural—and widespread—reaction to our rapidly changing world. Fear is a barrier to embracing change and achieving much more of our potential. If we are to thrive in perpetual change, we need a fundamental shift in leadership. We need leaders who recognize fear for what it is—a roadblock to growth—and help others face and move past fear to reach a much greater positive impact. It is a very different form of leadership; it can be challenging, but it will yield significant rewards.

Fear Is a Limiter

More and more people around the world are being driven by the emotion of fear. In this context, the fear is about the future. When people look into the future, they tend to focus on the threats and challenges ahead. The future becomes very scary—they don't want to go there. They just want to hold on to what they have. This fear is widespread, across generations, genders, and countries.

Why is this fear becoming so pervasive? It is a natural consequence of the long-term forces that are reshaping our global economy and society. These forces are creating mounting performance pressure. Competition is intensifying on a global scale, the pace of change is accelerating, things we thought we could count on are no longer there, and, because of growing connectivity, small events in a faraway place can quickly cascade into extreme, disruptive events that leave us scrambling to figure out what to do next. That's a lot of pressure, and it is continuing to mount.

A natural human reaction to mounting performance pressure is fear. It is an understandable emotion, and it is also very limiting. If we are driven by fear, we tend to shrink our time horizons—we only want to focus on the present, because future pressure seems so significant. We become more risk averse and more isolated because fear erodes trust.

Yet here's a paradox: The same long-term forces that are creating mounting performance pressure are also creating exponentially expanding opportunity. We can create far more value with far fewer resources and far more quickly than would have been imaginable a few decades ago. But if we are driven by fear, we can't even see those opportunities in the future, much less be motivated to pursue them. If we are going to unleash those exponentially expanding opportunities, we need to find ways to move beyond the emotion of fear and cultivate emotions that will help us to achieve much greater impact.

Moving Beyond Fear

What will help us to do this? One very powerful tool is an opportunity-based narrative. In this context, narratives are very different from stories. Stories are self-contained—they have a beginning, a middle, and an end. Stories are also about the storyteller or other people, real or imagined; they are not about you. In contrast, narratives are about opportunities or threats in the future that have not been addressed, and the resolution of the narrative hinges on a call to action to those being addressed by the narrative.

Most of the narratives we hear today are threat-based narratives focusing on some significant threat in the future. These narratives feed the fear.

What's an example of an opportunity-based narrative? There aren't many, but one that illustrates the potential is a narrative that Steve Jobs crafted for Apple back in the 1990s. The narrative focused on a new generation of technology that could help everyone achieve more of their potential, in contrast to previous generations of technology that took away our names, gave us numbers, and put us in cubicles doing routine tasks. This narrative had a call to action to the people outside Apple, a call condensed into the slogan "Think different." The message was that we would be able to tap into the opportunity created by a new generation of technology only if we were willing to think different. This narrative spoke to a deep aspiration that people had, and it is the reason Apple became the equivalent of a religion for many people.

Opportunity-based narratives help people move beyond fear and cultivate helpful emotions for a rapidly changing world. Perhaps the most powerful of these emotions is a specific form of passion—the passion of the explorer. If we study environments that have sustained extreme performance improvement, we will find that the participants in those environments have the passion of the explorer. People with this passion are excited about achieving more and more impact in a specific domain (it could be anything from gardening to nuclear physics), and they are driven to connect with others and seek help from them as they address opportunities for impact.

> Opportunity-based narratives help people move beyond fear and cultivate helpful emotions for a rapidly changing world.

If the opportunities we identify in our narratives are sufficiently large and inspiring, they can draw out the passion of the explorer in more and more people.

The Challenges Ahead

Yes, this will not be easy. We have developed institutional models and cultures in large organizations around the world that view the passion of the explorer as deeply suspect and something to be resisted.

The institutional model that governs most of our large organizations is a model of scalable efficiency. In this model, success is achieved by doing things faster and cheaper. The key to efficiency is to tightly specify all tasks and to ensure that they are performed in the same way throughout the organization.

In this institutional model, the passion of the explorer is deeply suspect. People with this passion take too many risks, they ask too many questions, and they deviate from the script too often. Instead of passion, we want people who like the work they do and who will do the assigned tasks reliably and efficiently. That's why so many leaders measure worker engagement and motivate workers with threat-based narratives. We're on burning platforms, and we need to work even harder and faster to keep our jobs.

At one level, it's hard to question this institutional model because it drove the growth and success of large institutions around the world for over a century. The challenge is that, in a rapidly changing world, this model of scalable efficiency is becoming less and less efficient, and that fact is feeding the fear of leaders and the people they lead.

The Big Shift in Institutional Models

We need to shift from an institutional model of scalable efficiency to an institutional model of scalable *learning*.

In a rapidly changing world, we need to shift from an institutional model of scalable efficiency to an institutional model of scalable *learning*. This will be a profound change, and it will not be easy.

Leading for Tomorrow

What is a scalable learning model? It is a model where the key to success is to find ways for everyone in the organization to learn faster. It shifts how we think about learning at a fundamental level. Most leaders today will say that the people in their organization are learning through training programs and process manuals. This form of learning involves sharing *existing* knowledge. In a rapidly changing world, however, existing knowledge becomes obsolete at an accelerating rate.

We need to embrace a very different form of learning, learning that involves creating *new* knowledge. That learning does not occur in a training room; it must be cultivated in the work environment as people encounter new and unexpected situations with increasing frequency. And it's not just for people in research labs or innovation centers; it's essential for people throughout an organization. It expands our focus from completing tasks more efficiently to finding ways to create increasing value for the organization and its stakeholders.

In the institutional model of scalable learning, the nature of work itself shifts in a profound way. Rather than simply performing tightly specified and highly standardized tasks, this work focuses on constantly evolving the tasks and adapting them to specific contexts so that greater value can be created and delivered.

As we shift to this new form of work, we will expand our horizon beyond skill building. Skills are valuable in specific contexts—how to operate this machine or perform that kind of calculation. This new form of work requires us to cultivate capabilities that are valuable in helping us to learn in *all* contexts. Capabilities include curiosity, collaboration, imagination, creativity, and reflection. We all have the potential for drawing out these capabilities, but our current work environments tend to ignore them, unless we are in the narrow silos of a research laboratory or innovation center.

Who would be best equipped to perform this kind of learning and work? People who have the passion of the explorer. They are constantly looking for new challenges and situations that will help

243

them create more value. They are excited by the opportunity to come together with others to have more meaningful impact for themselves and their stakeholders. People with the passion of the explorer are intensely cultivating the capabilities that will help them to learn more effectively.

Profound Change in Organization

Embracing the scalable learning institutional model will drive us to evolve work environments to help people learn more effectively. It will break down the hierarchical silos that exist in most large organizations, because we will discover that people learn faster when they come together with others who have diverse perspectives and backgrounds.

It will drive us to connect with people outside our own organization. We will see the evolution and scaling of very different forms of organizational ecosystems. Today, most ecosystems are shaped by a short-term transactional mindset—another organization has resources we need, so we find ways to transact with them to gain access to those resources. We will move from transactional ecosystems to performance ecosystems where the focus is on building longer-term relationships with a growing number of other organizations in ways that will help all participants to learn faster.

As we seek to learn faster, we will discover that learning is accelerated when people come together in small groups—let's call them impact groups. These are groups of three to 15 people who form deep, trust-based relationships with each other and are driven by a shared passion to have an increasing impact in a specific area. The groups are focused on action and impact, not just conversations. On one side, they support each other when actions fail to yield results, and on the other side, they are constantly challenging each other to find ways to achieve even greater impact.

These groups will remain relatively small because of the deep trust required among all participants. However, the groups will be driven to find ways to connect with other groups so that they can scale their learning and impact. These intra-group connections will become the key driver of the growth of performance ecosystems.

These new ecosystems will require a very different kind of platform: learning platforms. Once again, we need to stay focused on learning in the form of creating new knowledge. Many platforms today connect us with lectures and workshops where we can learn existing knowledge.

Now there's a big, untapped opportunity to create learning platforms focused on creating new knowledge. The primary design goal of these platforms is to help all participants learn faster by creating new knowledge. The core unit of these platforms will be shared workspaces where people in impact groups can come together and pursue initiatives designed to achieve greater impact. The platforms will then help to connect these impact groups into broader networks so that they can access a broader range of perspectives and capabilities and scale their learning even more.

The Big Shift in Leadership

These profound organizational changes will require major changes in leadership models. Today, the mark of a strong leader is someone who has the answer to all questions. No matter what the question is, we can rely on them to have an answer. If they don't have an answer, then maybe it is time to find a new leader who does have answers to all the questions.

This is one of the reasons we are seeing such a widespread erosion of trust in all our institutions. If their leaders claim to have answers to all the questions, there are two possibilities: One, they are

Beyond Fear: Building Institutions of Learning, Not Limitations

not aware of how rapidly and profoundly the world is changing, or two, they are lying. In either case, why would we trust an institution with this kind of leader?

The rapidly changing world we are confronting requires a very different form of leadership. In this world, the most effective leaders will be those who can look ahead and see exciting, emerging opportunities and who will pose inspiring questions about how to address those opportunities. They will freely admit that they don't have answers and ask for help from others to find the answers that will help to make these opportunities a reality.

This candor from leaders fosters a very different culture in our organizations. It will indicate that questions are not only OK, but they are essential to finding ways to address new opportunities. It will indicate that asking for help is not only acceptable; it is essential to coming up with better answers.

Rather than focusing on short-term challenges or threats in the future, these leaders will craft opportunity-based narratives that focus on the prospects their teams can address if they all come together and move beyond the practices of the past. Really large and inspiring opportunities can help workers move beyond the emotion of fear and draw out the passion that will excite them and motivate them to venture into unexplored territory.

Instilling this excitement and motivation will require a different approach to strategy. It's an approach that many of the most successful technology companies in Silicon Valley have pursued. Rather than focusing on a five-year plan, this strategy—let's call it zoom out/ zoom in—focuses on two very different time horizons.

The zoom-out horizon is ten to 20 years. Key question on that horizon is: What exponentially large opportunity could we be pursuing in this rapidly changing world? The zoom-in horizon is very different; it is six to –12 months. The key question on this horizon is: What two or three initiatives could we pursue in the next six to –12 months

Leading for Tomorrow

that would have the greatest impact in accelerating our progress toward the zoom out opportunity, and how would we measure progress at the end of six to –12 months?

This approach to strategy can be very powerful in overcoming fear. By focusing on very large and inspiring opportunities in the future, leaders can begin to cultivate excitement among their teams. But, even more important, by focusing on short-term initiatives that can make tangible progress in addressing these opportunities, leaders can overcome the natural skepticism that many people driven by fear will have regarding long-term opportunities. They will tend to dismiss them as fantasy until they see real short-term progress. Only then will they get excited about joining the effort to address the opportunities.

Focus on Small Moves, Smartly Made

We need to pursue profound and widespread change to succeed in the world that is changing around us. Yet we need to resist the temptation to embrace top-down, big-bang approaches to change. In this model of change, leaders bring together their teams, and announce that they are on a burning platform and that everything needs to change throughout the organization. But because it is a large organization, driving the change will take a lot of time and significant funding. This approach has a large failure rate because it draws out the immune system and antibodies that mobilize to resist the change. People in the organization who are driven by fear will naturally resist initiatives that require large funding and long time horizons before results can be achieved.

The most effective way to drive change in an environment driven by fear is to focus on scaling the edge, where small moves, smartly made, can set big things in motion. What does this mean? Rather than trying to change everything at once, leaders need to engage in the zoom-out/zoom-in approach to strategy. Identify and focus on an

Beyond Fear: Building Institutions of Learning, Not Limitations

> The most effective way to drive change in an environment driven by fear is to focus on scaling the edge.

exponentially large opportunity in the future. Identify a part of the organization that today is a relatively modest "edge" but that has the potential to scale by addressing this opportunity until it becomes the new core of the organization.

As leaders move to the zoom-in part of the strategy, they can explore ways to scale this edge of the organization with relatively modest resources. They need to find and bring together people on the edge who already have passion for the opportunity. As the edge starts to scale, it will draw more people and resources from the core organization as employees overcome their fear and see the progress that is being made.

Bottom Line: Address the Fear

In a world of accelerating change, leaders need to focus on the emotions that are shaping our choices and actions. The leaders who will be most successful are those who find ways to address the fear that is increasingly a barrier to change and cultivate the passion of the explorer. People with this passion will be excited about coming together and achieving more impact in pursuing very large opportunities.

Leaders who recognize this imperative and who adopt very different leadership models will succeed in addressing exponentially large opportunities on the horizon. By more deeply understanding the needs and aspirations of the people they are leading, these leaders will help everyone come together to achieve more of their potential. We need leaders who understand what it means to be human and unlock the potential that resides within all of us.

Chapter 20

AI Anxiety Is Real. How You Lead Through It Is a Choice

Morra Aarons-Mele

If 21st-century capitalism has a central tenet, it is that innovation rules and disruption drives progress. Innovation can be thrilling and transformative, but it is also stressful. Disruption demands abrupt change, and sudden change invites anxiety. Few disruptions have arrived with as much speed and force as artificial intelligence. The rise of generative AI has created extraordinary opportunities and equally extraordinary uncertainty. It is stretching our emotional, psychological, and organizational capacities in ways that few leaders have experienced before.

AI will augment our lives in amazing ways, and it will transform virtually every job. Many business leaders predict that AI, in the short term, at least, could eliminate large portions of the workforce. Just how AI disrupts our work lives depends largely on companies, such as Anthropic, OpenAI, Microsoft, and Meta, at the forefront of its development, and on our employers. AI technology companies, have the choice to build ethical technology that enhances the human experience or to deliver tools they know will replace human workers. How that pans out is an open question. The public narrative around AI and work is scary. I'm often shocked by the things CEOs say out loud about how AI will eliminate many of their employees' jobs and by the way the media ecosystem amplifies those messages.

That is anxiety-producing stuff. And it is a heavy burden for workers to bear.

Like trees in heavy windstorms, we can manage stress if we are flexible, and so leaders in every organization have choices to make too. We can choose to prioritize human well-being over trends and immediate rewards. We can choose to lead in a way that aligns with our values. We can choose to embrace the emotions that surface around huge and unpredictable change. Whether AI comes to augment our lives to or eliminate jobs, leaders now must make the choice to understand and manage what I call AI anxiety for themselves and their teams.

Most leaders I speak with use AI daily in their personal and work lives and see its potential to free us from routine tasks, allowing us to focus on strategy, creativity, and human connection. Many have come to rely on AI as a sort of companion and a coach. "I never have to stare down a blank page again," said one chief strategy officer to me joyfully. At the same time, most feel that AI threatens white-collar professionals in a way they've never experienced before. Many have also built a level of mistrust of AI, largely around corporate edicts to implement AI transformations in ways they believe technology is not ready for. They're dubious: Is AI a revolution or a hyped-up trend? They're also leading teams full of people who have differing opinions and fears about the tools, and they're expected to keep these teams motivated, aligned, and functional as AI is introduced.

As a result, these leaders are feeling anxious, and you might be too. But unpacking your anxiety can be a superpower during this time of rapid change. We're going to explore why AI provokes anxiety, and I'll share tools that can help you name and explore your own emotions and values. What you discover may not single-handedly change the trajectory of AI in your organization or society. But it will give you the ability to find clarity in who you are and how you want to lead and act, even when the future is uncertain.

Leading for Tomorrow

Why AI Makes Us Anxious

I've identified three common drivers of anxiety when it comes to AI: lack of control over the rate of change, loss of meaning, and uncomfortable emotions we prefer to avoid. Let's look at each of them more closely.

Anxiety Driver 1: Lack of Control over the Rate of Change

AI anxiety is often framed as irrational technophobia, but, in fact, it is deeply rooted in human biology. Our autonomic nervous system reacts strongly to sudden, uncontrollable change. When we face uncertainty and lack information or feel our agency slipping, our nervous system activates a threat response. Adrenaline, cortisol, and other stress hormones flood the body to prepare us for fight, flight, or freeze. AI arrives with the velocity of a force we cannot control, and the body responds accordingly.

The actual technology overwhelms us too. It can feel like AI is getting smarter by the day while we're. . .not. In response, while we may not be literally fighting or fleeing in the office, the flood of hormones in our system might show up in behaviors like overworking, ill temper, micromanagement, checking out—or just avoiding a stressful Tuesday or a dreaded standing meeting. Consider what happens when an organization announces an AI-first transformation. The words might be accompanied by hopeful language about efficiency and innovation, but they often trigger a physiological alarm. Even rumors of layoffs, a confusing new AI tool, or a poorly communicated policy can create the same biological cascade we would experience if we encountered a predator in the wild.

Here's an example, relayed by journalist Brian Merchant in his blog *Blood in the Machine*: A new executive "casually referred to a ChatGPT model she was fine-tuning as our 'Chief Marketing Officer' in front of my manager [the current CMO]. She claimed it was outperforming us. It wasn't—it was producing garbage. But the real harm

AI Anxiety Is Real. How You Lead Through It Is a Choice

was watching someone who'd given decades to his field get *humiliated*, not by a machine, but by a colleague weaponizing it."[1]

An interaction like this creates many emotions, among them a strong threat response. When we're publicly told we'll imminently be replaced, and there's not much we can do about it, it's no wonder our nervous system might respond by saying "Hold up. This feels dangerous."

Anxiety Driver 2: Loss of Meaning

The humiliated executive highlights another reason why generative AI makes us anxious: It undermines the values we hold and the meaning we find in work. I've heard from people who resent AI for siphoning off creativity and expertise or who think that it encourages sloppiness or laziness. We work for many different reasons; although money is important, humans highly value agency in our jobs, and we need to feel a sense of purpose. When we give over those decisions to AI, what happens to core values like self-reliance, learning, or usefulness?

Dr. Ziyaad Bhorat studies the long history of humans' angst toward automation; AI is just the latest example. Automation anxiety, he says, sees "those tools capable of performing tasks with less and less of our input as both exciting and unsettling, because it indicates a certain level of mastery and a corresponding level of dependency" on those technologies.[2] And that challenges not just our jobs but our purpose.

As Brian Merchant writes: "We recognize that AI is not sentient, that it's management, not AI, that fires people, but also that there are many ways that AI can 'kill' a job, by sapping the pleasure one derives from work, draining it of skill and expertise, or otherwise subjecting it to degradation."[3]

Bhorat proffers three important abilities that individuals and communities have already identified as worth protecting from AI: work, knowledge and understanding, and decision making.[4] He writes that work is worth protecting, as is the right to keep our skills from atrophying and from being substituted by machines. We will come to the importance of values later in the chapter.

The history of anxiety about people being replaced by machines stretches into antiquity. The word "sabotage" may conjure espionage or corporate drama, but it actually comes from the clumsy gait of workers in early industrial France, who wore wooden clogs called *sabots*. An apocryphal story goes that disgruntled laborers threw their *sabots* into machinery to protest automation that threatened their livelihoods.

And, of course, there were the Luddites. Contrary to myth, the Luddites weren't anti-technology; they were anti-exploitation. They objected to factory owners who used machines as an excuse to underpay workers, and they disliked what they saw as shoddier products emerging from automation. Writing in the 1960s, Hannah Arendt warned that automation might ultimately replace not just human labor but human *thinking*.[5] Arendt feared automation could "shatter the very purposefulness of the world."[6]

Anger against automation has deep roots. So does automation anxiety.

Only history can tell if the generative AI revolution will be different from others. But what makes AI feel so disturbing is how fast it's moving and how little control most of us feel we have about it. Remember that loss of control provokes a threat response in most people. As Enrique Rubio, founder of Hacking HR, puts it, "Everything that needs to happen to make sure the transition to an AI-driven world is smooth is moving *very slowly*" while the technology itself is moving very fast. We are overwhelmed, and our systems—government, education, public policy—aren't catching up.

AI has no off switch. As Rubio notes:

The wheel, the printing press, steam power, electricity, all these things were created with a vision of augmenting our physical capabilities, our muscle power, so that we didn't

AI Anxiety Is Real. How You Lead Through It Is a Choice

*have to do that with our own hands. This automation trig-
gered the cognitive revolution, too, because when you have
electricity, you can write longer than if you have a candle.
With AI, we're talking about augmenting human capabilities, but at some point, once you have identified the human
capabilities that you can augment, the question is, do you
need the human anymore?*

Anxiety Driver 3: Uncomfortable Emotions We Prefer to Avoid

Like any giant, existential change, AI is going to summon lots of messy emotions, and anyone who's ever tried to suppress or ignore an emotion knows that it just doesn't work. The emotions come out somehow, through pain in the body, unwelcome behaviors, burnout, poor decision making, or poor mental health. To work and lead in the age of AI, we have to get comfortable recognizing our emotions and understanding why they happen. Otherwise, we will not only be controlled by AI, we will be controlled by our emotions.

> To work and lead in the age of AI, we have to get comfortable recognizing our emotions and understanding why they happen.

Here are some common emotions that have come up in my interviews and coaching sessions with leaders:

- Anxiety over losing income and livelihood, a career you've worked hard to build

- Fear of irrelevance

- Loss of control and self-determination

- Anxiety your kids won't be able to get jobs or that all the money you're paying for college isn't worth it

- Overwhelm at the sheer pace of change

- Anger at confusing or unrealistic demands about implementing AI

- Frustration when AI doesn't live up to the hype

- Resentment at lost resources or shifting priorities

- Grief at the loss of excellence, professional skill, or a hard-won craft

- Loneliness because interacting with machines is replacing interactions with peers

- Mistrust in your organizational leadership because you suspect they are not telling you the whole truth about what their plans for implementing AI mean for your own job and the jobs of your team.

Understanding Your AI–Emotional Landscape

Before leaders can help their teams make sense of AI, they must understand their own reactions to it. Understanding our strong feelings doesn't mean that we can stop them. AI does not care about our emotions. There's a certain level of radical acceptance that must happen in the midst of overwhelming and uncomfortable change. As Jon Kabat-Zinn famously said, "You can't stop the waves, but you can learn to surf." Leading in the age of AI demands not just emotional intelligence, but the ability to summon emotions to the forefront, so we can understand them, and then let them go.

Leaders who can name their emotions—"This scares me," "This frustrates me," "I feel threatened," "I feel left behind"—are better equipped than others to respond strategically instead of reactively.

Anxiety Means You Care

I share something in common with NYU professor, author, and entrepreneur Tracy Dennis-Tiwary. We both think that anxiety is a valuable emotion. It's trying to tell us something. The future is always uncertain. "When we're anxious," says Tiwary, "we're really tuning into that uncertainty. But what does uncertainty mean? It doesn't mean disaster. It means that there's the possibility of both peril and reward, of danger and safety. When we're anxious, we apprehend at the same time that both are possible."

This is so true of AI anxiety, with its myriad of unknowns. Unknowns can cause anxiety, and that's OK. There are a few things that we can do here.

We can become more knowledgeable about AI. When we have strong emotions around something, we tend to avoid it. Many of us avoid diving into how AI actually impacts our work because we're scared about what we might find when we get up close. Dive in! Understand what you're dealing with now and consider what might happen in the future based on research, trends, and use cases.

We can welcome the anxiety. It's trying to tell us something. As Tiwary says, "Anxiety is the emotion that activates us to work, to avert disaster and to make our dreams come true." We've all had times in our lives when feeling anxious has motivated us to try harder, find new solutions, and stick with something hard. This is the gift of anxiety.

Most important, anxiety is a signal that something we care about is on the line. If you've ever been anxious before a major sporting event, performance, or starting a new job, you understand what this means. What is AI anxiety trying to signal to you?

What's Triggering My AI Anxiety?

Let's play detective.

AI—and anxiety—don't affect everyone the same way. Some of us are worriers from birth but excel when things get really hairy. Some of us happily buckle up for the ride during chaotic moments while others need a detailed schedule for every minute of the day. Building a better relationship with your anxiety starts with noticing

Leading for Tomorrow

or tuning in to what's setting you off. The first step is to understand what makes you anxious at work. You might find you are reacting in negative ways or that you use anxiety adaptively to feel motivated, get work done, and tackle hard tasks. (A friend who worked at a large tech company often joked that the cafeteria seemed very full on the days right after a layoff was announced. Employees wanted to keep their flexible schedules post-COVID; management requested they return to work. Layoffs made everyone anxious, thus luring them into the office for fear of being the next to get the chop.) Noticing can take practice for many of us because we're used to ignoring difficult emotions or acting out our feelings instead of actually feeling them.

Have you ever been working away, having a pretty good day, and then an email pops up in your inbox? Your heart races, your stomach flips, and your hands shake. You're certain that email is bad. Maybe you're scared to open it, and you pretend it doesn't exist. Or maybe you open it, freak out, and spend 30 minutes crafting a reply.

That email is an emotional trigger for you.

A trigger is a cue, situation, event, or information that activates anxiety. A trigger tells your mind there is a threat. Your body may react with that racing heart while your mind is busy creating anxious thoughts like "Uh-oh, that email is bad news. I'm going to be in trouble."

Leaders and managers are triggered all the time at work. We may learn to tune out triggers out or sometimes not even notice them in our subconscious. What sets us off could be anything: the way someone talks, the way someone acts, or the way a team member is habitually late.

Triggers can summon past trauma or difficult experiences. Over time, these triggers build up inside us and, as Yale psychologist Marc Brackett puts it, "accumulate in a debt of anger or anxiety." That debt often shows up in situations that, on the surface, have no apparent connection with the trigger: yelling at a colleague or family member,

AI Anxiety Is Real. How You Lead Through It Is a Choice

clenching your jaw, drinking too much, binge-watching TV. But the reaction that seems to come out of nowhere has an identifiable cause. Triggers cause us to experience emotions, some pleasurable and some downright squirmy.

Managing these emotions begins with noticing triggers—those moments when anxiety, worry, or anger flare unexpectedly. A trigger is simply a moment when the body senses danger before the conscious mind has fully processed the situation. Your trigger might be a headline predicting job loss, a comment from a colleague, a new organizational mandate, or even a casual remark from your teenager about how they used AI to complete their homework.

Noticing these moments is a leadership skill. If you are someone who has worried about money your whole life, for example, being asked to implement AI transformation might trigger intense anxiety about earning your livelihood and supporting your loved ones. For many of us, implementing AI might trigger feelings that we alone are not up to the job; we're not smart enough. I interviewed a tech executive who felt anger that millions of dollars were being spent on AI transformation while other urgent areas of the business were starved. Feeling overwhelmed or not understanding AI can trigger feelings of inadequacy or perhaps that we are too old or outdated to adapt to so much change. I have interviewed people in marketing, for example, who already feel overwhelmed by the intense transformation social media has created in their field and are now being asked to use AI as a coworker. This is a radical shift from everything they were trained to do.

The marketing leader whose CMO was humiliated? Well, he reported some weeks later:

Today, in the name of "AI efficiency," a lot of people saw the exit door and my CMO got PIPd. The irony here is twofold: one, it does not seem that the people who left were victims of a turn to "vibe coding," and I suspect that the "AI efficiency" was used as an excuse to make us seem innovative even during this crisis. Two, this is a company whose product desperately needs real human care.[7]

(A PIP is a performance improvement plan, often a common way of ushering someone out the door or being able to fire them for cause.)

The Values Beneath

As you become more aware of your emotional landscape, you will notice patterns that reveal what you value most. Anxiety often signals that something important is at stake. Fear of irrelevance may reflect a commitment to mastery. Anger may reflect a deep belief in fairness. Grief about the loss of a particular task may reflect a sense of identity connected to craft or creativity. Curiosity about AI's possibilities may signal a value of growth or innovation.

Recognizing the values underneath your emotions is a powerful leadership tool. Values provide clarity in the midst of uncertainty. Values help leaders choose actions that align with who they want to be, even when the environment is in flux.

> Values help leaders choose actions that align with who they want to be, even when the environment is in flux.

First, answer a handful of questions to help dig into your specific emotions:

- "How do I feel about AI in general? What excites me? What worries me?"

- "Am I anxious about losing relevance as a leader or am I excited to see what's next. . .or a little of both?"

- "Do I worry about pressure to cut jobs either now or in the future?"

AI Anxiety Is Real. How You Lead Through It Is a Choice

- "Do I trust my company to make good decisions when it comes to implementing AI?"

- "What feels uncertain about my company's AI strategy right now? How does that make me feel?"

- "How does my team feel about AI?"

- "Am I overwhelmed by the speed of change?"

You can sit with these questions and ask them to yourself or bring them to a coach, therapist, or mentor. Notice and log your body's signals: a tight chest, racing thoughts, or irritability. They may mean you should keep digging into specific feelings until they're a little less uncomfortable. Ultimately, the goal is to become more familiar with your emotions. We cannot act strategically or create clarity if we don't understand how we really feel about AI. Too often, we muddle through change, reacting to anxiety, fear, anger, and other emotions; our emotions are in charge. When we understand our strong feelings, we're in charge. Then consider the role of values. AI triggers anxiety about an uncertain future, but for a lot of us, the thought of AI taking over our lives also clashes with values we hold dear. Emotional flexibility is a skill that allows us to tolerate anxiety while still acting in alignment with our values. So, pause, name the emotion (something you'll get better at with the previous exercise), identify the value underneath it, and consider a constructive next step. For example, if you feel anger when your board demands rapid AI adoption at all costs, ask what value is being threatened. Is it fairness? Trust? Craft? Agency?

A Values Reflection

Imagine a world in which generative AI is a key part of your daily work, and replaces some of the humans you work with. Maybe it already has. Which of your values clash with AI use? Which ones align?

Leading for Tomorrow

Accountability	Equality	Order
Achievement	Ethics	Perseverance
Adaptability	Excellence	Personal fulfillment
Adventure	Fairness	Power
Altruism	Financial stability	Pride
Ambition	Freedom	Recognition
Authenticity	Future generations	Reliability
Balance	Gratitude	Resourcefulness
Being the best	Growth	Respect
Belonging	Honesty	Responsibility
Career	Hope	Risk taking
Caring	Humility	Safety
Collaboration	Humor	Security
Commitment	Inclusion	Self-discipline
Community	Independence	Self-expression
Compassion	Initiative	Self-respect
Competence	Integrity	Teamwork
Confidence	Intuition	Time
Connection	Job security	Trust
Contentment	Joy	Truth
Contribution	Justice	Understanding
Cooperation	Kindness	Uniqueness
Courage	Knowledge	Usefulness
Creativity	Leadership	Vision
Curiosity	Learning	Vulnerability
Dignity	Legacy	Wealth
Diversity	Loyalty	Well-being
Environment	Making a difference	Wholeheartedness
Efficiency	Optimism	Wisdom

261

Identifying your values helps create a strategic decision, guided not by emotions or impulsivity but rather aligned with values. For example, you might push for a phased rollout or deeper exploration instead of reacting defensively or ignoring the concern altogether.

To be clear, action isn't always the answer; sometimes it's enough just to give your emotions an audience and then tell them to simmer down. But sometimes emotions are a signal that behavior or plans do need to shift. If that angry voice in your head around the new AI policy won't go away, examine it. Consider the emotions AI is evoking in you and ask yourself: "Does this emotion demand action?" Sometimes yes, sometimes no. Regardless, you will gain clarity, and be ready to act when the time is right.

Action, too, can take many forms. Your AI action plan could involve using your heft to change policy or practice around AI implementation. It could involve your own upskilling or new learning about how to implement the new technology. It could involve committing to a series of honest conversations with colleagues and your team or investing in activities that emphasize human connection. But ultimately, taking committed action is the most powerful way to put anxiety to great use.

Author Brené Brown has said, "If you're not feeling unsettled, you're probably not paying attention."[8] Wow, does that ring true. The only way we "win" the AI race in favor of humanity is if we honor our most human trait: our emotions, unsettled and uncomfortable as they are. Innovation brings progress, and it also brings big feelings, so leading through AI means honoring your own. Remember: AI anxiety is a logical threat response to uncertainty and the speed of change, and if we listen to it, it can guide us to take the right actions.

Leading When You Cannot Promise Certainty

I was writing this chapter when, in the same week, Amazon announced plans to lay off 14,000 white-collar workers, citing "efficiency," and OpenAI adopted a for-profit structure that allows the

Leading for Tomorrow

AI behemoth to fund its vision to "benefit all humanity." Few people were buying OpenAI's professed altruism. My inbox was flooded with emails from journalists with subject lines like "How an AI Job Apocalypse Unfolds." I have no idea if there's a real job apocalypse, but I know the narrative around this news inflames AI anxiety. I imagined myself as a manager in a daily team standup, navigating the emotions in the air amid all the headlines. It didn't feel good.

Once leaders have developed awareness of their own emotions, the next step is guiding their teams. Doing this requires acknowledging a difficult truth: You cannot promise stability. You cannot promise that roles, tasks, or structures will remain unchanged. You cannot promise that AI will spare your function or industry.

But you can promise clarity and transparency. You can promise partnership, ongoing conversation, and a commitment to human dignity.

Step 1: Feel the Fear and Do It Anyway

During the pandemic, leaders learned that we had to figure out how to keep our teams gelled even when we had no idea what the heck would happen day to day. And many of us realized something beautiful: that showing a little more vulnerability and openness to the gray areas was exactly what our people needed. For a brief moment in time, leaders were allowed to talk about what they didn't know. They could admit to being anxious and scared. Although times of crisis demand many different leadership skills, research shows that those leaders who emphasized frequent, iterative, transparent communication, were open about what they did and did not know, and who shared news even when it wasn't great helped alleviate negative feelings brought about by the COVID-19 pandemic.[9]

No one knows exactly where AI transformation is heading. Nobody knows whether we will have our jobs in a year, or five years, or what the workplace will look like. If we give people false promises, they will

AI Anxiety Is Real. How You Lead Through It Is a Choice

sniff us out as frauds. We owe them better. And we need to provide a compass for teams who are as confused and anxious as we are.

It's powerful for your team to see you embrace anxiety and uncertainty and model moving from fear into action.

It's powerful for your team to see you embrace anxiety and uncertainty and model moving from fear into action. It normalizes their own feelings and increases trust in you as their leader. Doing this isn't as hard as it might seem. Remember that we can move through anxiety only when we accept its presence. Research by Ranjay Gulati at Harvard Business School and the Stanford Mind Body Lab shows that our internal narrative—our mindset—helps determine our ability to face uncertainty with courage.[10] Great leaders, from Winston Churchill to everyday heroes, have never denied their anxiety. Instead, they've modeled how to feel the fear and move forward anyway. They admit they are anxious, they understand why they're anxious, and they choose to move ahead nonetheless. Doing this allows everyone else to move through their strong emotions and into committed action.

How can you model flexibility in the face of uncertainty? You can do it through the language you use and the tone you set.

Transparency doesn't mean dumping your personal trauma. It means acknowledging the emotional reality we're all living through. The future is uncertain. People are scared. And that's OK to say out loud. We know from decades of research on psychological safety that honest, transparent conversations build trust. They create a sense of shared purpose.

That trust starts with basic things, like letting your team know that you, too, are human and uncertain and also that you are strong and committed to figuring this thing out. Saying something like "Wow, this thing seems to get smarter everyday" or "I noticed my kid using ChatGPT to do his homework, and it made me uncomfortable" helps everyone else breathe a little easier. This approach fosters connection and shared resilience. When you admit to someone, "AI scares me," and they know they can respond honestly, that's psychological safety. It says, "You're not the only one." Modeling emotional flexibility means showing that it's OK to be overwhelmed sometimes. That doesn't mean falling apart. It means acknowledging that you're navigating something hard and still showing up.

Lee Gonzales is director of AI Transformation at the online coaching platform BetterUp, and he is a software engineer by trade. He is bullish on the upside of AI transformation and marvels at what AI allows him to do in his work. "It's like science fiction" come to life, he tells me. Gonzales has a lot of AI anxiety. "I would say my concern and trepidation with AI is so great that I have pivoted my career" to address it.[11]

Under his direction, BetterUp hosts a monthlong AI training program for employees called Flight School that begins not with AI skills but with feelings—and an invitation for employees to talk openly about their hopes, anxieties, and questions regarding AI. Gonzales wants a future in which people become the "pilots" of their AI destiny, empowered, super-knowledgeable, and in charge of the technology rather than the reverse. Otherwise, we become "passengers" vulnerable to a future that he says will be "very bad."

Five Helpful Questions to Ask Yourself and Your Team About AI Adoption

1. "What do I love about AI?"

2. "What's one way AI could improve to help me do my job better?"

3. "What scares me about AI? Personally? For my kids? For society?"

4. "Is something about the way our (company/team/industry) uses AI that makes me anxious? Angry?"

5. "Does adoption of generative AI feel aligned with my values? Are there any ways it clashes with my values?"

AI Anxiety Is Real. How You Lead Through It Is a Choice

Step 2: Create a Container and Have Good Conversations

It's tough to talk about emotions and AI in the middle of a rushed standup or distracted check-in. These conversations can happen in an everyday context, but they need time and attention. They need a "container."

In psychology, a "container" is an environment, meeting, or conversation that safely holds big emotions. The idea is that people bring tough stuff, process it in the room, and leave it in the container. Every container needs a facilitator. That's you as the leader. You can create a container in regular meetings, or you can create special meetings or one on ones that help uncertain, anxious, or angry people move through their emotions in a safe and constructive way. You are not your team's therapist, but you can help your team through tough times—or, alternatively, you can bring in an expert like a coach or someone skilled in professional development. The container is not about going through punch lists or running through urgent to-do items. The container is where your team can process emotions and discuss hard things without fear of shame.

At the beginning of the pandemic, a leader I admired gathered her global team on Zoom as lockdowns first began. She opened the meeting like this: "I can't tell you 'You got this.' What I can do is hold space for us to be together right now, to talk and figure some things out." That's a simple, powerful container.

We have to talk about AI if we're going to use it well. Disruption and AI expert Charlene Li recommends listening for the question behind the question when we talk about AI. She writes, "Behind every 'How does this work?' is a more vulnerable question. Your employees may wonder if they're still needed, what their purpose is if AI replaces key tasks, and what value they have to your organization."[12] It's the leader's job to tease out these questions from

Leading for Tomorrow

employees, honor them, and attempt to answer them as best as we can, even if we hardly feel we have the answer.

How do we preserve human agency during AI transformation while we're managing anxiety on our teams? We have to talk about it. That's a powerful action we leaders must commit to. We can create a consistent space for these conversations. After an AI training, for example, open up a dialogue about identity, purpose, and value in an AI-augmented world, suggests Li.

Here are some questions to ask yourself when creating a container:

- "Am I grounded enough to have this conversation, and how can I ground myself?"

- "What can I tell my people that's true?"

- "What can't I tell them because I don't know, or what I know is confidential."

- "How can I make space for what's uncertain?"

- "Is this better done in one-to-one settings, or is it appropriate for a team meeting or retreat?"

In Lee Gonzales's Flight School sessions with teams, he brings in issues of emotion, identity, values, and fears right up top:

It's critically important that in this space, we're going to honor psychological safety. We're going to say it is OK to express your fears, your doubts, your trepidation, to be angry, to basically say whatever you need to say. . .in this ongoing, emerging transformation of everything, everywhere, all at once. If we don't give people the space to express their feelings. . . then that just sits quietly in the background. We have to address it, because that fear is very real.[13]

267

Conversations about emotions are followed by visioning sessions and exercises in which participants imagine how their jobs could improve with AI built in, and what possibilities lie ahead for professional growth and innovation.

This work is vulnerable because it touches people's identities. "People have an attachment to their identity, and that is so deep that if you can't lever into that first, the change will never, never, never actually persist or be deep enough."

Gonzales challenges software engineers to examine their fundamental identity: Is it that they write code, or is it that they solve problems? "We talk about mindsets, and we help people set the table for processing those feelings. We take them from passenger to pilot, and in that transition, we help them understand there's so much power and capability."

The majority of the company has been through Flight School, Gonzales says, and self-reported results show a 25 percent increase in people's propensity to share AI learning, experimentation, and use cases publicly, a 22 percent increase in reprioritizing and rethinking workflows, and an 11 percent overall shift in AI mindsets and adoption.[14] These results suggest that, for many people, successfully becoming a creative and sophisticated AI user requires a mindset shift, and it starts with addressing AI anxiety.

Flight School uses an AI prompt that asks employees to consider how their values might shape the way they integrate AI into their work and lives. If a hard-earned mastery of craft is a strong value for someone, then retaining a sense of professional pride is crucial, even as AI plays a role in work. This thought "journey" with AI, Gonzales says, shows people the art of the possible with prompts.

Like many companies, BetterUp wants people to use AI to make work more efficient and to make more money. The problem, Gonzales warns, is that too many leaders think they can skip the emotions step. As he told me in an interview: "Every executive on the planet right now is going, 'I'm not seeing the bottom line, we're not making more profits, we're not delivering more product to market faster. . .' Why is that? And I think that it's because they didn't address the mindset first."

Step 3: Take Committed Action

Of course, it's not enough to uncover the emotions around AI transformation and do nothing. Your people may not expect you to promise them their jobs for life, but they expect you to have their backs in the midst of change. Plus, taking action and getting curious are two of the best ways to manage AI anxiety.

And so, before you have open conversations, offer a clear next step. The haphazard way that AI is being implemented in many organizations weakens trust, which is a strong value for many of us. As leaders, we can help buttress trust even when we have little control over macro decisions.

> As leaders, we can help buttress trust even when we have little control over macro decisions.

For example, you can get curious with your team. Illustrate how you're going to figure out this AI thing together. Maybe that's shared learning sessions, or hackathons, or time together to just ask vulnerable questions and hash things out. Maybe it's setting up a system to track, measure, and share how AI is making work better and ways that it's frustrating.

Learning is based on curiosity. If the situation warrants, you can equip people to learn new skills. In your container, you can be honest about potential consequences and intervene early to give people the tools they think they might need to stay employed. HR expert Enrique Rubio told me: "What worries me is that some companies already know which jobs are likely to disappear, but they are not saying anything. They are not giving people time to prepare or explore other options. They are not offering skill-building support or even a

AI Anxiety Is Real. How You Lead Through It Is a Choice

heads-up." Instead, says Rubio, they are waiting until the last possible moment to deliver the bad news. That kind of silence causes harm. It erodes trust. If someone leaves now to pursue a new opportunity, that is difficult. But it is far better than being told that their role will be replaced by AI with no alternatives. For most people, this reality is not imminent, but taking positive action makes us feel less anxious.

After discussing values, we can be clear about how we will take action that supports our values if something is unacceptable. Knowing that the ubiquity of gen AI might conflict with our values of professionalism and craft, for example, teams can set up shared norms around guardrails for AI use in their jobs. They can build in oversight and accountability and ensure that humans are making the final decisions. Rubio suggests telling managers what they can use AI for, "but establish that ultimately they are responsible for decisions and work product. AI cannot make final decisions."

Continue to Make Space and Repeat the Process, Over and Over

AI anxiety can't be solved in one conversation, and your team will continue to have strong feelings. I encourage you to make time for these conversations consistently and meaningfully. Doing this could be a gift not just to your team but to yourself. After all, when was the last time you felt you had space to think your thoughts? Space to have a real conversation. Space to sit with what is making you and your colleagues uncomfortable! Writing in the *Harvard Business Review*, Saïd Business School fellow Megan Reitz and researcher John Higgins write that the very best leaders allow themselves and their colleagues to inhabit spacious mode,

> *in which people pay attention more expansively, without hurry, making them more receptive to relationships, interdependencies, and possibilities. . . .Spacious mode leads to*

critical benefits in the workplace, *such as gaining insight into challenges, thinking strategically, spotting opportunities, building relationships, and sparking joy and motivation.*[15]

Your container can do that.

The media often refers to the "AI arms race," and indeed, the race to "win at AI" preoccupies our government, our companies, and our leadership mandates and OKRs (objectives and key results). Few are taking any time to pause and reflect. AI dominance might be a race, but we know that the very best competitors care for their minds and bodies while competing. They reflect and review their performance. Oftentimes they slow down to get stronger.

Understand the emotions AI surfaces, identify the values underneath your emotions, and choose actions that align with those values. Start with yourself, then create containers where people can talk honestly, ask vulnerable questions, and take committed action together—reskilling, setting norms, and mapping what you know about the future together. Be transparent about what you know and don't know, keep humans accountable for decisions, and help people shift from AI passengers to AI pilots. Most of all, make space and repeat the process, so you normalize emotions, build trust, and sustain a shared purpose through ongoing disruption. If there were ever a change that needed some good, spacious conversations, AI transformation is it.

As leaders, we have the power to slow down for just a bit and make space, for uncomfortable emotions and for anxieties, yes, but also to pause and consider what's possible for a better future.

Notes

1. Brian Merchant, "AI Killed My Job: Tech Workers," *Blood in the Machine* [Blog], June 25, 2025. www.bloodinthemachine.com/p/how-ai-is-killing-jobs-in-the-tech-f39

AI Anxiety Is Real. How You Lead Through It Is a Choice

2. Ziyaad Bhorat, "Automation Anxiety: And a Right to Freedom from Automated Systems and AI," Carr Center for Human Rights Policy, Harvard Kennedy School, October 2, 2023, issue 2023-02. www .hks.harvard.edu/sites/default/files/2023-11/23_DiscussionPaper_ Bhorat_R.pdf. Quotes from an email interview with the author, July 23, 2025.

3. Merchant, "AI Killed My Job."

4. Bhorat, "Automation Anxiety," and email interview with author.

5. https://escholarship.org/content/qt7416q0c6/qt7416q0c6_noSplash_ cd1e81789281226812202b459840f09d.pdf?t=rc6fl4

6. Ibid.

7. Merchant, "AI Killed My Job,"

8. Lulu Garcia-Navarro, "Brené Brown on How to Lead with Vulnerability at Work," *The Interview* [a podcast from the *New York Times*], September 6, 2025. www.youtube.com/watch?v=6t6-npk5_9U.

9. Sreejith Balasubramanian and Cedwyn Fernandes, "Confirmation of a Crisis Leadership Model and Its Effectiveness: Lessons from the COVID-19 Pandemic," *Cogent Business & Management* December 2021 9, no. 1 (2022). https://doi.org/10.1080/23311975.2021.2022824

10. Ranjay Gulati, "Now Is the Time for Courage," *Harvard Business Review* (September–October 2025). https://hbr.org/2025/09/now-is-the-time-for-courage

11. Morra Aarons-Mele, "Exploring AI Anxiety with a Leader in Charge of AI Transformation with Lee Gonzales," *The Anxious Achiever* [podcast episode 274], December 2, 2025. https://podcasts.apple.com/us/podcast/exploring-ai-anxiety-with-a-leader-in-charge/id1480904163?i= 1000739260612

12. Charlene Li, "Addressing AI Fears Head On," LinkedIn, July 21, 2025. www.linkedin.com/pulse/addressing-ai-fears-head-on-charlene-li-pb0je/

13. This and the next quotes from Gonzales are from Aarons-Mele, "Exploring AI Anxiety with a Leader in Charge of AI Transformation with Lee Gonzales."

Leading for Tomorrow

14. Lee Gonzales, "How AI Flight School Is Driving AI Transformation at BetterUp," LinkedIn. www.linkedin.com/posts/leegonzales_i-have-shared-with-you-before-how-we-here-activity-7369821390553669632-idz7/. Also, Aarons-Mele, "Exploring AI Anxiety with a Leader in Charge of AI Transformation with Lee Gonzales," and emails between Aarons-Mele and Gonzales.

15. Megan Reitz and John Higgins, "The Best Leaders Encourage 'Spacious Thinking,'" *Harvard Business Review*, July 1, 2025. https://hbr.org/2025/07/the-best-leaders-encourage-spacious-thinking

AI Anxiety Is Real. How You Lead Through It Is a Choice

Chapter 21

300 Years of Market Shocks, One Clear Lesson

Safi Bahcall

All apex innovators are alike; every doomed company is doomed in its own way.

One advantage of having written a book that has traveled far beyond the industry I cut my teeth in, biotechnology, is that over the past few years, leaders of markets whose histories and dynamics I knew little about—retail, aviation, defense, banking, investment management, legal services, entertainment, computer hardware, and so on—have invited me to get to know them and their companies better, to ask questions, and to help them figure out, for their industry, a question that I have always found fascinating: Why do some companies triumph during turbulent times, emerging as the apex innovators of their field, launching new businesses and conquering new markets, while others collapse into a puddle of regrets and recriminations? And most important, what can they as leaders do to end up as an example of the former and not the latter?

Rapid change separates not only companies into two groups—those who ride the wave of change and those left behind—but nations as well. For example, three centuries ago, China, under the Qing dynasty, and the Indian subcontinent, under the Mughal empire, dominated the world economy and trade, with just over half the world's GDP. The population of China was roughly 300 million; the Indian subcontinent 150, million. At the time, all of Western Europe totaled less than 60 million people; Great Britain, fewer than 15 million. Yet in 1842, four steam-powered British warships defeated the entire Chinese navy, ending 3,000 years of the Chinese dynasty. Not long after, the British East India Company ended nearly 1,000 years of Islamic rule in India.[1]

Fast forward two centuries. The biggest wealth creation in business over the past two decades, before AI, has been cloud services. Imagine the roughly trillion dollars of corporate spend on metal boxes and software subscriptions being funneled to just one or two service providers. A decade ago, you might have guessed that the natural owner of such a business might be the company with the best cloud engineers on the planet, which was, at the time, Google. Or the company with the most business-to-business IT relationships in the industry, which was Microsoft. Or any one of the other giants of enterprise IT—IBM, Oracle, SAP, Cisco. Yet the company that won that race was a company that sold diapers online: Amazon.

How did Amazon do it?

Experimentation at Pace and Scale

In my work with companies and my research into the rise and fall of companies and nations, I have seen many reasons large organizations fail to adapt to market shocks, whether they are technology changes (steam power, electricity, internet, hardware, software), regulatory changes (airline deregulation), or unexpected new entrants (Google into mobile OS; Amazon into cloud). I've divided those reasons into five broad categories—fear, focus, framework, friction, and fantasy (5Fs). Every company I've spent time with has some unique combination of aspects of each, strong in certain areas, weak in others.

However, in true Tolstoyan spirit, while every struggling company is different, every success story has one thing in common. That has been true from England and steam power to Amazon and cloud, Nvidia and chips, and the emerging story with OpenAI and machine learning. To me, it is the most important lesson for leaders from 300 years of market shocks.

When looking across industries and markets, the apex innovators are the ones who are able to run experiments at pace and scale without dropping the ball on their core franchise.

> Apex innovators are the ones who are able to run experiments at pace and scale without dropping the ball on their core franchise.

All four elements of that sentence matter. Each is less simple than it seems.

1. **Experiments:** Companies often fail to understand the nature of an experiment—what's a good experiment, what's a bad experiment, what's a good fail, what's a bad fail. If your management team can't clearly articulate those differences, if there's no clear framework for sourcing, curating, and funding experiments, if failed experiments are routinely punished, you have a problem.

2. **Pace:** If an experiment requires a PhD-level business plan with net present values, internal rates of return, and a marketing plan, sourcing plan, and Gantt chart, you will never achieve the pace of experimentation needed to adapt to a rapidly changing landscape. If, in contrast, your team can test a hypothesis with five days and $500, you have a chance.

3. **Scale:** What happens after an experiment works? Most large companies have mastered the art of growing a franchise. A smaller number have figured out how to create an organization

277

that can, in parallel, run experiments well. But many of even the best of those have yet to master the final step: scaling a positive outcome. Scaling requires transformation. And the first rule of transformation is this: You can't delegate transformation. That's a mistake I've seen sink many good CEOs.

4. **Franchise:** Growing a franchise requires reducing risk: delivering on time, on budget, on spec, consistently, with quality, to customers. Running experiments requires increasing risk: a willingness to try, repeatedly, experiments that will fail. If your experiments don't fail, they're not experiments; they are public displays of confirmation bias.

Managing both franchises and experiments simultaneously requires two parallel structures with two different sets of objectives and incentives. When companies drop the ball on the first, their franchise, they lose the means to fund the second, their experiments. When churn increases, margins decrease, and franchise growth stalls, it is a strong signal: Both structures will soon disappear.

Amazon has never let up on business experiments (popup stores; My Habit flash sales; auctions; restaurants; Haven health; Dash button; Fire phone; tickets; destinations; and of course—Prime, delivery trucks, AWS, and on and on). Yet it does so without sacrificing its franchise retail business, which has always run on a razor-thin operating margin that demands extraordinarily high efficiency.

Build the System for Experimentation

There is no magic wand you can wave to excel in running experiments at pace and scale. It requires building a system that addresses the root causes (again, the 5Fs: fear, focus, framework, friction, and

Leading for Tomorrow

fantasy) of why so many innovation efforts stall or simply devolve into theater: boxes on org charts, applause lines at town halls, and not much else.

This brief chapter is no place for the details of a new system, but here's one quick tip. Sometime soon someone on your team or in your company or just passing through will suggest an unexpected idea that challenges everything you are sure you know about your business, your customers, your markets. You will find yourself thinking "That's the dumbest idea I've heard in months."

Here's the suggestion. Keep that thought to yourself and let what passes through your lips, instead, be a simple question: "Interesting. What experiment might we run to test that idea?"

Note

1. For more on the connections between the history of science and technology, national innovation, and world history, see Safi Bahcall, *Loonshots: How to Nurture the Crazy Ideas That Win Wars, Cure Diseases, and Transform Industries* (St. Martin's Press, 2019), chapter 9, "Why the World Speaks English," and references therein.

Chapter 22

Escape Velocity: How to Break Away from the Logic of Your Past Success

Frans Johansson

Some 300 years ago, soon after having developed his revolutionary theory of gravity, Isaac Newton proposed a fascinating thought experiment. Imagine firing a ball from a canon perched atop a high mountain, he said. If the ball was fired with low velocity, it would fall back to Earth. This much was obvious to everyone. And if fired with more velocity, it will travel farther before landing. Also obvious.

But here is where it started to get interesting: Fire the ball with enough speed, and it will reach a state where it will continuously "fall" toward Earth while also moving forward fast enough to miss the curve of the planet, thus entering orbit. This was less obvious. Even today, the notion that the Space Station, for instance, is continuously falling seems strange to most people. Over time, however, even these objects will fall back down to Earth due to atmospheric friction slowing them down—unless they can somehow maintain their speed.

The real breakthrough insight, however, came when Newton imagined firing the ball at a *very* high speed. In such a case it would break free of Earth's gravitational pull entirely and reach escape velocity. Easily said, but harder to pull off in reality. Although we have launched close to 60,000 objects into orbit over the past six decades, the number of objects that have reached escape velocity can be counted in the hundreds. The remainder are trapped by gravity, doomed to circle Earth until they slow down enough to crash and burn. In physics, this trap is called a gravity well and it is defined as the space around a massive object where everything is pulled inexorably toward its center. To escape, you need enough speed—enough thrust—to overcome that invisible pull.

Breaking Free of the Gravity Well

In business, most companies also find themselves trapped in a gravity well created by the company's own success: entrenched processes, legacy revenue streams, cultural habits, institutional expectations, and desire to provide predictable returns. These companies maintain orbit velocity, circling the same industry, customers, and opportunities over and over. Profitable perhaps, maybe even admired by the market, yet unable to break free. Once they've made it into orbit, they can no longer escape it. They are stuck waiting only for the inevitable fall back to Earth.

But some companies do manage to break free. Take Amazon. By the early 2000s, their engineers were spending most of their time rebuilding the same basic components—servers, storage, databases—every time they wanted to launch a new feature. They solved this problem by building a shared layer of infrastructure that every team could use, a foundation that eliminated the repetitive drudgery. At first, this was purely an internal fix—a way to free Amazon's own developers to focus on innovation. But when Amazon released a version of its software tools externally, something unexpected happened: Developers everywhere loved it. The tools that helped Amazon move faster internally were solving the same problem across the entire tech world.

At a 2003 offsite at Jeff Bezos's house, the team made a decision that defied logic to nearly everyone else: A company known for selling books would now build a business selling computing power.

Leading for Tomorrow

The analysts saw a distraction, but Amazon's leaders had never believed they were in the retail business; they believed they were in the *technology* business, and retail just happened to be the first application. Amazon Web Services—AWS—was the embodiment of that belief. Today, AWS generates over $100 billion in revenue and is by far its most profitable division.

"I cannot tell you the number of times I got asked, with a quizzical look on people's faces, 'But what does this have to do with selling books?'" Adam Selipsky, CEO of AWS, told *Fortune* in 2022.[1] The answer, of course, was *nothing*.

Amazon is an example of a company that managed to escape the exceptional gravitational pull of its mega-successful retail business. The company illustrates not only that it is possible to break away from the gravity well of the legacy business, but also just how profitable this can be. For the past 20 years, our team has explored this dynamic while working with well over 500 organizations and their leaderships along with close to 10,000 teams from virtually every industry around the world. Through this work, we have not only observed what keeps companies stuck to their past but also what enables organizations to break free from it.

The concepts of escape velocity and orbital velocity provide a fresh lens for understanding how organizations navigate fast-moving markets. "Escape velocity" refers to the conditions required to break free from the existing logic of a company's business and industry. "Orbital velocity," by contrast, describes the conditions at which a company maintains its trajectory around its chosen strategic path. Leaders often struggle to distinguish between the two: Too much focus on incremental improvements can leave an organization in perpetual orbit unable to break free, while too aggressive an attempt at escape without the right conditions can lead to failure.

In this chapter, I explore the relevance of escape velocity for today's organizations, illustrating how understanding it can guide

Escape Velocity

choices in a business universe filled with accelerating change. The surprising insight is that the key differentiator between staying put and catching a ride to the future lies in very human, but rarely practiced, behaviors.

Accelerating Change

Reaching escape velocity is more important than ever, something that appears to be increasingly recognized by leaders everywhere. The reason why is because the increasing speed of change is forcing organizations to ask a very different set of questions. Twenty-five years ago, the question I heard most from leaders around the world was straightforward and remarkably similar: *"How do we create our next killer product?"*

> The increasing speed of change is forcing organizations to ask a very different set of questions.

The iPod had just changed music. The iPhone was about to change everything. Companies scrambled to follow suit and create products that could transform markets. But beneath the surface, a revolution was already underway. Within a few years, the question I kept getting had changed. Suddenly leaders were asking: *"How do we create our next killer business model?"*

Why the shift? Because products alone no longer guaranteed success. Global competition, commoditization, and fast-moving markets meant that *how* value was captured often became more important than the product itself. The focus turned toward networks, platforms, and ecosystems. Owning the interface—not the factory—became the new playbook.

Dell disrupted PCs with a direct-to-consumer, build-to-order model. Airbnb and Uber upended entire industries without owning a single hotel or taxi. Meta and Twitter amplified network effects to a global scale. Salesforce reinvented business software with SaaS subscriptions, proving that the business model itself could be revolutionary. And yet today I rarely hear either of those questions much. Today leaders are asking something completely different: *"Is the world outside our organization moving faster than we are?"*

The question is asked because the implication is terrifying: Even as the company has increased its speed of execution, it might not be enough. They are still in the same place or, worse, are falling behind. This is the organization caught in the gravity well, captured by the logic of its past successes and unable to reignite the growth and results that got it into orbit in the first place. The real challenge today isn't just building a product or inventing a business model. It's adapting—sensing change and responding before it's too late. Because if the world is moving faster than you, even your best products and business models can't save you if your organization is unable to change fast enough to make use of them.

It turns out that most leaders today fear that the answer to their question is *yes*. The world is moving faster than they are. Which immediately leads to another question: *What can they do about it?*

Escape Velocity Through M&A

Perhaps the most common approach we hear from CEOs today is their attempt to buy their way out of the gravity well. The logic is seductive: If you are stuck, acquire something faster, newer, more innovative, and ride the rocket someone else has already built. Mergers and acquisitions are one of the few visible, decisive levers CEOs have at their disposal, and so it is not surprising that they return to them when looking to make a move or feel that they have run out of options. It is also a move that a board, analyst, or investor can understand. If the acquisition does end up working out, it has the possibility of showing results faster than other approaches.

Escape Velocity

And sometimes this works. There are moments when acquisitions can accelerate growth or expand the reach of a business that has already achieved momentum. We'll return to those examples in a bit. But generally speaking, acquisitions rarely generate true escape velocity. Instead, they tend to reinforce a company staying in orbit. Why? Because every deal must make sense within the logic of the current system—approved by the same leaders, justified by the same analysts, supported by the same shareholders. Each of these forces pulls the company back toward the center of gravity. The gravitational pull of the core business—its metrics, incentives, and worldview—remains intact.

When you study companies that have broken free of their pasts—companies that have reached escape velocity—you find that almost none did it through acquisition. Their breakthrough moments came instead from developing internal capabilities powerful enough to overcome inertia. Table 22.1 outlines a range of organizations, each with its own gravitational pull, its own moment of escape, and the source of the thrust that carried them forward. These companies come from a range of industries and geographies, chosen mostly because many of them will be fairly well known to the reader. The purpose of the table is not to provide a comprehensive overview of the landscape but to illustrate just how important internal capabilities are in order to escape a company's gravity well.

One thing becomes immediately apparent: Escape velocity rarely comes from simply acquiring another company, no matter how logical that appears to be. It comes from the hard, disciplined work of building and exploiting internal capabilities. For not a single one of these fairly well-known examples was the escape velocity a function of a major acquisition. Instead, internal capability provided the machine and fuel. AWS started as an internal project to help internal developers; it ended up becoming by far their most profitable division. Netflix had already disrupted the world of video rentals once, but the idea that it had to do so again was all from internal capability.

286

Leading for Tomorrow

Company	Gravitational Pull (What they were bound by)	Escape Velocity Moment (When they broke free)	Primary Driver (M&A or internal capability)
Adobe	Boxed software licenses	Transition to SaaS (Creative Cloud)	Internal capability
Amazon	Online retail	AWS launch	Internal capability
Apple	Personal computers	iPod to iPhone	Internal capability
Disney	Dependence on third-party distribution (theaters/cable)	Disney+streaming platform	Internal capability augmented with M&A
NVIDIA	Graphics hardware for gaming	GPU repositioned for AI/deep learning	Internal capability
IBM	Hardware/mainframes	Shift toward services, software, and enterprise solutions	Internal capability
Microsoft	Software licensing (Windows/Office)	Cloud-first/mobile-first strategy under Nadella	Internal capability augmented with M&A
Fujifilm	Photographic film/analog imaging	Pivot into healthcare, diagnostics, semiconductor materials	Internal capability

(continued)

Company	Gravitational Pull (What they were bound by)	Escape Velocity Moment (When they broke free)	Primary Driver (M&A or internal capability)
Siemens	Traditional industrial hardware and automation	Digital platform "Siemens Xcelerator" and software/services push	Internal capability
Best Buy	Consumer electronics retail conventional format	Transforming retail floors into tech service hubs with digital integration	Internal capability
Netflix	DVD rental business	Self-disruption: pivot to streaming and original content creation	Internal capability
Zoom	Enterprise video conferencing (Cisco/WebEx)	Cloud-native video platform	Internal capability/ founder left
Bumble	Tinder and traditional dating apps	Women-first dating platform	Internal capability/ founder left

Escape velocity rarely comes from simply acquiring another company.

Even when acquisitions later amplify this type of growth, the core capability that made escape possible was homegrown. Even in these cases, M&A did *not* act alone. It worked because the incumbent already had sufficient internal capability to integrate, scale, and leverage the acquired asset. M&A was an amplifier, not the sole engine. For instance, when Disney acquired Marvel and later Lucasfilm, it dramatically expanded the content/IP library and enabled Disney to become a platform-era entertainment company. Disney was able to use M&A to shift its center of gravity from theatrical distribution to streaming. When Microsoft acquired LinkedIn, it helped the company accelerate its existing push toward a new business model based on cloud and networks. Some other observations also stand out:

- **Contrary to popular belief, incumbents can absolutely escape the gravity well.** This is great news. Fujifilm started its journey into medical imaging in the 1980s and was able to expand its healthcare presence significantly, growing beyond its original market of film. IBM has managed to resist the pull of gravity at least twice—once from hardware to services and then again to software.

- **In some cases, the engine to reach escape velocity emerged outside the incumbent walls.** Founders like Eric Yuan of Zoom or Whitney Wolfe Herd of Bumble carried deep experience from established firms, Cisco and Tinder, respectively, and used it as a launchpad to create new businesses. They both cited repeatedly in interviews that they were blocked (in different ways) from pursuing their ideas. Their success raises a provocative question: If their former organizations had cultivated cultures that valued these insights—if they had created environments open enough for new ideas to thrive—might those breakthroughs have happened from within?

In nearly every case, the force that a company had to escape was the very thing that once made it successful. For Apple, it was the

In nearly every case, the force that a company had to escape was the very thing that once made it successful.

personal computer. For Amazon, online retail. For Disney, traditional distribution. For Netflix, DVD rental business. Their escape velocity moment came when they stopped optimizing the old engine and started building a new one. But if M&A is not the answer, we must look toward internal capabilities and get a handle on which ones really make a difference.

Escape Velocity Through Internal Capability

A consistent difference between companies that reach escape velocity and those that don't is where they place their trust. The former rely on their people's actions and behaviors to break new ground; the latter depend on technology, organizational design, channel strategy, and other mechanisms to do so. While these latter elements are all important, if you let them lead your efforts to break away, you will almost certainly fail—because the choices you make in these areas will only reinforce your current orbital path. To truly escape it, your people must lead the way through their actions and behaviors. But which actions and which behaviors?

Our firm has worked with organizations from every industry to introduce a number of simple, repeatable behaviors on platforms that drive rapid adoption. We call these behaviors MOVES. Aside from enabling companies to quickly scale new ways of working, they can also be tested and measured. Our analysis shows that companies that break away use similar MOVES that can be grouped into four overarching capabilities (outlined in Figure 22.1). Together these capabilities provide the best chance for companies to escape the logic and gravitational pull of their current operations and create new growth vehicles.

Leading for Tomorrow

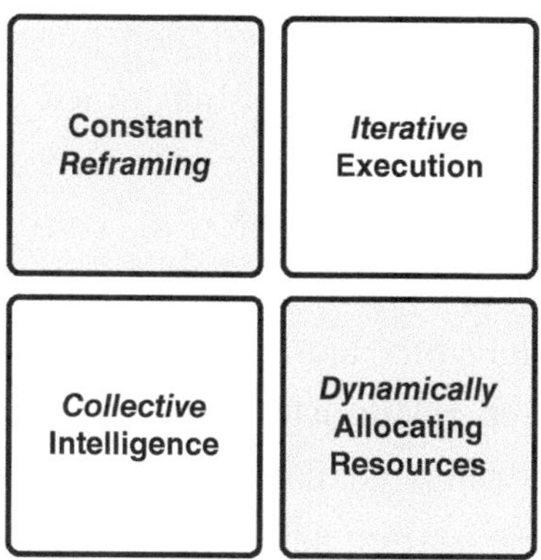

Figure 22.1 The MOVES Capabilities

Constant Reframing

Every leader, team, and organization must constantly be willing to reframe what success is, and how they intend to achieve it, because of the accelerating speed of change. This is especially true for organizations that wish to escape their own gravitational pull. Why? Because the seeds for such a breakout are almost always present within current activities and operations. These often-hidden seeds—whether a niche customer base, an experimental prototype, an unexpected use case, an unofficial workaround, or a stashed-away consumer complaint—rarely align with current goals, priorities, or stated outcomes. Recognizing and acting on them requires the ability to reframe these elements to understand the new opportunity and then dare to pursue it.

Take NVIDIA. For years, the company focused obsessively on rendering the most realistic graphics possible for gamers, building chips that could perform thousands of calculations simultaneously. What NVIDIA didn't realize was that the same architecture powering virtual worlds was also ideally suited for teaching machines to see, listen, and think. The seeds of the company's next revolution were already in their hands; it just had to redefine what success meant. When researchers began using NVIDIA GPUs for deep learning, the company didn't dismiss it as an anomaly; they reframed their purpose from powering games to powering intelligence. That shift turned a gaming company into the backbone of the AI era.

This capability is not only required at a senior, strategic level. Ideally, people everywhere should be asking themselves whether they are solving the right problem, or whether there is another way to think about an asset, relationship, or technology. In the startup world, these reframes often go hand in hand with pivots and survival. Slack, for example, started as a gaming company with a mediocre game. Its internal messaging system, however, became the foundation of the company's real growth engine.

In larger corporations, this behavior cannot be counted on to occur spontaneously; it requires practice and reinforcement. It's not enough for leaders to ask teams to shift their thinking; people need the experience and capability to both conceive and execute these reframes. This makes it easier for an organization to align around new opportunities. We've seen companies reframe simple existing products and customers, representing a fraction of their operations, into billion-dollar verticals in just a few years. At Apple, engineers had been prototyping iPad-like devices for years. But it was only when they reframed the use case for their multitouch interface technology and applied it to a mobile phone that the company could rally behind a transformative product.

Iterative Execution

Most organizations still operate under the assumption that accurate planning and forecasting are the keys to executing strategy and capturing opportunities. Yet we frequently see three-year strategic plans that are effectively out of date within just two quarters. The illusion of control shatters quickly in a world of accelerating change. Consider generative AI, for example. A question on everyone's mind today is deceptively simple: Will AI, on the whole, cut jobs or create them? But even experts with deep experience cannot agree on the answer. And if they disagree on something so fundamental, how much practical value does all this planning really have?

Instead, organizations should focus on resolving the key uncertainties in a plan as quickly as possible before committing significant resources. Fundamentally, there are only two ways to address the uncertainties inherent in innovation: Either place many bets in the hope that some will succeed or iterate intensively on a single bet.

While the most effective approach is often a combination of the two, most organizations struggle to place more than a few new bets at a time. This means that iterative execution becomes the real differentiator. At NVIDIA, for instance, when researchers began using its gaming GPUs to train neural networks, engineers ran countless experiments—rewriting code, reshaping chip architectures, and building small prototypes that failed as often as they succeeded. Each iteration revealed another insight: GPUs weren't just for rendering pixels; they could recognize patterns and learn.

The ability to shift from long-term planning to iterative execution is absolutely critical when aiming to reach escape velocity. Such efforts often require significant resources, and justifying that spend becomes easier once early failures have been worked through, but the idea still proves valid. The more frequently an organization iterates, the higher the likelihood it will discover what works. The faster it iterates, the faster it learns.

Dynamically Allocating Resources

Once an investment has proven its potential, however, many companies face the opposite challenge: They hesitate to fully pursue the implications of that bet. Even after validating a new opportunity, organizations often struggle to shift resources, attention, and priorities toward areas of growth. This reluctance is rarely about a lack of vision; it is often cultural or structural. Teams need to be ready, aligned, and empowered to move decisively. The ability to swiftly reallocate capital, talent, and focus is a key determinant of whether a promising insight will actually transform the business or fade into unrealized potential. Without this capability, the very investments meant to fuel growth can become stagnant experiments, trapped by inertia, bureaucracy, or fear of risk.

Once NVIDIA had validated its insights around AI, the company moved to double down with conviction. It invested billions into creating a full AI ecosystem—chips, systems, developer tools, and partnerships that amplified one another. The launch of DGX servers, CUDA libraries, and global programs like NVIDIA Inception ensured that startups and researchers alike would grow on its hardware. This was not diversification; it was concentration. Jensen Huang and his team focused their energy on the one initiative they had seen enough evidence to believe would explode in the future. By daring to leave the gravitational pull of gaming behind, they could reallocate priorities, resources, attention, and even corporate reputation toward an entirely new trajectory. The genius wasn't in predicting the future perfectly; it was in recognizing, early and decisively, that the seeds of that future were already in their hands—and committing fully to it.

Again, this capability cannot sit solely with the executive leadership team. If the culture does not value these shifts, the organization will either fracture, because it has a difficult time accepting winners and losers in the resource game, or, perhaps even worse, instinctively resist change. Budget lines revert to legacy products. Innovation gets smothered by meetings, metrics, and approvals. On paper, the company may appear to be investing in the future. In reality, it is protecting the past. True transformation requires both decisive leadership and a culture that can flex, reallocate, and act on validated bets without fear or hesitation.

Collective Intelligence

Reaching escape velocity is not solely about reframing, iterating, or shifting resources; it also requires doing all of those things in a creative manner. Opportunities are discovered when breaking down silos between functions and divisions and/or by combining technologies and assets in new, unique ways. The ability to iterate, particularly under tight resource constraints, improves when your team has a diversity of perspectives, networks, and backgrounds. And it is easier to double down if you are sure you are making the right decision; the chances of that happening go up when you bring together people from different points of view.

> Reaching escape velocity is not solely about reframing, iterating, or shifting resources.

To break free, in other words, organizations must unleash what I call the Medici Effect: the power that arises when diverse perspectives collide, recombine, and generate insights no single individual or even team could foresee. Capturing this intelligence requires looking beyond functional, regional, or divisional boundaries, and even outside the company itself. Ideas from unexpected places—another department, a different geography, a partner ecosystem, or a customer—can be the spark for entirely new directions.

But capturing diverse perspectives is not enough. People must be able to actively seek them out and recombine them into actionable insights. Doing this requires both curiosity and discipline: the willingness to explore ideas that initially feel foreign or misaligned, and the ability to translate them into experiments, prototypes, or strategic shifts.

At NVIDIA, researchers began to experiment with using GPUs for scientific computing in the mid- to late 2000s. One of the early pioneers was Andrew Ng at Stanford, who discovered that GPUs could train neural networks dozens of times faster than CPUs. At the same time, researchers at the University of Toronto were exploring deep learning and needed massive computational power—they too turned to NVIDIA GPUs. It was the ideas emanating from an intersection of different disciplines, perspectives, and functions that set the stage for NVIDIA to eventually break free from gaming and reach for the stars (again).

For companies aiming to escape their own gravitational pull, collective intelligence is a multiplier: The more perspectives captured, the richer the opportunity space, the higher the probability of breakthrough innovation. Without a culture that actively values diverse insights, organizations risk repeating the same patterns, defaulting to familiar approaches, and ultimately protecting the past rather than creating the future.

The Future

Every successful organization has had to figure out how to launch itself into orbit and stay there. Far fewer organizations have successfully figured out how to escape from this orbit without crashing back down to Earth. The time has come for this to change. When every company faces the pull of its own gravity, the true advantage lies not in prediction but in propulsion and acceleration. We know more about what it takes to reach escape velocity—and sustain it—than ever before. The answer resides with the capabilities we have built. It's time to start building them.

Note

1. Geoff Colvin, "How Amazon Grew an Awkward Side Project into AWS, a Behemoth That's Now 4 Times Bigger than Its Original Shopping Business," *Fortune*, November 30, 2022. https://fortune.com/longform/amazon-web-services-ceo-adam-selipsky-cloud-computing/

About the Editors and Contributors

About the Editors

Scott Barry Kaufman is a humanistic psychologist exploring the depths of human potential. He is the director of the Center for Human Potential and founder of Self-Actualization Coaching. Scott has authored 11 books, including *Rise Above, Choose Growth* (with Jordyn Feingold), *Transcend, Wired to Create* (with Carolyn Gregoire), and *Ungifted.* He received a PhD in cognitive psychology from Yale University and has taught at Columbia University, Yale, New York University, the University of Pennsylvania, and elsewhere.

Scott hosted *The Psychology Podcast* for 11 years, accumulating over 30 million downloads and earning a spot on *Business Insider*'s list of "9 podcasts that will change how you think about human behavior." He is among the top 1 percent of the most cited scientists in the world, and, in 2015, *Business Insider* named him one of "50 groundbreaking scientists who are changing the way we see the world."

Chris Shipley is an author, entrepreneur, mentor, and catalyst, working at the intersection of innovation, technology, and leadership. She has documented, influenced, and predicted the impact of technology on business and society for 40 years as a journalist, industry analyst, and business strategist. As the executive producer of the DEMO conference for over a decade, Chris identified and introduced to the market game-changing companies such as WebEx, salesforce.com, VMWare, Audible, and Roku.

Today, Chris focuses on the human and organizational challenges caused by technology-driven change and economic disruption. She is the author of four books, most recently as coauthor with Heather McGowan of *The Adaptation Advantage*, which explores issues of identity and leadership in the future of work, and *The Empathy Advantage*, which argues for much-needed organizational and leadership changes in a postpandemic world.

About the Contributors

Dr. Jennifer Aaker is a behavioral scientist whose work explores how purpose, meaning, and technology shape well-being. The General Atlantic Professor at Stanford Graduate School of Business and a recipient of the Distinguished Scientific Achievement Award, MBA Professor of the Year Award, and the Paul D. Converse Award, Jennifer's work shapes technologies and lives that amplify human values, designing an AI-powered future that fuels human flourishing. Jennifer's research has been featured in *The Economist*, *The Wall Street Journal*, *The New York Times*, *The Atlantic*, and *Science*. She is the coauthor of the global bestsellers *Humor, Seriously* and *The Dragonfly Effect*, translated into over 20 languages. Her goal is to help leaders cultivate purpose, connection, and joy in their work and lives.

Morra Aarons-Mele is on a mission to make work better for everyone, especially high achievers who feel like they don't fit the mold. Through her writing, workshops, and coaching, Morra helps leaders identify their strengths, honor their neurodivergence or mental health challenges, and build healthier ways of working. An anxious achiever herself, Morra believes that taking your mental health seriously is a leadership strength. A former political consultant, she founded and sold the firm Women Online/The Mission List, ran campaigns for organizations from Obama for America to the Gates Foundation to the CDC, and has spent her career helping major institutions change minds and behaviors.

Morra hosts *The Anxious Achiever* podcast and is the award-winning author of *The Anxious Achiever*. She lives in Boston with her family and menagerie.

Scott D. Anthony is a clinical professor of strategy at the Tuck School of Business at Dartmouth College, where his research and teaching focus on disruptive change. Before moving to academia, he spent more than 20 years at Innosight, a growth strategy consulting company cofounded by Harvard Business School professor Clayton Christensen. Scott is a prolific writer. His most recent book, *Epic Disruptions: Eleven Innovations that Shaped Our Modern World*, explores 11 transformative breakthroughs that have changed the world. His previous books include *Seeing What's Next*, *The Little Black Book of Innovation*, *Dual Transformation*, and *Eat, Sleep, Innovate*. Thinkers50 honored Scott with its innovation award in 2017 and named him the world's ninth most influential thinker in 2023. Scott has a BA in economics from Dartmouth College, an MBA from Harvard Business School, and an Executive Master in Change from INSEAD.

Safi Bahcall is a physicist, former public company CEO, biotechnology entrepreneur, and best-selling author of *Loonshots: Nurture the Crazy Ideas that Win Wars, Cure Diseases, and Transform Industries*. Safi received his BA from Harvard summa cum laude, completed his PhD in physics at Stanford, and served for three years as a consultant at McKinsey and Company. In 2001, he founded a biotechnology company developing new drugs for cancer. He led the company's IPO and served as its CEO for 13 years. In 2008, he was named E&Y New England Biotechnology Entrepreneur of the Year.

In 2011, he worked with President Obama's Council of Science Advisors (PCAST) on the future of national research. He currently works with CEOs and leadership teams on innovation and strategy and is completing the research for his next book.

Chip Conley is a hospitality pioneer, best-selling author, and midlife visionary. He founded the boutique hotel company Joie de Vivre Hospitality, transforming an inner-city motel into one of the United States' most inventive hotel brands. Later, he joined Airbnb as Head of Global Hospitality & Strategy, guiding the startup into a global powerhouse. Drawing on those experiences, he founded the Modern Elder Academy, the world's first "midlife wisdom school," dedicated to reframing aging as a time of growth, purpose, and creativity with campuses in Baja, Mexico, and Santa Fe, NM. Chip writes and speaks about the intersection of business, psychology, and meaning. His eight books include *PEAK*, *Emotional Equations*, *Wisdom@Work*, and *Learning to Love Midlife*. He motivates individuals and organizations to embrace curiosity, wisdom, and intergenerational collaboration.

Nancy Duarte is CEO of Duarte, Inc. and the author of six best-selling books that have shaped the field of business communication. Founded in 1988, Duarte, Inc., has advised the world's top brands and executives, transforming those insights into training delivered globally. A renowned persuasion expert, Nancy pioneered the integration of story patterns into business communication, making her a sought-after voice for leaders navigating change. Her work has been featured in *Fortune, Forbes, Wired, Fast Company, The Wall Street Journal, The New York Times*, and CNN. She speaks at organizations like Apple, Google, Microsoft, LinkedIn, and Pfizer. Her TED talk has been viewed over 3.5 million times.

About the Editors and Contributors

Nancy contributes regularly to the *Harvard Business Review, MIT Sloan*, and *Forbes*, and her ideas are taught at Stanford, Harvard, and leading business schools worldwide. Recognized as an international expert, she continues to redefine how leaders inspire action.

Amy C. Edmondson is best known for her groundbreaking work on psychological safety in the workplace. She is the Novartis Professor of Leadership and Management at the Harvard Business School, a chair established to support the study of human interactions that lead to the creation of successful enterprises that contribute to the betterment of society. Recognized by the biannual Thinkers50 global ranking of management thinkers since 2011, Amy was ranked #1 by that organization in 2021 and 2023. Amy was inducted into the American Academy of Arts and Sciences in 2024 and has published over 60 scholarly articles and seven books. Her most recent book, *The Right Kind of Wrong*, won the *Financial Times* and Schroders Business Book of the Year. She earned her PhD in organizational behavior, AM in psychology, and AB in engineering and design from Harvard University.

Hal Gregersen has dedicated his extensive career to creating cultures of fearless inquiry and helping leaders transform their organizations into innovative powerhouses. He is a senior lecturer in leadership and innovation at MIT's Sloan School of Management, a former executive director of the MIT Leadership Center, a fellow at Innosight, and a cofounder of the Innovator's DNA consulting group. Hal is the author of the Nautilus award-winning book, *Questions Are the Answer: A Breakthrough Approach to Your Most Vexing Problems at Work and in Life*. He coauthored, with Clayton Christensen and Jeff Dyer, *The Innovator's DNA: Mastering the Five Skills of Disruptive Innovators*, a guide to cultivating the discovery skills that CEOs and entrepreneurs rely on to build and guide

About the Editors and Contributors

sustainably creative companies. He is ranked as one of the world's 20 most influential management thinkers by Thinkers50 and is the winner of the 2017 Distinguished Achievement Award for leadership.

John Hagel has spent over 40 years in Silicon Valley as a management consultant, author, speaker, and entrepreneur. His most recent ventures, Beyond Our Edge, LLC and the Center for Growth, deliver strategic consulting and programs built on his lifetime of work in transformation, growth, and leadership. He is the author of eight books, most recently, the acclaimed *The Journey Beyond Fear.* Throughout his career, John has collaborated with leaders of major institutions worldwide. As a partner at Deloitte, he led the global Center for the Edge. He was a partner at McKinsey & Company, where he helped lead its Strategy Practice and helped establish the firm's Silicon Valley office. He also served as Senior Vice President of Strategy at Atari, Inc. and founded two Silicon Valley startups. John teaches at Singularity University and serves on the Board of Trustees of the Santa Fe Institute, a leading center for research on complex adaptive systems.

Jonathan Haidt is on a mission to help people understand each other, live and work near each other, and even learn from each other despite their moral differences. A social psychologist at New York University's Stern School of Business, his research uncovers the intuitive foundations of morality and how morality varies across cultures, including the cultures of progressives, conservatives, and libertarians. Since 2018, he has been studying the contributions of social media to the decline of teen mental health and the rise of political dysfunction. He is the author of several *New York Times* best-selling books, including *The Anxious Generation: How the Great Rewiring of Childhood Is Causing an Epidemic of Mental Illness; The Righteous Mind: Why Good People Are Divided by*

About the Editors and Contributors

Politics and Religion; and *The Coddling of the American Mind: How Good Intentions and Bad Ideas Are Setting Up a Generation for Failure* (coauthored with Greg Lukianoff).

Sophie Hamilton explores how AI can help unlock human potential, support artists and innovators, and open the doors to creativity for everyone. In her roles at Spotify, where she leads business development, and Stanford University Graduate School of Business, she shares her work on humanity in the age of AI with audiences around the world—from Google and the United Nations to the most intimidating group of all: middle schoolers. At Stanford, Sophie is authoring a body of research with Dr. Jennifer Aaker, centered on architecting AI for better sustainability outcomes within ourselves, teams, and the planet. She lectures on this topic in corporate and educational settings.

Sophie has helped raise over $1 million for cancer research and partnered with global brands like Nike and Mastercard to build more inclusive futures.

Frans Johansson's ideas and insights offer an indispensable perspective on the issues of the day that impact business, global competitiveness, and innovation. His views and ethos are articulated in his books, *The Medici Effect*, which proves the power of innovation at the intersection of diverse fields, industries, and disciplines; and *The Click Moment*, which rewrites the rules for success in an increasingly unpredictable world. His fifth company, Medici Next, works with global brands, including Disney, Nike, Novartis, Pfizer, Under Armour, and HSBC, among an array of diverse industry leaders. Over the last 15 years, Frans has brought his books to life, inspiring audiences worldwide with his provocative, often counterintuitive ideas while impelling action with methods and tools now implemented by over 5,000 teams worldwide.

303

Whitney Johnson is the CEO and cofounder of Disruption Advisors, a leadership development company that helps organizations operationalize a growth mindset in their leaders and teams. A cofounder of the Disruptive Innovation Fund with Harvard's Clayton Christensen and an award-winning stock analyst on Wall Street, she now applies her understanding of momentum and growth in stocks to people and teams. Her *S Curve* model gives leaders and their teams a shared language to create positive change across their organization. Whitney was named a 2021 Top #10 Business Thinker by Thinkers50 and is a globally recognized thought leader, keynote speaker, executive coach, and consultant. A LinkedIn Top Voice since 2019 with 1.7 million followers, Whitney is the author of the best-selling *Smart Growth: How to Grow Your People to Grow Your Company*. In 2025, she received the ATD Talent Development Thought Leader Award, recognizing her pioneering work in leadership and talent development.

Tom Kelley helps organizations unlock creativity, build human-centered cultures, and lead innovation. For more than three decades, he helped lead IDEO, the design and innovation firm known for its human-centered approach and creative problem solving. He is the author of the best-selling books *Creative Confidence* and *The Art of Innovation*. Tom is the founder and advisor at Design for Ventures (D4V), a Tokyo-based VC firm that works closely with early-stage Japanese entrepreneurs and has supported more than 60 startups. His work in Tokyo led to a feature story on the cover of *Forbes Japan*.

Tom is committed to supporting the next generation of leaders and served as the first Executive Fellow at UC Berkeley's Haas School of Business, later holding the same title at the University of Tokyo. He has spoken in more than 30 countries on creativity, design, and human-centered leadership.

About the Editors and Contributors

Rita McGrath, one of the world's top experts on strategic inflection points, is consistently ranked among the top 10 management thinkers in the world by the prestigious Thinkers50. She is a trusted partner and advisor in the C-suites of many of the country's biggest and most well-known companies—especially as they work to grow, evolve, and reinvent themselves. Rita is known for her energy, positivity, storytelling, and ability to connect with audiences. She is the best-selling author of five books on leadership, business, and organizational management, including *Seeing Around Corners: How to Spot Inflection Points in Business Before They Happen,* and is a sought-after corporate speaker, a longtime educator at Columbia Business School, and the author and host of the popular podcast and newsletter *Thought Sparks,* available on YouTube.

Jacqueline Novogratz is the founder and CEO of Acumen, a global organization that fights poverty and builds dignity through patient investment in companies and leaders. She pioneered the concept of patient capital and, through Acumen, has impacted more than 700 million lives across Africa, South Asia, Latin America, and the United States. Under her leadership, Acumen manages over $500 million in investments and has trained nearly 2,000 social innovators through Acumen Academy. A serial social entrepreneur, Jacqueline cofounded Rwanda's first microfinance bank and founded the Philanthropy Workshop and Next Generation Leaders program while at the Rockefeller Foundation. She began her career in international banking with Chase Manhattan Bank. She is the author of *The Blue Sweater* and *Manifesto for a Moral Revolution* and has been recognized by Forbes as one of the "100 Greatest Living Business Minds." She holds an MBA from Stanford and a BA from the University of Virginia.

About the Editors and Contributors

Jean Oelwang is the founding CEO of Virgin Unite, an entrepreneurial foundation that builds leadership collectives, incubates ideas, and reinvents systems for a better world. As part of her work over the last three decades, Jean has helped corporations put the well-being of people and the planet at their core, including working with over 25 Virgin businesses across 15 industries to help embed purpose in all they do. Over the last 20 years, she has worked with partners to lead the incubation and start-up of several global initiatives, including The Elders, The B Team, The Carbon War Room (successfully merged with the RMI), The Africa Partners Collective, Ocean Unite (now ORRAA), The Caribbean Climate-Smart Accelerator, 100% Human at Work, The Virgin Unite Constellation, Generations Unit, and The Planetary Guardians, where she is the founding CEO. Jean spent 17 years living and working on six continents to start and help lead mobile phone companies. She was the joint CEO of Virgin Mobile in Australia before starting Virgin Unite.

April Rinne is a change navigator: She helps individuals and organizations rethink and reshape their relationships with change, uncertainty, and a world in flux. She is a trusted advisor to well-known startups and companies, financial institutions, non-profits, and think tanks worldwide. April is the author of *Flux: 8 Superpowers for Thriving in Constant Change*. A graduate of Harvard Law School, April has been weaving a story about how to thrive amid flux for as long as she can remember, drawing on her history as a futurist, advisor, global development executive, microfinance lawyer, investor, mental health advocate, and inveterate traveler (100+ countries). She harnesses her very personal experiences with flux, including the death of both of her parents in a car accident when she was 20. Through her travels and tragedy, vision and values, global perspective and grounded sense of purpose, April helps

About the Editors and Contributors

others better understand how we see, think about, struggle with, and ultimately forge positive relationships with change.

Sanyin Siang helps future-forward leaders optimize their unique strengths and build super teams for thriving in uncertain, ambiguous times. CEOs, boards, sports industry leaders, tech founders, and executive teams seek out her insights on activating human-centric leadership. At Duke University, Sanyin leads its Coach K Leadership & Ethics Center at the Fuqua School of Business and is a professor at its Pratt School of Engineering. Recognized by Thinkers50 as the world's most influential executive coach and mentor (2019), she was inducted into the Coaching Legends Hall of Fame in 2023. She shares her thought leadership with more than 1 million followers on LinkedIn and through the Coaching for the Future Forward Leader Advice Column for *MIT Sloan Management Review* and The Last Word Column for *Dialogue Review*, The Launch Book, and her newsletter: https://leadershipplaybook.substack.com

Brian Solis is a globally recognized independent digital analyst and anthropologist. In his role as head of Global Innovation at ServiceNow, Brian sets the strategic direction and programming for ServiceNow's Innovation and Executive Briefing Centers in Silicon Valley, New York, London, Paris, Sydney, and Singapore. He is an award-winning author of eight best-selling books including *X: The Experience When Business Meets Design; What's the Future of Business*; and *The End of Business as Usual*. In his latest book, *Lifescale: How to Live a More Creative, Productive and Happy Life*, Brian tackles the struggles of living in a world rife with constant digital distractions. His model for "Lifescaling" helps readers overcome the unforeseen consequences of living a digital life to break away from diversions, focus on what's important, spark newfound creativity, and unlock new possibilities.

About the Editors and Contributors

Lisa Kay Solomon brings both strategic rigor and human warmth to helping others build the futures they are excited to live in. A Futurist in Residence and lecturer at the Stanford University's Hasso Plattner Institute of Design (the d.school), Lisa is a strategic foresight designer and award-winning innovator who believes we're all capable of imagining and designing better futures. Her popular classes help students build the skills they don't yet know they need.

Lisa coauthored the best-selling books *Moments of Impact: How to Design Strategic Conversations that Accelerate Change* and *Design a Better Business*. Her LinkedIn Learning class "Leader as Futurist" has reached over 130,000 learners worldwide, and she is the host of a popular new podcast called *How We Future*." Lisa is on the board of The Long Now Foundation and has built multiple programs and workshops that infuse long-term thinking into classrooms and boardrooms.

Zeynep Ton focuses her work on helping organizations design systems that delight customers, provide meaningful and well-paying frontline jobs, and drive productivity and growth. She is a professor of the practice at the MIT Sloan School of Management and the cofounder and president of the nonprofit Good Jobs Institute. She has received numerous teaching awards at MIT Sloan and Harvard Business School. Her research has been published in leading journals and has been widely featured in the media.

Zeynep is the author of two books: *The Good Jobs Strategy: How the Smartest Companies Invest in Employees to Lower Costs and Boost Profits* and *The Case for Good Jobs: How Great Companies Bring Dignity, Pay, and Meaning to Everyone's Work*. Originally from Turkey, Zeynep came to the United States on a volleyball scholarship to Penn State, earning an engineering degree, and later a DBA from Harvard Business School.

About the Editors and Contributors

Caroline Webb specializes in showing people how to transform their life and work for the better by applying insights from the behavioral sciences (behavioral economics, psychology, and neuroscience). Her book, *How to Have a Good Day: Harness the Power of Behavioral Science to Transform Your Working Life*, was hailed by Forbes as one of their "must-read business books" and by Inc. magazine as one of the "best 15 leadership and personal development books of the past five years." Caroline was named one of the top 50 executive coaches in the world on Thinkers50's inaugural "Coaches50" list.

During her 12 years at McKinsey & Company, Caroline cofounded McKinsey's leadership practice and specialized in helping leaders achieve transformational change in their organizations and teams. She also founded and remains a faculty member of McKinsey's flagship leadership development course for senior female executives. Caroline is originally from the United Kingdom and has degrees in economics from Cambridge and Oxford universities.

Chris Yeh lives by his personal mission: help interesting people do interesting things. He is the coauthor, with Reid Hoffman, of *Blitzscaling*, the book that explains how to build world-changing companies like Amazon, Alibaba, and Airbnb in record time, and the *New York Times* bestseller *The Alliance*, with Reid Hoffman and Ben Casnocha, that teaches managers how to recruit, manage, and retain entrepreneurial employees. A writer, investor, and entrepreneur, Chris has had a ringside seat in the world of startups and scaleups since 1995. His writing and speaking help founders, venture capitalists, corporate leaders, policymakers, and everyday people better understand how the internet has changed the way we work together to build amazing organizations. Hundreds of companies, from garage-dwelling startups to Fortune 50 titans, have tapped his knowledge and insights to accelerate and transform their businesses.

About the Editors and Contributors

About Silicon Guild and Thinkers50

Silicon Guild

The Silicon Guild is a group of thought leaders and best-selling authors who write about the ideas shaping business, society, and culture. In confusing, uncertain, and anxious times, members of the Silicon Guild bring voices of clarity, humanity, and community into critical conversations. The now-global Guild seeks to contribute to and elevate research, wisdom, and creative voices to an array of humanistic needs within business and society. The Guild and its publishing imprint are also part of the broader BLK SHP (Black Sheep) cultural creative movement, composed of leading creative thinkers and writers, artists, entrepreneurs, social entrepreneurs, business and society leaders, and patrons—the Medicis of this era.

Thinkers50

Thinkers50, built on the core values of independence, integrity, and accessibility, is admired globally for objective market intelligence, positioning Thinkers50 as the authority in management ideas.

Every two years, Thinkers50 salutes the leading business and management ideas of our age with its Ranking of Management Thinkers and Distinguished Achievement Awards, called "The Oscars of management thinking" by the *Financial Times*. The Thinkers50 annual Radar list identifies emerging thinkers with the potential to make a significant contribution to management theory and practice, and the Thinkers50 Hall of Fame recognizes and celebrates the legacy of thinkers whose lifetime's work has had a lasting influence on business and management.

Acknowledgments

From the Editors

Every book is the work of many, and perhaps none more so than this one. From the moment Thinkers50 and Silicon Guild conceived of this collaboration, scores of people have stepped into the mix to make this book a reality. Special thanks to Des Dearlove at Thinkers50 and Rita McGrath and Allie Chipkin at the Silicon Guild, who were the catalysts for this project. Wiley's excellent acquisitions editor, Jeanene Ray, and an initial planning group, which added, for a time, Caroline Webb to our ranks, focused the lens to explore the intricacies of human-centered leadership as the world turns increasingly to automation.

Twenty-three world-class thinkers, authors, and thought leaders stepped up to contribute their insights and research to this anthology, each bringing a unique perspective, deep experience, and mountains of support as the project evolved from idea to reality. Curious about the topic and how their contributions would weave into a unified narrative, these busy contributors responded to every email and edit with enthusiasm and grace. We are grateful for their trust in us to edit their work, and for every kind encouragement they offered along the way.

This book has benefited from so many behind-the-scenes contributors. Development editor extraordinaire Kelly Talbot, Wiley's managing editor Michelle Hacker, content refinement specialist Saswat Mishra, and chief detail wrangler Raven Buckler ensured that we delivered an excellent manuscript on time. We are grateful to the talented design team who listened to our ideas, then came up with a much better cover concept, and to the copyeditors and production team who turned these collected words into a beautiful book.

Much like the future this book explores, this project was truly a human-centered experience. We steeped this work in curiosity, collaboration, and the very human capacity to imagine and create a more transcendent world. And among the greatest gifts of this project was the joy of working together and with these amazing collaborators.

—Scott Barry Kaufman
New York, NY

—Chris Shipley
Redwood City, CA

December 24, 2025

From the Contributors

This book exists because two people believed with deep conviction that leaders need new language, new courage, and new ways of seeing what's possible. Chris Shipley and Scott Barry Kaufman contributed chapters *and* momentum to this book. They held the center of gravity for a complex, human undertaking in service of something larger than themselves.

Chris brings a rare combination of strategic clarity and generative optimism. She sees patterns before they're obvious, and she invites others into the future without fear. Scott brings an ability to hold intellectual rigor and curiosity in the same breath.

Together, they created the conditions for all of us contributors to do our best thinking.

Chris and Scott's stewardship reminded us that leadership is not about control or certainty but about convening people around a purpose that makes the world a better place. For that, we are profoundly grateful.

Amy Edmondson	Jacqueline Novogratz	Rita McGrath
April Rinne	Jean Oelwang	Safi Bahcall
Brian Solis	Jennifer Aaker	Sanyin Siang
Caroline Webb	John Hagel	Scott Anthony
Chip Conley	Jonathan Haidt	Sophie Hamilton
Chris Yeh	Lisa Kay Solomon	Tom Kelley
Frans Johansson	Morra Aarons Mele	Whitney Johnson
Hal Gregersen	Nancy Duarte	Zeynep Ton

January 1, 2026

Acknowledgments

324

Index